THE WEST BANK AND GAZA: ISRAEL'S OPTIONS FOR PEACE

Report of a JCSS Study Group
The Jaffee Center for Strategic Studies
Tel Aviv University

The Jaffee Center Study Group on The West Bank and Gaza: Israel's Options for Peace

Head of Center

Aharon Yariv

Deputy Head of Center and
  Project Coordinator

Joseph Alpher

Editors

Joseph Alpher
Shai Feldman

Jaffee Center for Strategic Studies

Yehuda Ben-Meir
Abraham Ben-Zvi
Ze'ev Eytan
Shlomo Gazit
Dore Gold
Mark Heller
Efraim Karsh
Anat Kurz
Ariel Levite
Shemuel Meir
Yoram Peri
Aryeh Shalev

The Washington Institute for
  Near East Policy

Martin Indyk
Harvey Sicherman
Steven Spiegel

The Institute for Technological
  Forecasting, Tel Aviv University

Jona Bargur
Gideon Fishelson
Yoel Raban

External Participants

Moshe Brawer
Bruce Maddy-Weitzman
Yitzhak Reiter

The Jaffee Center for Strategic Studies (JCSS)

The Center for Strategic Studies was established at Tel-Aviv University at the end of 1977. In 1983 it was named the Jaffee Center for Strategic Studies in honor of Mr. and Mrs. Mel Jaffee. The objective of the Center is to contribute to the expansion of knowledge on strategic subjects and to promote public understanding of and pluralistic thought on matters of national and international security.

The Center relates to the concept of strategy in its broadest meaning, namely, the complex of processes involved in the identification, mobilization and application of resources in peace and war, in order to solidify and strengthen national and international security.

★ ★ ★

American Board of Advisors

Joint Statement of the two Boards of Advisors

As individuals long concerned about Israel's need to achieve lasting peace and security with its neighbors, we agreed to serve as an informal Board of Advisors to the Jaffee Center for Strategic Studies' Study Group on *The West Bank and Gaza: Israel's Options for Peace*. This study is all the more timely as a result of recent developments at the Palestine National Council meeting in Algiers and the subsequent decision by the United States Government to open an official dialogue with the Palestine Liberation Organization.

Having reviewed the Study, we regard it as an impressive effort to produce an objective, sober, balanced analysis of the complex issues surrounding the future of territories occupied by Israel during the 1967 War, issues which remain central to Israel's future and to that of the region. This analysis constitutes a significant contribution to the public debate in Israel and in the United States. It merits a wide readership and the most thoughtful consideration, which we hope it receives.

Cyrus Vance believes an additional option, encompassing a broader three-party framework analogous to the Benelux arrangement in Western Europe, also needs to be explored.

SPONSORS

The American Jewish Congress is the principal sponsor of this study, and the Anti-Defamation League of B'nai B'rith is the co-sponsor.

FUNDING

Major funding for this project was provided by a committee comprised of Emmanuel Sella, Jerome Brody and Murray Koppelman, New York. Additional funding was provided by Lester Crown and the Hon. Philip M. Klutznick, Chicago, Ill.; Ernest Alson, Knoll International Holdings, Inc. Foundation, and Alan Slifka, New York.

JCSS INTERNATIONAL BOARD OF TRUSTEES

TABLE OF CONTENTS

	Page
Foreword	1
Preface	5
Executive Summary	11
I. Option One — Status Quo	21
Definition	21
Ramifications	22
The Palestinians	22
Israeli Arabs	24
The Arab States	27
Israel's Security	28
The Israeli Domestic Setting	31
Demography, Geography and Economy	35
The United States	37
The Soviet Union	40
Conclusions	42
II. Option Two — Autonomy	45
Definition	45
Ramifications	50
The Palestinians	50
Israeli Arabs	52
The Arab States	53
Israel's Security	55
The Israeli Domestic Setting	58
Demography, Geography and Economy	60
The United States	62
The Soviet Union	63
Conclusions	64
III. Option Three — Annexation	67
Definition	67
Ramifications	68
The Palestinians	68
Israeli Arabs	70
The Arab States	72

Israel's Security   75
The Israeli Domestic Setting   78
Demography, Geography and Economy   80
The United States   82
The Soviet Union   86
Conclusions   88

IV. Option Four — A Palestinian State   91
Definition   91
Ramifications   92
The Palestinians   92
Israeli Arabs   96
The Arab States   98
Israel's Security   101
The Israeli Domestic Setting   106
Demography, Geography and Economy   109
The United States   111
The Soviet Union   113
Conclusions   114

V. Option Five — Unilateral Withdrawal from Gaza   119
Definition   119
Ramifications   121
The Palestinians   121
Israeli Arabs   122
The Arab States   123
Israel's Security   125
The Israeli Domestic Setting   127
Demography, Geography and Economy   128
The United States   130
The Soviet Union   132
Conclusions   132

VI. Option Six — A Jordanian-Palestinian Federation   135
Definition   135
Ramifications   138
The Palestinians   138
Israeli Arabs   140

The Arab States   141
Israel's Security   143
The Israeli Domestic Setting   146
Demography, Geography and Economy   148
The United States   149
The Soviet Union   150
Conclusions   152

VII. General Conclusions   155

Appendices   159
1. Military Strategic Background: War Dangers,
   Security Arrangements, and the Arab-Israel Military
   Balance, 1982-1987-1992   161
2. Israeli Public Opinion on Security and the
   Palestinian Question   184
3. Maps: The Arab and Jewish population of the West
   Bank and Gaza   194
4. The West Bank and Gaza: Geographic and
   Demographic Background   199
5. The Palestinian Diaspora   206
6. The Israeli Arabs: Basic Data   207
7. The Economic Ramifications of the Options   210

About the Members of the Study Group   230

Foreword

The events of 1988 in the Israeli-Palestinian sphere added impetus to the need, perceived by many of us, to weigh Israel's options with respect to the future of these territories. A comparative study of all relevant options was long overdue. This document comprises a comprehensive attempt to meet the challenge.

It is fitting that the Jaffee Center undertake this enterprise. JCSS is Israel's only independent academic "think tank" that focuses entirely on problems pertaining to Israel's national security. We have in the past produced a number of studies, by individual researchers, such as Mark A. Heller's *A Palestinian State: The Implications for Israel*; and *The Autonomy — Problems and Possible Solutions* and *The West Bank: Line of Defense*, both by Aryeh Shalev. These examined the ramifications of establishing a Palestinian state in the West Bank and Gaza, analyzed autonomy as defined by the Camp David agreements, and assessed the strategic importance for Israel of the West Bank. Prepared in the late 1970s and early 1980s, these studies in many ways laid the research foundations at JCSS on the issues that form the backbone of this report.

If we had a sound basis upon which to build, we also approached the task with a sense of heavy responsibility in view of the situation we confronted. The ongoing uprising in the territories, the Palestinian National Council decisions of November 1988 and their reception on the Arab and international scene, the initiation of a US-PLO dialogue, and the deep divisions within the Israeli public that were so jarringly demonstrated by the November 1988 elections — all reflect, for Israel, the dangers entailed in the political deadlock on the Palestinian issue. This, in turn, presages a further escalation in violence, international pressures, economic difficulties, and the danger of war. Therefore it was incumbent upon us to study all the existing possibilities for breaking the deadlock.

That is what we have tried to do in this report. Certainly critics will abound. For some, our study group report will not be "patriotic" enough; for others it will not be "liberal" enough. Yet I

1

feel certain that the openminded reader will find that an honest, painstaking and persistent effort has been made to remain as impartial as humanly possible under the present circumstances. Throughout our efforts, we sought to ensure objectivity through reliance on a stringent quality control process: repeated and very thorough discussion in a large and heterogeneous forum. Our study group meetings were frequently arduous and extended; at times participants were carried away by their convictions and emotions. But in the end all accepted that objectivity must be paramount.

A number of acknowledgements are in order. I would like to express my sincere gratitude and appreciation to the entire JCSS study group for its hard work, and especially to my deputy, Joseph Alpher, the project coordinator, whose dedication, perseverance and wisdom guided the project in the proper direction and brought it to fruition. To several additional persons, a specific word of thanks. Henry Siegman, Director of the American Jewish Congress, planted the seed. It was he who first approached us with the suggestion that we compare the strategic advantages and disadvantages for Israel of different solutions to the Palestinian problem. He and AJCongress President Robert K. Lifton offered to mobilize financial resources and recruit additional sponsors for such a project, and willingly accepted our principal conditions: no interference in our research process, and a commitment to endorse our findings, whatever they be, as worthy of Israeli and American public consideration. When the Anti-Defamation League of B'nai B'rith joined as cosponsors, they too accepted the same restrictions on their involvement. All have been true to their word.

During the second, integrative stage of our work the study group drew on the knowledge and experience of a number of distinguished Israelis who took part in a day-long workshop to discuss the options. They are Avraham Ahituv, former head of Israel's General Security Service; Hanan Bar-On, former deputy director general of the Foreign Ministry; Meron Benvenisti, Director of the West Bank Data Project; Yisrael Har-El, Chairman of the Council of Settlers of Judea, Samaria and Gaza; Alouph Har-Even, Director of the Van Leer Institute; Lieutenant General (res) Moshe Levi, former Chief of Staff of the Israel Defense Forces; Major General (res)

Avraham Rotem, former IDF Director of Military Training; and Haim Tsadok, former minister of justice. Many additional members of Israel's defense community, active and retired, were interviewed during the course of research for the security aspects of the project. A number of distinguished economists took part in a separate workshop that discussed economic ramifications: Professors Pinhas Zusman and Ezra Sadan of the Hebrew University in Jerusalem, Dr. Oded Leviatan and Dan Zacai of the Bank of Israel, and Professor Zeev Hirsh of Tel Aviv University. All these persons deserve our sincere thanks for their wise and frank advice; none bears any responsibility whatsoever for our analyses and conclusions.

Tova Polonsky, Shulamit Reich and the JCSS administrative staff deserve special thanks for the efficient logistics they provided, at times under trying conditions. Tsira Shwartzman and *Kolmos Translating and Publishing* labored energetically to provide real-time, high-quality translations. Dyonon Printers of Tel Aviv University produced the many drafts of this report instantaneously and efficiently. *The Jerusalem Post* and *Ma'ariv* volunteered many of their services in order to produce the Study Group Report.

It is our sincere hope that this product of our labors will be of use to those who intend to brave the stormy waters of the Arab-Israel conflict — that they may reach the safe shores of peace.

Major-General (res) Aharon Yariv
Head of Center

December 1988

Preface

In keeping with the Jaffee Center's primary goal of enriching the public debate on Israeli security issues, this study group report is directed not only at leadership elites, but at all interested persons: Israelis, Palestinians, Americans, and all other friends (and enemies) of Israel. It concentrates on an analysis of those options that Israelis think about — those that are on the agenda of significant sectors of the Israeli political scene. Each of these options is analyzed from every aspect that is relevant to Israel's overall strategic concerns, with each researcher asking, "if this option is implemented, how will it affect Israel from the standpoint of my expertise, e.g., security, Israeli public opinion, American-Israeli relations, demographic factors, Arab reactions, etc? How will those ramifications redound on the option's feasibility and advisability for Israel?" This approach reflects the basic assumption that only after going through this intellectual process can Israelis and others address new ideas and concepts for a solution.

Thus, during the early meetings of the study group, two lists were compiled. The first is a list of six "options." Some of these might be called strategies, or partial options, or (as in the case of the status quo) "non-options." We settled for the term options. The six were selected not because they appear to be beneficial, or pleasant, or feasible — indeed, some involve acts or choices that appear to be morally repugnant — but because they are on Israel's current political agenda, and Israelis (and their friends) need to be informed as to the ramifications for Israel of adopting them. It was also recognized that the list of options must be short enough to produce a manageable research project. Hence we concentrated on the principal options. They are the status quo, autonomy, annexation, a Palestinian state, unilateral withdrawal from Gaza, and a Jordanian-Palestinian federation.

The definitions devised for the options are necessarily rather one-dimensional; a minimum of variants is mentioned, and no new territorial borders (of which there could be infinite variations) are drawn. Obviously any option (except the status quo) could be

5

carried out in stages, in terms of time and space. But such variations are impossible to capture in a single, workable definition. The options are analyzed in this report in completely random order, so as to avoid any implication as to the study group's preferences. And the descriptive terms West Bank, territories, administered territories, and Judea and Samaria, are used interchangeably.

The second list comprises the issue-areas according to which we analyzed each option. There are eleven: the Israeli domestic setting, Palestinian reactions, effects on the Israeli Arab community, the Arab states, demographic and geographic aspects, terrorism, sociopolitical ramifications for the Israel Defense Forces, security and war risks, American reactions, the Soviet response, and economic aspects.

Some of these are obvious choices. A few require brief explanation. The Israeli Arab community, for example, was singled out and isolated from Israeli society as a whole because, in looking at the Palestinian issue, it was impossible to ignore that community's special status: some 18 percent of Israelis are Palestinian Arabs who enjoy full voting rights in a democratic Israel. As a collective, they are particularly sensitive to the nature of a solution; and their proportion within the Israeli population is expected to increase. Similarly, it seemed justified to take a special look at sociopolitical ramifications of the options for the IDF. In the Israeli reality the army, which bears the security burden of a solution, is in fact a microcosm of Israeli society, and its functioning is affected accordingly. The sociopolitical ramifications are included in the sections on the Israeli domestic setting.

On a broader scale, the attempt to assess ramifications for the Israeli domestic setting reflects a recognition that a given option — however objectively beneficial to Israel it may appear to some — must also be judged on the basis of its acceptability to Israel's democratic society, where the public is the ultimate arbiter. This criterion, we felt, was at least as valid a tool for assessing an option's feasibility as, say, its acceptability to Palestinians or to the Soviet Union.

Our investigation of economic ramifications resulted in findings that required a somewhat special presentation. The available

6

data, and their analysis, led us to the conclusion that none of the six options affected Israel's economy in a markedly different way. The significant variant of a Palestinian solution in economic terms is not the political characterization of a solution, but rather the degree to which Israel's borders with a Palestinian entity are open or closed to the movement of goods, workers and investment capital. The inquiry itself produced some useful thoughts on ways to gauge these economic effects of a solution. These are presented in Appendix 7.

The ramifications of the options for Western Europe, Japan and the international community were not analyzed in a separate section. Rather, they are referred to, where appropriate, in conjunction with US, Soviet and economic issues.

The eleven issue-areas are grouped under eight uniform headings within the "ramifications" section of chapters I through VI, which correspond with the six options.

The core of this study group is the Jaffee Center's research team. It was supplemented by outside experts in accordance with specific disciplinary needs. No political criteria were invoked. Regarding two issue areas, the participation of additional institutions was solicited. Thus the Washington Institute for Near East Policy prepared initial drafts of the assessments regarding America's likely reactions to the six options. Similarly, the Interdisciplinary Center for Technological Analysis and Forecasting at Tel Aviv University was mobilized to study the economic ramifications of the options. In this way a genuinely heterogeneous study group, embodying a wide variety of political views, was created. The challenge was to see if we could, together, analyze and argue the issues as objectively as possible, and produce conclusions we all agreed on.

During the first phase of the project, all six options were defined and analyzed by specific researchers, each from his or her own disciplinary standpoint. These analyses were discussed and refined at length by the team as a whole. In the second phase, the format of the project was reordered, producing a draft organized around the various options, by integrating all analysis relevant to each of the options. In this way each option could be discussed separately with regard to all the strategic ramifications that apply

7

to it, and conclusions could be drawn with regard to that option. This produced, in effect, the six main chapters of our study, each of which addresses all the ramifications of one of the six options.

A number of explanations are in order concerning the specific contents and approach of this book. Though one aspect of our research was carried out by Americans, this is essentially an Israeli-centered study: it asks, "what's good for Israel?" and only looks at the advantages and disadvantages for other parties of the various options insofar as they affect Israel. Moreover, it examines only possible solutions for the Palestinian-Israeli conflict — not for the Arab-Israel conflict as a whole. It assumes that the problem of the West Bank and Gaza has become the decisive dimension, though not the only aspect, of the overall Arab-Israel dispute. Obviously, this is a difficult distinction to make, as all the issues are closely intertwined. Our objective here was to generate a manageable research project, given the constraints of time, resources and logistics.

Thus, for example, while we predicated the need for Arab states to help in resettling Palestinian refugees, we did not ask which Arab states would do so, or under what circumstances. It was further assumed that the prospect of a Palestinian solution would generate positive change in the Arab states' attitude toward Israel, but that this element would have to be addressed in a separate context. Similarly, while we recognize Syria's possible role in preventing or inhibiting a Palestinian solution, we do not investigate the possibilities or modalities of a Syrian-Israeli war, or a Syrian-Israeli peace, in and of themselves. And even in looking at the Israeli-Palestinian conflict, the study group concentrated on Israel and the territories of Judea, Samaria and the Gaza Strip. The non-institutional Palestinian diaspora is only referred to insofar as refugee resettlement is recognized as a key component of a settlement. Nor is the disposition of East Jerusalem discussed; this highly emotive and complex issue must be dealt with separately. Despite these necessary limitations, we feel that our conclusions can stand by themselves.

In the course of our research and discussions, a great deal of useful background data and assessments was produced, which could not be directly integrated into the concise report we sought to produce. Some of these assessments have been worked into Chapter I on the status quo, as they indeed describe current realities. Some of the data are presented in the appendices. Readers are advised to peruse these sections at the outset, even if afterwards they look only at those additional options that interest them in particular.

★   ★   ★

A final note on responsibility is in order. This report reflects a broad measure of consensus among the members of the study group. All participated as individuals. Naturally, not every member feels comfortable with every judgement, or endorses every conclusion. However, they all support the general thrust of the report.

EXECUTIVE SUMMARY

The *intifada* — the uprising waged by the Palestinians in the West Bank and Gaza since December 1987 — and the diplomatic initiative launched by the PLO in late 1988, have added impetus to Israel's need to weigh its options with respect to the future of these territories. A comparative study of all relevant options was long overdue. *The West Bank and Gaza: Israel's Options for Peace* comprises the first attempt to meet this challenge. Six primary options comprise the core of this investigation. They were selected for analysis on the basis of one main criterion: they are currently on the Israeli public agenda.

The Status Quo

The first option studied is for Israel to maintain the status quo. Since the absence of change in the legal and political status of the West Bank and Gaza allows the IDF's disposition of forces to remain unchanged, Israel would continue to enjoy the strategic depth provided by the West Bank, with associated advantages for warfighting and deterrence. The status quo also allows Israel to await the appearance of desirable partners for peace, possibly with fewer concessions required.

Yet these advantages are increasingly offset by the progressive deterioration in Israel's strategic standing entailed by the continuation of the status quo. Elements of this deterioration include the likely growing radicalization of Palestinian Arabs and a possible intensification of the *intifada*; radicalization among Israeli Arabs; an enhanced unilateral Palestinian statebuilding effort in the West Bank and Gaza; an increasing likelihood of deterioration in Israel's relations with the Arab world, and specifically with Egypt; growing domestic discontent and societal polarization in Israel; and increased strains in US-Israeli relations and in Israel's ties with Western Europe. The result may be a considerable erosion in Israeli deterrence, and the specter of an eventual Arab-Israeli war.

In the short-term, the potential costs of the status quo will be largely determined by the intensity of the *intifada*, by the extent to

11

which the PLO pursues a moderate political stance, and by the reactions of Israel and the Bush administration. Of these key elements, only the nature of Israel's reaction is under its own control. Hence it is difficult to assess Israel's strategic fortunes as a consequence of adherence to the status quo. Given that the status quo has proven to date to be quite resilient, it may be equally possible for Israel to "muddle through" for an undetermined period of time. Yet the potential dangers this entails for Israel and for the region require that Israel make a concerted search for alternatives.

Autonomy

The second option is the establishment of autonomy in the West Bank and Gaza. Two principal versions of this option were considered. The first is a narrow autonomy similar to that developed by Israel in the course of the Camp David autonomy talks, that would be applied to all Arab residents of the two regions, but not to the land of those territories. Nearly all local matters that involve Arabs exclusively would be managed by the autonomous administration. The second variant is a "deep autonomy" offering the Palestinians extended self-rule — including national symbols such as a flag and anthem — control over all state lands not occupied by the IDF or by Jewish settlements, and joint control (with Israel) over water, customs and immigration (of both Jews and Arabs). An additional variation on either of these two would involve unilateral imposition by Israel of elements of autonomy, without prior negotiation with Palestinians.

In Israel, the Camp David autonomy option as a settlement agreed with the Palestinians would enjoy wide domestic acceptance, among Jews as well as Israeli Arabs. The security risks entailed in this option are minimal: since the IDF would be able to retain its present order-of-battle in the West Bank and Gaza, its capacity to withstand strategic threats would not diminish. In addition, the autonomy option would be supported by the United States and is unlikely to be opposed by the Soviet Union, provided that Palestinian acceptance is obtained. But the Palestinians would reject this option even as an interim arrangement, as long as

12

a post-autonomy transition to sovereign independence were not agreed and specified in advance, as part of the autonomy agreement.

The second variation to this option, the establishment of deep or comprehensive autonomy, would not encounter fewer difficulties. Deep autonomy would not pose greater security threats to Israel than would the narrow variant, and the external reaction to its establishment — particularly in Washington — is likely to be even more supportive. But in Israel, autonomy schemes will elicit domestic opposition in direct proportion to the extent of self-government provided by them, and to the extent to which they would otherwise resemble state independence. Thus, opposition within Israel to an autonomy that comprised many elements of sovereignty could be considerable. Yet by the same token, a broader autonomy is unlikely to elicit greater Palestinian acceptance; for the Palestinians, the critical factor is not the extent of autonomous authority provided — though greater autonomy would be welcomed — but whether they receive a prior commitment that it will eventually, at an agreed date, lead to statehood.

As for unilaterally-imposed autonomy, in the current atmosphere of *intifada* it most likely would neither encourage better Arab-Israeli relations nor reduce friction and violence. Quite the contrary, it might be understood as a sign of Israeli weakness. It would be nearly impossible to find local Palestinians willing to cooperate in good faith. Indeed, unilateral autonomy could well bring to power extremist Palestinians who would exploit it to bring about renewed escalation. Moreover it may be perceived by the United States as a deviation from the Camp David agreements and an attempt to derail the American-Palestinian dialogue that commenced in mid-December 1988.

Annexation

The third option considered in this study is the annexation of the West Bank and Gaza to Israel. In view of the presence of over 1.5 million Palestinians in the territories, Israel — assuming it wished to remain a Jewish-Zionist state — would have to either deny them political participatory rights, or eventually "transfer" most of them from the West Bank and Gaza to the surrounding Arab states.

Annexation is technically feasible; Israel requires no partners in order to carry it out. It offers Israel the ability to formalize its strategic presence throughout the Land of Israel, fulfilling the commitment of some Israelis to the concept of Greater Israel. But implementation of this option would end a decade-long trend of Arab accommodation with Israel, and would begin a spiral toward war, possibly with Soviet support for Arab belligerents. It presages a violent Palestinian reaction involving escalating and unrestrained terrorism. The United States and many others would likely see this as an attempt to preempt the peace process. The US would disassociate from Israel, minimize the "strategic relationship" and apply extreme sanctions. Annexation may induce Washington to expand its dialogue with the PLO, and to discuss with the Soviet Union the possibility of joint action designed to compel Israel to reverse its decision, and perhaps to try to impose a solution to the Israeli-Palestinian conflict. American Jewry, Israel's most important strategic ally, would be increasingly alienated. Economic damage to Israel would encompass not only a drastic reduction in American aid, but also the indirect effects of trade and tourism boycotts, and possibly the cost — in human lives and in billions of dollars — of a war with the Arab countries.

Annexation would also generate a crisis within Israeli society and the Israel Defense Forces, and would bring about accelerated radicalization among Israeli Arabs. And it would place upon Israel an unbearable demographic and economic burden. While a large scale "transfer" of Palestinians from the territories would alleviate the demographic problem, it is bound to exacerbate all other negative ramifications of annexation to an intolerable level.

A Palestinian State

The fourth option considered is the establishment of an independent Palestinian state in most of the territory of the West Bank and Gaza. Israel and the PLO would agree that the Palestinian refugee problem would be solved by settling most of the refugees in Arab states, and the PLO would cancel the Palestinians' claim to

14

the "right of return." Security provisions for Israel would include demilitarization of the territories, alterations to the pre-1967 borders, and the deployment of limited Israeli forces for early warning, air defense, and absorbing an initial Arab military move into the West Bank from the east. Israel would also retain control over West Bank air space. While some Jewish settlements located within the new borders and IDF deployment zones could be retained, others would probably be evacuated. The two countries would collaborate on sensitive issues of mutual importance such as internal security and counter-terrorism, and disposition of water resources.

The creation of an independent Palestinian state offers a greater possibility of resolving the Palestinian issue on terms acceptable to the Palestinians than does any other option considered. It more closely approximates the goals of the *intifada* and the PNC's unilateral declaration of independence than any other option. But it entails serious risks for Israel. While the option could enjoy acceptance among the majority of Palestinians, it involves a danger that, in the long term, the Palestinian state would attempt to realize the Palestinians' aspirations for Greater Palestine (the "right of return") by terrorism, subversion and/or by catalyzing an Arab war coalition against Israel (the "strategy of stages"). It also projects the danger of Palestinization of Jordan, whereby a Palestinian state on the West Bank would collaborate with Jordan's large Palestinian population to engineer a Palestinian takeover of Jordan and elimination of the Hashemite Dynasty. Meanwhile, Palestinian extremists would likely opt for terrorism in an effort to prevent the establishment of a Palestinian state.

As a hedge against the danger that the Palestinians would attempt to invoke terrorism and subversion against Israel, the establishment of elaborate internal security arrangements in the West Bank following Israel's withdrawal would be an absolute prerequisite. Moreover, to ensure stability, extensive international economic aid would be required by the new state: some $1.5-2 billion per annum for the initial years to maintain its present standard of living, and an initial investment of $2-2.5 billion in essential infrastructure.

Most Arab states are likely to accept this option, with Syria and

15

Libya remaining the most probable opponents of any separate Palestinian-Israeli accord. The Soviet Union would be highly supportive of this option, and is likely to attempt to constrain Syrian efforts to torpedo its implementation. Washington is likely to accept any deal concluded by Israelis and Palestinians, even if the Palestinian state is not its preferred option.

A Palestinian state is virtually the only choice of Palestinians. However, under existing circumstances most Israelis would regard this option as unacceptable, and it is highly unlikely than an Israeli government would contemplate its negotiation and implementation. Negotiations with Palestinians over statehood would elicit widespread opposition, some of it violent, among those Israelis who consider any Palestinian state option as an existential threat to the State of Israel. Actual implementation, requiring the forced evacuation of settlements, would result in further divisiveness among the public and within the IDF. Certainly without extensive transition stages to test Palestinian intentions, and confidence-building measures to improve the regional environment, Palestinian statehood is potentially extremely risky from a security standpoint, and is as dangerous for the fabric of Israeli society as is annexation.

Gaza Withdrawal

The fifth option considered is a unilateral Israeli withdrawal from most of the Gaza Strip. The withdrawal would be followed by a complete severance of ties, including, possibly, a hermetic sealing of the border between Israel and the Strip. In order to prevent terrorist infiltration from Gaza and ensure Israel's security, the border would be fenced and mined. A few Jewish settlements in the Strip would be dismantled, but most — located near the border with Egypt — would remain in territory held by Israel which would serve as a security zone separating Egypt from the Gaza Palestinian population. The inhabitants of the Gaza Strip would be free to choose whatever political framework they wished, including a PLO-led Palestinian mini-state.

Unilateral withdrawal from Gaza would allow Israel to divest itself of a small section of territory in which over half of the inhabitants are refugees, and the rate of population growth is very high. The option would encounter limited Israeli domestic opposition, and is likely to be acceptable to Israeli Arabs as well. Implementation of this option would not present Israel with major military threats that are materially different from those presented by the continuation of the status quo. Most external parties — the Arab states, the superpowers — would not object strenuously to Israeli implementation of this option.

Yet Israeli unilateral withdrawal is likely to be perceived as a retreat, and an abdication by Israel of its responsibilities, in the face of cumulative Palestinian pressure. Hence it might result in some loss of Israeli deterrence, thereby producing increased unrest among Palestinians elsewhere. In addition, the option would amount to the creation of a Palestinian mini-state in Gaza that would constitute a precedent-setting realization of the Palestinian state ideal and would receive international recognition, yet would owe Israel nothing in return through negotiations or agreement. The Gaza mini-state would be destitute; its GNP could fall overnight by 75 percent. It could turn into a Lebanese-style base for terrorism and chaos; it would probably generate unrest in the West Bank, and would quickly constitute a source of friction between Egypt and Israel. Overall, this appears to be a very risky option.

Jordanian-Palestinian Federation

The sixth option considered is the creation of a Jordanian-Palestinian federation in most of the territory of the West Bank and Gaza Strip. Jordan would be predominant in such a federation, with responsibility for defense, internal security and foreign affairs resting in Amman. As in the case of the fourth option — a Palestinian state — security arrangements would be established to mitigate potential strategic threats following Israel's withdrawal. Most important among these measures would be the complete demilitarization of the West Bank, security arrangements for Israel on the East Bank, and the deployment of Israeli forces for early warning, air defense, and absorbing an initial Arab military move into the West Bank from the east.

17

(Jordan, the PLO and some Israelis frequently refer to a *confederation* option. Yet they have different agendas in mind: King Hussein and most Israelis mean a federative structure of the type described here, in which Hussein controls security; the PLO means a genuine confederation between two independent states in which the King would be little more than a titular ruler. Here the option is analyzed as it appears on the Israeli agenda, and presumably on Hussein's covert agenda. The Palestinian variant is subsumed within the analysis of option IV, a Palestinian state.)

Like the creation of an independent Palestinian state, this "Jordanian option" would allow Israel to end its control over more than 1.5 million Palestinians. But given the envisaged predominant Jordanian role in maintaining internal security in the West Bank, and the fact that demilitarizing the area is likely to be far easier once it constitutes only part of a sovereign state's territory, this option seems to meet Israel's security requirements more efficiently. Moreover, Jordan would be effectively removed from membership in an Arab war coalition, thus further safeguarding Israel against strategic threats from the east. Indeed, Jordan and Israel would share a number of strategic interests that could contribute to peace and stability, such as resettlement of the Palestinian refugees.

For these and other reasons, on the Israeli domestic scene this option is potentially more acceptable than Palestinian statehood, although it too would elicit strong opposition from many quarters. Demographically and economically this option could be beneficial to the Palestinians. With appropriate economic aid, Jordan could take responsibility for the resettlement of a large number of refugees from Gaza and the West Bank. The United States is likely to support this option, but the Soviet Union is likely to accept it only if the PLO does so.

Yet the Jordanian-Palestinian federation option is not currently feasible, primarily because it is unacceptable to most of the Palestinians. Since the Palestinians believe that they can eventually achieve sovereign independence, they would oppose implementation of the federation option, employing terrorism against Israeli and Jordanian targets, as well as against Palestinian "collaborators." Given Jordan's refusal to conclude an agreement that does not receive the Palestinians' blessing, and in view of Jordan's progressive withdrawal during 1988 from responsibility for the West Bank, the option is not currently being advocated even by Jordan. Yet in view of Jordan's fundamental strategic interests, the Hashemite Kingdom will seek to be involved in any future Palestinian settlement, whatever the circumstances.

Even if the option were feasible, it is not entirely clear that it would be to Israel's long-term strategic advantage. Demographically, the Palestinians would constitute an overwhelming majority in a combined East-West Bank state. Should they later move successfully to establish majority rule in the federation, Israel would be faced with a far more potent Palestinian successor state along its eastern border, that is not committed by treaty to coexist with it. Hence, if and when this option does reemerge as a viable possibility, its many advantages for Israel would be valid only to the extent that long-term Hashemite rule is predicated. Thus Israel would have to weigh this option carefully against the risk of eventual Palestinian dominance over the East Bank — a risk that also exists in option IV, a Palestinian state. Finally, this option also involves heavy short-term risks, since Syria is likely to invest considerable effort to torpedo its implementation.

General Conclusions

The central conclusion of this study is that under existing conditions and in their present form, none of the options currently on Israel's agenda seems to offer a reasonable avenue for dealing with the West Bank and Gaza. The unilateral options (annexation, withdrawal from Gaza) are feasible, but could prove disastrous. The negotiated compromise options (autonomy, Palestinian state, Jordanian-Palestinian federation) bear some promise of mitigating the conflict, but are totally unacceptable to one or both sides. Under these circumstances — and barring the emergence of a major new leadership initiative, superpower intervention or some cataclysmic event — Israel must, in the immediate term, cope with the status quo and seek ways to ameliorate it. Otherwise it is liable to degenerate into a situation that produces international, regional and local pressures on Israel to accept a Palestinian state solution under disadvantageous conditions.

Looking beyond the status quo, however, our analysis of the six options points to the desperate need, and the possibility, for creative thinking on the Palestinian issue both in Israel and among the Palestinians. Both sides must develop new and more promising courses of action for solving the Israeli-Palestinian conflict. In so doing, many of the beneficial aspects that we have found in the six options could be given expression, and the harmful aspects avoided. A new option would also have to reflect the imperative or constant components, such as massive international and inter-Arab participation in refugee resettlement and economic development, without which no settlement seems likely or worthwhile.

The Jaffee Center study group has developed such a proposal for a Palestinian-Israeli peace process — one that, it believes, should be on the Israeli agenda. JCSS has done so on a completely independent basis — without the sponsorship, counsel or participation of any of the American research team, persons and institutions involved in this report. The Jaffee Center's ideas on the peace process are embodied in the companion booklet to this volume, *Israel, the West Bank and Gaza: Toward a Solution.*

I. Option One — Status Quo

Definition

This option implies the absence of change in the legal and political status of the territories that prevailed through 1988. Israel would continue to rule over the West Bank and Gaza, more or less along existing lines. The Palestinians' resistance to Israel and Israeli control would continue, albeit at varying degrees of intensity. For the purposes of assessing the status quo, Palestinian political initiatives, such as the PNC's unilateral declaration of independence in November 1988, are not considered to have affected Israel's legal and political status in the territories.

Israel's pursuit of this option could reflect merely the absence of an alternative political decision. Thus it could derive from an Israeli national political paralysis with regard to the adoption of any decision that changes the status quo, and/or from the absence of negotiating partners for any settlement minimally acceptable to Israelis. For Israel's political leadership, this might be the easiest option to adopt, since any alternative decision to change the status quo could generate acute tension inside the country.

But reliance on the status quo could also reflect a genuine assessment on the part of certain Israeli political actors that time is in Israel's favor: that Israel could and should outlast the Palestinians and compel them to accept a settlement under favorable terms. Alternatively, advocacy of the status quo might reflect the expectation that the passage of time would allow Israel eventually to annex the territories, or would even constitute, in and of itself, a gradual process of de facto annexation. The status quo also reflects the preference of Israelis for whom the notion of continued occupation provides a sense of physical security, despite external and internal developments. Finally, it corresponds with the preference of those national-religious elements within Israeli Jewish society who rely upon divine intervention to create a Greater Israel.

Ramifications

The Palestinians

Perpetuation of the political and territorial status quo satisfies the needs and aspirations of none of the Palestinian constituencies, either in Judea, Samaria and Gaza or in the Arab countries. Its only redeeming features for them are that it requires no contractual Palestinian concessions to Israel, and that Palestinians are united in opposing the status quo.

Were the status quo to continue — without even the beginnings of a political process aimed at negotiating an alternative — there is little likelihood that the *intifada* would cease. The Palestinians view the uprising as some kind of collective rite of passage that has broken down longstanding inhibitions and psychological obstacles to active resistance at the popular level. Hence it may go into temporary "remission" at some time, but it would almost certainly reerupt — particularly if provocative Israeli acts, such as massive settlement or deportations, were employed. In such circumstances the sense of political and economic deprivation would intensify even more; traditional social restraints, which are already disintegrating, would utterly collapse, and Israel would lose the minimal capacity for indirect rule that it still retained. This could produce greater radicalization among Palestinian youth — particularly underemployed university graduates and unemployed laborers.

Regardless of the sensitivity of Israeli actions, the mere fact of continuing occupation necessarily aggravates Palestinian frustration. Combined with the increasing "proletarianization" of Palestinian society in the territories, this almost certainly means further radicalization, especially among the "overqualified" young (those with education but without the opportunity for appropriate employment), but also among less politically-conscious laborers whose access to the Israeli labor market (their primary source of income) is constantly interrupted by strikes and curfews, and merchants who have gone bankrupt (because of the absence of Israeli consumers and drastically diminished buying power in the local market). In this sense, the *intifada* may have a built-in escalation mechanism; failure to revive pre-December 1987 "normality" produces a constant stream of new recruits for street violence.

The Palestinian organizations are likely to continue to be constrained by considerations associated with the *intifada*'s image as a popular uprising, as well as by the PLO's need to abide by the American demand that it refrain from terrorism as a condition for maintaining their dialogue. Additional constraints comprise Israel's security measures and the preventive measures taken by the neighboring Arab states. However should the PLO's political initiative fail, the organization may lose its standing in the territories, hence its capacity to prevent a terrorist escalation and to balance Islamic fundamentalist influence. Growing frustration may then be expressed in increased militancy and terrorism, and involve more widespread use of lethal weapons, producing a higher cycle of violence. In general, the relative role of terrorism within the general civil revolt in the West Bank and Gaza can be expected to increase. This will likely manifest itself in self-initiated and small-cell action, rather than in organizationally-orchestrated terrorism.

The most likely vehicle for radicalization is a messianic religious movement. By late 1988 Islamic fundamentalism was already a dominant force in the Gaza Strip, and was beginning to mount a challenge for leadership in the West Bank. The rise of Islamic fundamentalism could cause the further diminution of the Palestinian Christian population, which is centered around Jerusalem. It constitutes only about five percent of the Palestinian Arab population, but it is a significant factor in manifesting world Christian links to the Holy Land.

If the Arab Christians enjoy fairly ready opportunities for emigration, the Muslim majority does not. Neither Jordan nor the Gulf states are prepared to absorb them, even assuming they wished to leave.

The PLO has been increasingly pressured to exploit whatever opportunity the *intifada* has created, and to forestall undesirable developments in the future — chaos, religious radicalism or even despair and exhaustion in the territories. This response manifested itself during 1988 in the most serious and sustained campaign for a political settlement — along the lines envisaged by the PLO — in the history of that organization. If sustained, the campaign would pose a serious challenge, internationally and domestically, to an Israeli government's political ability to maintain the status quo.

Should the PLO's political initiative fail, however, and given the prospect that the *intifada* may degenerate into aimless violence, some local elements may intensify their desire for a political settlement with Israel. But there is almost no likelihood that a local leadership would dare to realize this aspiration in defiance of both the fundamentalists at home and the PLO abroad.

All told, then, continuation of the status quo suggests increased radical fundamentalism, Palestinian protest and terrorism in the territories and abroad, and Palestinian pressure upon the Arab states to take action. Of course, by maintaining the status quo Israel does derive a certain advantage in forcing the Palestinians to take the initiative — provided, of course, that Israel is prepared to respond in kind.

Israeli Arabs

The Israeli Arabs regard themselves as part of the Palestinian people, and they evince solidarity with the desire of the Arabs in the territories to establish an independent Palestinian state there. Yet most of them do not see themselves as being part of the political solution of the Palestinian problem, since as far as they are concerned their political fate has already been decided: to be a national minority in a state possessing a Jewish majority, aspiring constantly to enhance that status and obtain equality of rights and opportunities. Their identification with the struggle of the Arabs in the territories is not their paramount national concern. But that struggle holds out the potential of more acute ideological and political radicalization in line with the unfolding situation in the region. Incipient signs of violent activity stemming from identification with the *intifada* were already perceptible in the Israeli Arab sector in 1988.

The continuation of the political status quo in the territories is troublesome for Israeli Arabs both on a national-ethnic level, and because it slows their full integration into Israeli society. Hence they have a vested interest in finding a political solution in the territories that will satisfy the Palestinians, while easing the burden of internal conflict that they feel — between identification with the state, and identification with their fellow Palestinian Arabs.

A radicalization process began among Israeli Arabs long before the *intifada*. It may be characterized as an intensification of the struggle for equal civil rights, together with a certain blurring of the boundary between civil rights and national or autonomous rights. Its principal manifestation is the division of the Israeli Arab body politic into three principal sectors: 1) Moderates, who support the Palestinian struggle but whose primary aim is to enhance their political, social and economic integration into Israeli life; in the November 1988 elections their vote (for Zionist parties) totaled 42 percent of the total Arab vote. 2) Radicals, who generally advocate the establishment of a Palestinian state led by the PLO alongside Israel, and militantly pursue equality of rights. Some of these activists openly advocate the evolution of Israel into a binational state. In the 1988 elections their vote, for the Israeli Communist list, the Progressive List for Peace, and the Democratic Arab Party came to 58 percent of the Arab vote. 3) Extreme nationalists, who do not recognize Israel's right to exist, and usually call for the boycotting of elections (the percentage of Arabs who voted has dropped from around 80 percent in the 1960s, to 70 percent in 1988 — a partial indicator of extreme nationalist influence).

An Arab Follow-up Committee, composed of the National Committee of Heads of Arab Local Authorities, together with the Arab members of Knesset from all parties, has since 1984 become the supreme political body in the Arab sector; it has been dubbed "the parliament of Israel's Arabs." It is this forum that sets reactive guidelines to various political developments and decides on the character of all protest activities. It has organized a number of expressions of solidarity with the Arabs in the territories.

Continuation of the status quo would intensify the radical and nationalist trends, particularly among the younger generation of Israeli Arabs. In accordance with PLO strategy, it would also bring

25

about closer ties and political cooperation between the Palestinians on both sides of the Green Line, as well as a more intense drive to establish a large Arab party or political bloc at the expense of support for Zionist parties — thus potentially affecting the balance of forces in the Knesset. One of the more significant political reactions of Israeli Arabs to the *intifada* during 1988 was the decision of an Arab member of Knesset, Abd al-Wahab Darawsha, to leave the Labor Party in protest over his inability to influence security policy in the territories despite the fact that the defense minister was from his own party. Darawsha's success in establishing the Democratic Arab Party symbolized a growing chasm between the country's Arab citizens and the Zionist parties.

In general, there is no guarantee that the relative restraint evinced by Israeli Arabs thus far would persist if the status quo continued. The moderate Israeli Arab camp, which essentially seeks full integration into the state as it exists today, could weaken progressively — it lost seven percent of the total Arab vote in the November 1988 elections, after nearly a year of the uprising. Whether developments in the territories cause Israeli Arabs to participate in violent events depends on a broad range of circumstances and Israeli reactions. The central question is: how intolerable would the situation in the territories be from the Israeli Arab public standpoint? Past experience indicates that emotionally charged events, such as an attack on Islamic holy sites or terrorist activity by Jewish underground groups, are liable to spark violent mass solidarity protests in the Israeli Arab sector. Certainly if the *intifada* were exacerbated, widespread violent protest activity could erupt in Israel's Arab sector, particularly if, on a parallel, the demands of Israeli Arabs for greater integration and equalization of rights were not accommodated. An Israeli failure to respond in kind to what is perceived as PLO displays of moderation would also further radicalize Israel's Arabs.

In short, were the status quo to be characterized by a decline in the *intifada*, coupled with successful Israeli measures to encourage integration of Israeli Arabs, then the situation would entail little disadvantage for Israel. However, to the extent that unrest continues in Judea, Samaria and Gaza, that the PLO is perceived as moderating its positions, and that Israeli Arab demands for equality are not dealt with effectively, then the status quo could generate extensive violent activity

26

and increased radicalization among Israeli Arabs, to the detriment of Jewish-Arab relations inside Israel.

The Arab States

With the *intifada* remaining at its late-1988 level, the Arab states' relations with Israel would remain unchanged. The Arab majority coalition of moderate, pro-western states that claim to seek political accommodation with Israel would try to prevent the continuation of the status quo by galvanizing the political process. At this level, the *intifada* is also unlikely to affect inter-Arab alignments, and Syria is likely to remain relatively isolated on the inter-Arab scene. However, an intensification of the *intifada* would spell serious damage to existing de jure and de facto arrangements between Israel and the Arab states. In addition, Syria would be better positioned to mobilize support for its stance; pressures on Iraq to defect to the Syrian camp could be considerable, though this is highly unlikely in the near term.

In the past, Jordan regarded the continuation of the status quo as preferable to any other option except for the return of the West Bank to Jordanian sovereignty. Yet it now views the status quo as increasingly and inherently destabilizing, hence fraught with danger. The Hashemite Kingdom interprets the *intifada* as evidence that if the conflict is not soon resolved, radicalization will prevail in the territories, and right-wing influences will gain more power inside Israel. In the absence of progress on the political level, Jordan's status in the West Bank would continue to weaken, probably irreparably. For Jordan this spells the possibility that eventually, the Hashemite throne would be undermined, either by an Israeli attempt to help establish Palestinian statehood in the East Bank, or by the forcible "transfer" of embittered, highly politicized Palestinians from the West Bank and Gaza to the East Bank. The *intifada*, as a clear manifestation of Palestinian radicalization, thus appears to Jordan as the first stage of its nightmare scenario.

Syria would be content with the status quo in that it allows Damascus to continue to strive for strategic parity with Israel, without the urgent need to seek to derail any of the less favorable options — and hence to confront Israel — before parity has been achieved. In its calculations, Syria may also reason that continuation of the *intifada* would gradually weaken Israel's position — thereby tilting the strategic balance in Damascus' favor — by eroding Israel's international standing and increasing tensions within its society. In addition, Damascus probably calculates that with the passage of time after the end of the Gulf war, both Iraq and Iran may be persuaded to contribute toward a confrontation with Israel.

Cairo would be unhappy with the continuation of the status quo, and a negative Egyptian reaction is likely if responsibility for the absence of progress toward peace is placed solely with Israel. Should Jerusalem fail to respond to sustained signs of PLO moderation, Israeli-Egyptian relations might indeed deteriorate. Furthermore, should the *intifada* escalate — generating a corresponding escalation of Israeli countermeasures, Egypt would find it increasingly difficult to sustain simultaneously its relations with Israel and its standing in the Arab world. This too would lead to a deterioration of Egyptian-Israeli ties, though not to Egypt's active participation in a war coalition against Israel. Nevertheless, should a deterioration of the status quo result in a war on Israel's northeastern front, Egypt might be passively supportive of the Arab cause, forcing Israel to devote part of its military resources to protecting its southwestern flank.

Israel's Security

Under the status quo, a number of particularly negative developments in the realm of national defense are likely to continue. First, Israel has exhausted its human and economic-budgetary resources that can be devoted to national defense. Secondly, after 41 years of struggle and war, Israeli society is showing increasing signs of national fatigue. Third, the Jewish state has lost its national consensus on some major aspects of security policy, and the IDF's image and standing have been seriously tarnished. The net effect of these developments is growing concern over Israel's ability in the long term to withstand an attack by a future wall-to-wall Arab war coalition. Should these developments maintain their present course, Israel's survival might depend on the Arab side's fear that Israel might retaliate with unconventional weapons.

The more immediate security difficulties entailed in the status quo are related to the possible continuation of the *intifada* in the West Bank and Gaza. From a purely military standpoint, Israel has adjusted to the *intifada* and can deal with the present level of unrest for an indefinite period. In budgetary terms, and particularly in reserve service days required, the extra burden placed by the *intifada* on the IDF is tolerable. Israel's record of successful anti-terrorist activity, with very minor impact on life within Israel, is also likely to continue.

The IDF, however, is incurring considerable intangible costs as a consequence of the *intifada*. The first involves the moral damage represented by the frustration that Israeli soldiers increasingly express toward Palestinian civilians as a consequence of the complex situations in which they find themselves. The second is the *intifada*'s contribution to the deterioration of Israel's national consensus on defense matters. And finally, the *intifada* has introduced distortions to the IDF's priorities, forcing the consumption of energy and manpower for a mission that should not be at the top of the IDF's agenda. Our assessment, nevertheless, is that the IDF can withstand these costs.

Under existing conditions, Arab motivation to launch a war aimed at recapturing the lands controlled by Israel since the 1967 war, is limited. While there does continue to exist a fundamental Arab desire to eliminate Israel, in the aftermath of the peace concluded between Egypt and Israel only Syria and the Palestinians may be described in these terms. But the Palestinians' collective energy is currently absorbed by the *intifada* and the consequent PLO political initiatives. Only if the uprising and the initiatives fail to produce positive political results might the Palestinians revert to an effort to catalyze another Middle East war — an effort that would have a low probability of success in view of Jordan's anticipated lack of enthusiasm. Syria, on the other hand, remains interested in regaining the Golan Heights, while Israel, other Arab states, and the major external powers remain indifferent to the Syrian problem.

29

In addition to these inter-Arab divisions, another element mitigating against war under the status quo is the Arabs' assessment of the risks and opportunities entailed. While Egypt remains outside the Arab war coalition and the IDF is well positioned militarily — and capable of delivering a painful counterpunch — the remaining Arab states are not enthusiastic about the notion of war. Arab fears that Israel might exploit a future war to expel Palestinians from the West Bank and Gaza to one or more of the surrounding Arab states, might prove a further deterrent to war.

Only two developments might alter this picture and generate a riskier environment. Neither is currently of high probability. First, the end of the Iran-Iraq War could in time bring about an attempt by Iraq to reassert its leadership of a radical Arab coalition. This could increase the likelihood of participation by Iraqi expeditionary forces in an Arab attack on Israel. Secondly, the ceasefire in the Gulf could generate an increase in Iranian militancy, particularly reflected in a willingness to conduct terrorism and insurgency.

A second possible negative development within the status quo situation is the damage suffered by Israel's deterrent profile, in terms of leadership and decisionmaking, as a consequence of its inability to put an end to the *intifada*. In this sense, a determined and rapid repression of the uprising — provided it did not generate negative side effects — would contribute to Israel's deterrent posture. Yet the more extreme and sustained the measures Israel takes, the more it jeopardizes US support — and this has potential negative consequences for Israel's consensus and its overall deterrent posture.

Two specific new developments — both of low probability — within the status quo could actually lead to war. First, an escalation of the *intifada* could induce Israel to adopt extremely repressive countermeasures. (An attempt to expel a large number of Palestinians to Jordan, for example, might result in clashes along the Jordan River, with Egypt reacting by canceling or suspending its peace agreement with Israel.) Secondly Syria could attack on the Golan Heights, with the objective of surprising the IDF and securing early gains, possibly in order to catalyze a post-war political process. An escalation of the situation in the West Bank and Gaza that generated increased friction between the

30

United States and Israel along with further deterioration of Israel's national consensus, could cause the Syrians to assess that an opportunity for attack had been created.

But in purely military terms, Israel would be able to withstand such a war successfully. It would be able to rely on the near-ideal positioning of its forces; the very limited capacity of Arab forces, with the exception of Syria, to achieve strategic surprise; and the fact that, notwithstanding Israel's present dissensus with respect to its policies in the West Bank and Gaza, Israelis would quickly rally round the flag were a significant external threat to appear.

From a security standpoint, then, the status quo provides no immediate existential threat to Israel. But it is replete with dangers.

The Israeli Domestic Setting

From the domestic Israeli standpoint this is, at first glance, the simplest option. No momentous national decision is required; nor is there a need to consider delicate procedures for executing such a decision. Further, the status quo of 1988, troublesome as it was for Israelis, could continue to be borne by them for some time to come — not easily, and not without human, moral and material sacrifices; but Israelis, their defense forces and their economy have proven their adaptability and endurance. By late 1988 the IDF had settled into a pattern of relatively low-cost control in the territories; a movement to boycott military service in the territories remained a tolerable fringe phenomenon; and the economy had made adjustments for the absence of Palestinian Arab laborers and markets. The election results of late 1988 appeared to demonstrate that many Israelis were prepared to maintain the political status quo with regard to the Arab-Israel conflict.

But there is another side to this assessment. A large part of the Israeli body politic has, during the past ten years, developed a sense of urgency regarding the need to resolve the Arab-Israeli dispute, as it has reacted to a series of developments that it perceived in a highly negative light: the rise of the radical Right (the Tehiya Party in 1981, Rabbi Kahane in 1984, a combination of extreme Right and ultra-orthodox factions in 1988); the settlement

31

movement in the administered territories since 1977, and the concomitant emergence of the Jewish settlers as an aggressive, organized and demanding lobby; the consequences of the 1982 invasion of Lebanon; the growing saliency of the Arab-Jewish demographic balance within Greater Israel; and finally the *intifada*. Accordingly, this large sector of Israeli society sees in the status quo an ongoing danger to its and its country's future. It assesses that the status quo will, in fact, generate change for the worse: in the very image of the State of Israel, in the nature of Israeli society, and in rendering inevitable another Arab-Israeli war. This sector of public opinion is becoming increasingly convinced that the situation is turning Israel into an uncomfortable place to live in, and that the country is running out of time in which to right its course.

In this sense, under the best of circumstances this option would generate increased polarization in Israeli society, as well as radicalization of the Israeli Left.

This internal crisis would deepen yet further were the Israeli government to direct the IDF to invoke harsher measures than previously employed against Palestinian Arab civilians. The situation could easily deteriorate into a vicious circle of violence and repressive action. This would be perceived by the Israeli Left and Center as unwarranted oppression, causing followers of movements like Mapam, CRM and Shinui-Merkaz to consider refusing to obey certain orders. Were a government to implement the demands of Tehiya and other right-wing parties — to shoot or deport every stone-thrower and arsonist, to deport teachers and students of universities identified with the PLO, to remove all judicial restraint or review regarding security- related activities in the territories, and to deport even Jews caught "collaborating" — then some Labor Party circles might join the call to disobey orders, and perhaps even boycott military service in the territories. Such a development would pose a direct challenge to the integrity and viability of the IDF. A government decision to renew large-scale Jewish settlement in the territories would, obviously, exacerbate Israeli internal tensions yet further. This would also happen were a significant sector of the Israeli public to become convinced that the PLO had abandoned its armed struggle and was opting sincerely for a compromise political settlement.

A wise government does not give an army orders it cannot reasonably obey. Certainly this applies to an army like Israel's, in which virtually all citizens serve. One consequence of such a situation could be for the government to establish special units — possibly even outside the framework of the IDF — to carry out its policies in the territories, hoping thereby to deflate popular and even IDF protest over its policies. Alternatively, it might simply tolerate acts of terrorism carried out by Jewish settlers against Palestinian Arabs as deterrence or punishment for disturbances. In fact, some of these steps could encourage even greater friction with the IDF, together with popular discontent among the Israeli Left and Center. This in turn could lead the government to adopt measures that could be perceived by many as a threat to freedom of the press, to the role of the courts in the rule of law, and to other Israeli democratic institutions.

As this analysis implies, the situation of the IDF as an occupying army is unique, both because the IDF is unique and because a large portion of Israeli public opinion does not consider the army to be occupying foreign soil at all. For 20 years Israel's self-perception as a "nation in uniform," and the degree to which the IDF and Israel's democratic foundations were interlocked, appeared to immunize the IDF from politicization as long as it was able to manage daily life in the territories with a minimum of force and involvement. But due to the very same perceptions the *intifada* — by generating a considerable quantitative increase in the IDF presence in the territories and spotlighting Israel's own internal debate over the Palestinian question — has threatened to heighten the IDF's sensitivity to political influences.

Thus, under status quo conditions, the intensity of the *intifada* would be the primary determinant of the extent to which IDF morale, motivation and professionalism were affected. Ultimately, civilian sectors that volunteer in large numbers for elite duty, like kibbutz youth, could change their positive perception of the IDF — although, significantly, this had not happened after a year of the uprising. Still, anticipation of such developments has already led the IDF to expand special units, like the Border Police, for duty in the territories. These problems could escalate should the PLO sustain the political initiative it launched in late 1988, thereby causing more Israelis to believe that there may exist a negotiated alternative to the status quo.

On the other side of the political spectrum, some Jewish settlers in the territories have sought to push the IDF toward more aggressive prevention and punishment of Palestinians. This too is a potential cause for increased friction within the army and between the army and society.

The status quo, then, virtually assures that the IDF, and particularly its professional officer corps, would have to live with a degree of friction both internally and externally. Whatever the duties the army is asked to carry out, they would be borne more easily to the extent that the government giving the orders represents a broad Israeli consensus, rather than a narrow political coalition of the Left or the Right.

Certainly if only a small portion of this forecast reached fruition, both Israel's national societal fiber and Israel-Diaspora relations would be sorely tested. Nor would this sort of national deterioration necessarily be the consequence of premeditated government decision. It seems almost inevitable that the continuation of the status quo would produce situations that cause a general escalation of fear, hatred and repression. For example, an Arab firebomb attack on an Israeli settler schoolbus, killing dozens of Jewish children, could result in a terrible emotional outburst, characterized by demands for revenge. The government might order severe punitive action against the Arabs involved — the demolition of an entire Palestinian village and the deportation of its inhabitants. This would inevitably generate Arab and international protest, and a more violent level of *intifada*. While atrocities could take place under alternative scenarios for solutions, too, the status quo assures a degree of immediate friction between Palestinians and Jewish settlers not necessarily present in other scenarios. Were the government to balk at punishing the Palestinians in this way for the incident, it would have to use the IDF to forcibly repress settler vigilante groups. Either way, Israeli society would be eroded, while Israel would move closer to a war with its Arab neighbors that would be perceived by half the Israeli population as a consequence not of Arab belligerence, but of Jewish obstinacy.

34

The advantage of the status quo for Israeli society, then, is that it is Israel's ongoing option; it already exists. It requires no imaginative or risky decisionmaking. For many Israelis, it satisfies the maxim "better the devil you know." The disadvantage is that the longer the status quo persists, the heavier the toll on Israeli society, the greater the erosion of the quality of life, and — for many Israelis — the less pleasant a country to live in will Israel be.

Demography, Geography and Economy

Under status quo conditions, Israel can expect to confront growing social and economic problems among the Arab population of the administered territories in coming years. These would arise from the general overpopulation of the territories, the growing rate of urbanization and growth in the labor force, an extreme dearth of natural resources, and the absence of any development program aimed at overcoming these disadvantages.

The population of Palestinian Arabs in the territories is expected to increase by 34-40 percent by the year 2000; this, incidentally, corresponds with the present rate of increase in neighboring Jordan and Syria. (The Israeli Arabs' natural increase is expected to make them at least 23 percent of the Israeli population by the year 2000.) This represents a higher rate of increase in the territories than that of the previous 21 years, because emigration to the Gulf has dropped decisively since a high of 20,000 per annum during the 1960s and '70s. With the dwindling of emigration, the productive age groups are now assuming their normal share in the population, and this will soon be reflected in a rise in natural increase. Thus the age group 20-49, which formed 28 percent of the population of Judea and Samaria in 1967, is expected to rise to 36-38 percent by the year 2002. This substantial rise in the absolute number of Palestinians in productive age groups will result in considerable growth in the number of births, even if there is a downward trend in the average annual birth rate (as official statistics predict).

Accordingly, the labor force in the territories is already rising; in recent years, the annual rate of increase has been 15,000, and this figure should be higher during the 1990s. Needless to say, without new jobs, these new breadwinners present a potential source of considerable friction and dissent.

Were the *intifada* to persist, Arab resistance to integration into the Israeli economy would grow, producing some renewal of subsistence agriculture and a drop in the movement of labor and goods between the territories and Israel. In this sense, to the extent that Israel succeeds in quelling violent unrest, it may confront a growing economic burden in maintaining the territories. To the extent the violence continues, Israel's immediate problems center more in the security and political spheres than in the economic realm, but the Palestinians in the territories — cut off from both the Israeli labor market and Arab export markets for their agricultural produce — would suffer growing economic deprivation.

The damage to the economy of the territories caused by the uprising during 1988 was considerable: an approximate drop in GNP of 30 percent, and a rise in unemployment of some 25 percent. In contrast, Israel's GNP suffered only by about 2.5-3 percent, caused mainly by a decline in trade with the territories and a fall in construction and in tourism that can be attributed to the effects of the *intifada*. Thus the uprising caused a partial separation of the two economies.

Israel can adjust and find ways to compensate for some aspects of this damage (e.g., by importing construction workers from Portugal to replace striking West Bank laborers). But once it does so, the eventual ramifications for the economy of the territories will be amplified. Were Israel to prevent massive unilateral transfer payments and the development of local employment infrastructure, the economic damage in the territories would be even greater. On the other hand, the greatest risk for the Israeli economy implied by the status quo is the possibility of tourism and trade boycott actions, for example by the EEC (Israel's economy is highly dependent on foreign trade), and/or cuts in US aid.

The United States

In assessing an Israeli government's pursuit of the status quo — whether out of design or due to paralysis — Americans would not be immune to Arab actions and dissenting stands taken by major Israeli opposition groups. During 1988, Israel's indecisiveness was excused — even by many critics — because of the November elections. But after early 1989 continuing unrest in the territories, answered by sporadic repression but no effective Israeli political proposals, would begin to lead to a steady, if gradual, erosion of American intimacy in the relationship.

While it is not clear precisely how, if at all, the relationship will be affected by the advent — on December 15, 1988 — of the US-PLO dialogue, it seems likely that a new foreign policymaking team in Washington might pursue a more reserved approach toward Israel. This would reflect arguments by bureaucrats that it was necessary to stand up for the Palestinians in order to fortify the new dialogue and to protect US relations with the Arab states. Pentagon officials looking for excuses to cut programs in a restricted budgetary environment would take advantage of Israel's declining popularity to reduce them. The result over time would be a gradual drifting apart between the United States and Israel. Officials in the administration who believed that a substantial basis for US-PLO negotiations had been created, would increase their influence. Meanwhile, Arab-Americans who are attempting to reduce US support for Israel and gain greater sympathy for the Palestinians would be strengthened in their efforts.

In the American Jewish community, there would be a broadening of dissent as uneasiness with Israeli policy intensified. American Jews would certainly become more worried and significant sectors would gradually become less deeply committed to Israel. Confusion and division would increase; the noise level and media attention would rise. US Jews would begin to see their community as the effective center of world Jewish life, with religious and emotional dependence on Israel decreasing. Involvement in Israel, travel to Israel, and contributions to Israel would slowly decrease over time.

Congress, as usual, would be sensitive to American Jewish attitudes. Assuming the basic continuation of the status quo, there would be a slow increase in murmuring about foreign aid, resulting within a few years in a decline in economic assistance, perhaps of several hundred million dollars. These cuts would be explained as necessitated by Gramm-Rudman strictures, but the real cause would be the erosion of backing for Israeli policies.

The late 1988 "who is a Jew" controversy demonstrates that tensions between American Jews and Israel are possible and could accelerate. They would certainly increase if the law were passed by the Knesset. In turn, if tensions between Israel and the American Jewish community intensified, for whatever reasons, the conflict would be interpreted by both Congress and the administration as a sign of declining domestic support for Israel, thereby increasing the possibility of leverage being exercised on Jerusalem by either or both branches. In this sense, American Jewry has the power to validate a reduction in the support Israel enjoys in Washington.

Thus, as the status quo continues, the possibility of Israel's stature declining would accelerate. The risks entailed were both illustrated and exacerbated by the initiation of the US-PLO dialogue. In general, Israeli insistence on maintaining the status quo while others are perceived as taking reasonable initiatives toward a resolution of the Palestinian-Israeli dispute, risks a further erosion of Israel's image and standing in the United States. Moreover, should Israel continue to refrain from presenting credible alternatives to the status quo, it would risk being presented by Washington with alternatives tailored by others. Israeli rejection of such proposals may strain US-Israeli relations, and Jerusalem's reputation as a peace-loving, democratic state might begin to collapse in the United States.

The extent of the damage would of course depend upon the nature of the Arab initiative and the content and duration of the Israeli response. At a minimum, alongside campus unrest, anti-Israel demonstrations and turmoil in the Jewish community, Congress might well move toward at least a precipitous and symbolic cut in aid to Israel of perhaps several hundred million dollars. Although the same figures might apply in the absence of dramatic Arab moves, this cut would be more likely and more immediate in the wake of Israel's refusal to respond to an Arab peace initiative. Within the administration, officials who had vigorously defended a close relationship with Israel would either lose influence or change their minds. This could be critical in a young presidency, because once positions are taken or power established early in an administration, officials are difficult to dislodge and to dissuade.

There are two conditions under which an Israeli status quo policy would result in a solidifying of the US-Israeli relationship. First, if the current US-PLO dialogue were to break down and result in American disillusionment with the PLO, then the administration's faith in Israeli judgment would be enhanced, although Americans would still be searching for some way to reopen the peace process. Secondly, if the Arabs attacked Israel in an unambiguous way, then Israel would receive widespread and intense bipartisan support. In this case, Israel's insistence on a status quo policy would be seen as justified in most quarters, although there might be isolated grumbling that a more flexible Israeli approach would have avoided conflict. A war that emerged out of a crisis atmosphere and whose precipitator was more ambiguous might yield a more muted American response both on the governmental and popular levels. However, Israel would likely still be regarded as the injured party, unless it was seen as the initiator as in 1982.

Conversely, there is one additional condition within the status quo under which US pressures upon Israel would grow: widespread loss of life. If the victims were Arabs (e.g., Israeli soldiers or settlers massacre Arab villagers), then immediate pressure would descend on the Israeli government. There would be a sense in Washington of "enough is enough." If the victims were Jews, there would be expressions of outrage and sadness from the American government, and public sympathy for the Palestinians would decline. However, there would also be a sense, especially in the Executive Branch, that something must be done; the status quo cannot continue.

Thus, if Israel pursues a status quo policy it will leave the initiative to the Arabs to determine the level of its relations with

Americans — including many American Jews. With the exception of an Arab attack or some large-scale atrocity, a gradual erosion of relations with the United States would occur under this option. The erosion would be accelerated to the extent that a Palestinian peace initiative was widely viewed in America as positive, serious, sincere and helpful.

Still, some basic elements of the American-Israeli "special relationship" would remain intact. US frustration with Israel would grow, especially if the Palestinians were seen as acting positively, but many American leaders would still see Israel in the traditional light of a democratic and vibrant country. More would begin to see her as misguided, which could well lead to an American temptation to deal more energetically with the USSR or to produce a "peace plan" of its own.

If the status quo continues and the Middle East situation deteriorates progressively, a variety of circumstances could encourage the administration to embark on an ambitious peace initiative, perhaps in conjunction with the USSR and even the PLO. The trigger contingencies might include growing understandings with the Soviet Union on regional conflicts, European pressures for action, a Syrian-Israeli crisis or war, widespread casualties in the territories, dramatic progress in the US-PLO dialogue, or a threat to the stability of King Hussein's regime. The Israeli government might oppose the US initiative. Thus, in this case the ultimate result of a status quo policy could be a major deterioration of US-Israel relations.

The Soviet Union

The USSR is not happy with perpetuation of the status quo. It seeks to promote a negotiated settlement. In this sense, Moscow would probably go to some lengths to prevent Syria, its only remaining close ally in the Arab-Israeli sphere, from embarking on a belligerent course. It may even exert pressure on Damascus to step into line with the Soviet view on the issue of a political settlement.

Two major considerations underlie this Soviet position. First, Moscow is keenly aware of Syria's military inferiority vis-a-vis

Israel, and the consequent likelihood of the USSR being drawn into the conflict, with all its adverse implications for Soviet regional and global interests. Secondly, the USSR is reluctant to risk curtailment of the evolving detente in Soviet-American relations.

Gorbachev has carried the Soviet emphasis on the political course a step further, spelling out directly and unequivocally what his predecessors used to imply in more schematic and complex jargon. In Hafiz Assad's two meetings with the Soviet leader (June 1985 and April 1987), the Syrian president learned of Gorbachev's approach. "Reliance on military force in settling the Arab-Israeli conflict has completely lost its credibility," Assad was told by his Soviet counterpart. Gorbachev also dismissed Syria's quest for strategic parity as lacking "any meaning," and as "diverting attention from the question of attaining security and peace in the Middle East."

The Soviet Union is also likely to continue to exert pressure on the PLO to sustain its move toward moderation, so that the PLO can become a full partner to a negotiated settlement of the Arab-Israeli dispute. Moreover the USSR would probably resist any American attempt to monopolize the Arab-Israeli political process. But it would willingly join in an attempt coordinated with it. If in the pre-Gorbachev era the USSR proved willing to cooperate with the United States whenever the latter was ready to bring Moscow into the political process (e.g., arranging Security Council Resolution 242 of November 1967, the Geneva Conference in December 1973, the Vance-Gromyko Statement of 1 October 1977), it is likely to be at least as cooperative at this stage of *perestroika*, which has already generated increased superpower collaboration in dealing with third world conflicts. Without relinquishing the longstanding Soviet desire to get the West out of the Middle East, the Gorbachev years have certainly witnessed a greater rhetorical readiness to cooperate with the US. If translated into action, this could form a better basis for superpower collaboration.

Finally, the continuation of the status quo is unlikely to impede the improvement of Soviet-Israeli relations. Quite the contrary: Moscow's awareness of the damage done to its regional standing by the severance of diplomatic relations with Israel following the June 1967 war has led it to develop direct and indirect channels of

41

communication with Israel and even to make occasional concilia-tory gestures toward it. The scope and intensity of Soviet-Israeli interaction were considerably enhanced after Gorbachev assumed office, culminating in 1987-88 in the posting of Soviet and Israeli consular delegations. Moreover, while condemning the strong measures invoked by Israel against the *intifada*, Moscow has not been deterred from reiterating its willingness to reestablish diplomatic relations with Israel once a negotiating process on an Arab-Israeli settlement is underway within the framework of an international conference.

Thus, unless it deteriorates considerably, the status quo does not threaten to involve the Soviet Union in activity directly and immediately detrimental to Israel.

Conclusions

This option remains feasible for the time being, as it requires no active partners. This in itself is an advantage for Israel's political decisionmakers, particularly if they assess that further waiting by Israel will eventually produce desirable partners for peace, with fewer concessions required. The status quo also offers clear geostrategic advantages for warfighting. While it strengthens the Israeli political camp that favors eventual annexation, there is at least one political lobby in Israel — a portion of the settlers in Judea, Samaria and the Gaza Strip — that prefers this option as a fall-back position. (The settlers assess that annexation, their preferred option, would produce negative internal consequences, principally in their relations with Israeli society-at-large and with the Jewish Diaspora.)

But these advantages are increasingly offset by the negative developments that the status quo generates. Indeed, nearly all indicators point to progressive deterioration in Israel's standing the longer it maintains the status quo, with the *intifada* con-tinuing at its 1988 level or increasing in intensity. The Palestinian Arabs in the West Bank and Gaza are likely to become increasingly radical; Israeli Arabs may begin to move in this direction as well. Israeli internal discontent could grow, breeding political extrem-ism, with highly negative moral ramifications for society. Relations with the US would experience increasing stress, possibly resulting in aid cuts. This is particularly likely should the PLO's political initiatives of late 1988 fail to elicit an appropriate Israeli response. As Israeli deterrence is eroded, and US support decreases, the danger of war could grow, particularly if Iraq were to join an Arab war coalition.

While Israel has continued to register positive progress in its international and strategic relationships even while the *intifada* rages, this has derived not a little from the expectation that Israel would soon (i.e., after the November 1988 elections) take initiatives vis-a-vis the Palestinians, and from the perception of PLO intransigence and overall Arab reluctance to deal with Israel as a political equal. As these images change, Israel's international stock could decline accordingly.

Moreover, the status quo appears to be working to the advantage of the Palestinians' unilateral statebuilding effort; certainly, continuation in one form or another of the *intifada* may produce a kind of de facto Palestinian autonomy, under an indigenous leadership that owes Israel nothing in return for its achievements.

In the short term the most acute determinants of the ramifications of the status quo appear to be the intensity of the *intifada* and Israel's reaction to it, and the degree to which the PLO sustains a moderate political stance acceptable to many Israelis and the US administration. Neither of these variables is wholly under Israel's control. Hence it is difficult to assess whether there is a "breaking point" at which Israel's strategic fortunes would suddenly begin to plummet as a result of adherence to the status quo. Given the fact that the status quo has already proved more resilient than many pessimists predicted at the start of the *intifada*, it may equally be possible to "muddle through" for an undetermined period of time.

On the other hand, it is in the nature of the status quo that it is not permanent. Eventually, it must change, and this probably means for the worse. Meanwhile, the likelihood increases that Israel will be confronted by superpower initiatives potentially detrimental to its interests.

Given these dangers of deterioration, Israel should make a concerted effort to find a viable alternative to the status quo.

Meanwhile, it should search for ways to alleviate the worst effects of the current situation.

II. Option Two — Autonomy

Definition

The autonomy option still officially espoused by the Israeli moderate Right is the version developed by the Begin government on the basis of the Camp David autonomy framework, and presented by Israel in negotiations with Egypt and the US (herein referred to, for the sake of simplicity, as Camp David autonomy). Other Israeli political figures have indicated a willingness to contemplate a far more comprehensive autonomy, but they choose not to enunciate it clearly prior to actual negotiations. In any event, it should be born in mind that autonomy as proposed by Israel was envisaged officially as an interim step, and not a total solution. Further, the options of Camp David autonomy, or a more extensive version, that are described here are negotiated options (with Palestinians, and with the concurrence of Egypt and Jordan). But some or all aspects of autonomy could conceivably be applied unilaterally, without preliminary agreement with the Palestinian residents of the territories.

The varieties of autonomy may be seen as a continuum that comprises four functional variants: the scope of authority delegated by Israel to the Palestinians; the duration of the autonomy period; the extent of territory assigned to the autonomous entity (i.e., whether autonomy would apply to all or part of Judea, Samaria and Gaza); and the degree to which Israel and the Palestinians agree in advance as to the nature of the stage that will follow autonomy. Our analysis of the autonomy option will focus upon three points on this continuum: Camp David autonomy; a more comprehensive autonomy, herein referred to also as "deep autonomy;" and unilaterally-imposed autonomy.

According to the Camp David autonomy that is examined in this option (as interpreted by its Israeli proponents), self-rule would be applied to all the Arab residents of Judea, Samaria and the Gaza District, but not to the land of those territories. Jews living in these areas would not be included in the autonomy, but no additional Israeli settlements would be permitted, and nearly all local matters that involve Arabs exclusively would be managed by the autonomous administration. Issues not subject to that administration would comprise internal and external security (with the exception of a local police force), water resources and state lands, and customs, all of which would remain under Israel's responsibility, and some of which could be subject to joint administration. Israel's military presence in the territories would be reduced to that deemed necessary only for routine security and initial defense against attack. The nature of the autonomy agreement would be such as to permit, after three years of its operation, the convening of new negotiations over the final status of the territories, without prejudging their outcome. In this sense, this is a temporary option — one that does not provide a final settlement for the West Bank and Gaza. Assuming that agreement with Palestinian representatives could not be reached on the final status, autonomy might continue indefinitely.

This is the only option for a Palestinian solution of any kind that has actually been the subject of negotiation between Israel and an Arab partner (Egypt, from 1979 to 1982), and that is still on Israel's political agenda. Hence a brief recapitulation (based on close consultation with Israelis and Americans who were involved in the process) is in order regarding the nature of consensus achieved in those negotiations, and the areas of disagreement.

The central areas of complete agreement were few, and for obvious reasons. Israel's basic concepts for the autonomy held that it would not involve the delineation of borders or the application of sovereignty, and that it would last for a fixed period of time, after which any and all proposals for the next stage could be negotiated. Egypt, in contrast, viewed autonomy as a prelude and a preparatory stage to Palestinian state independence. Hence Israel and Egypt were able to agree in principle only that the autonomy be administered by an elected council, and that it not be granted powers of a sovereign nature. The two sides agreed on a preliminary basis to the concept that the autonomy council could, under certain circumstances, legislate alterations in existing laws. Israel also agreed not to increase its exploitation of West Bank water resources, and that the autonomy council would control the use of private lands.

46

But Israel and Egypt were unable to agree on a wide variety of issues that touched upon their fundamental concepts of the autonomy. The United States, in a conciliatory role, often proposed compromise formulae. These too were rejected by both parties in the course of three years of negotiation, although it is not inconceivable that both sides would ultimately have accepted them had they neared agreement in principle. The principal areas of disagreement comprised the following:

— Israel sought to give the autonomy council minimal administrative authority; it would be a 15-person executive. Egypt called for a 100-member body with maximum authority, including the right to legislate. The US compromise proposal suggested a 50-member council.

— Israel interpreted literally the phrase "autonomy for the inhabitants" in the Camp David framework, while Egypt pointed to the phrase "full autonomy" as referring to the territory of the West Bank and Gaza, and not just the inhabitants.

— Israel insisted that its military government remain the ultimate source of authority during the autonomy period, even if the government apparatus were no longer physically present in the territories, and that the scope of the autonomy's jurisdiction be defined in advance; Egypt wished to transfer the source of authority to the autonomy council, to cancel the military government, and to leave the scope of jurisdiction open. The US suggested that the autonomy agreement become the source of authority.

— Israel proposed a measure of joint control over water resources and state lands, and demanded exclusive control over immigration of Jews and Arabs into the autonomous region; Egypt demanded that control over these realms be assigned to the autonomy authorities. The US proposed joint control over water and immigration, and distribution of the state lands between the autonomy authority and Israeli settlements and security installations.

— Israel wished to exclude East Jerusalem Arab residents from the autonomy, while Egypt wished to include them; the

US proposed to permit the East Jerusalem Arabs to participate in elections for the autonomy council.

— Finally, with respect to the Camp David agreements' stipulation that Israel be responsible for external security, and that its forces be removed from the cities and be deployed in agreed security zones, Israel insisted on its ongoing authority to move its forces at will within the West Bank and Gaza; Egypt insisted that any Israeli force movements within the autonomous region be subject to the approval of the autonomy council. The US suggested that only Israeli troop movements for the purpose of countering an external military threat be subject to exclusive Israeli decision.

All this, during nearly three years of negotiations that did not even involve Palestinian representatives (who refused to participate).

In assessing the option of Camp David autonomy, we assume that Israel would continue to pursue an autonomy of the nature it proposed in these abortive negotiations — with possible modifications in the direction of the American compromise proposals. This would reflect a number of considerations. For one, Israel could argue that this is the only framework for a Palestinian settlement recognized by international treaty, i.e., the Camp David Accords (though the other signatories, Egypt and the US, interpret the autonomy provisions differently). Indeed, an Israeli government might even argue that it is *bound* to pursue this course. As a corollary, this autonomy framework offers legitimization for Israel's presence in the territories, and for its ultimate right to claim sovereignty. Lastly, this proposal defers any decision about the ultimate fate of the West Bank and Gaza Strip for a number of years, during which an Israeli government might reason that it could improve its overall position, while in the short term it was not relinquishing any land of Greater Israel to Arab rule.

As for the circumstances in which this variety of autonomy might be applied, the fact that it was once the subject of serious, though abortive, negotiation among Israel, Egypt and the US suggests that these political conditions could conceivably repeat themselves. This does not seem likely, however. Indeed, even the Egyptians — the only Arab party that agreed to discuss Israel's autonomy proposals — have declared repeatedly in recent years that Camp David autonomy is a dead letter.

The variety of comprehensive or deep autonomy analyzed here would differ from Camp David autonomy in a number of significant aspects. In terms of delegation of authority, it would offer the Palestinians extended self-rule, including such national symbols as a flag and anthem — though without any implication of automatic genuine sovereignty; control over all state lands not occupied by the IDF or by Jewish settlements; and joint control (with Israel) over water, customs and immigration (of Jews and Arabs). The autonomy agreement itself would be the source of authority. In all other aspects this deep autonomy would be similar to the Camp David variety: it would apply to all Palestinians throughout the territories; negotiations regarding the final status of the territories would be postponed to a predetermined date, whereupon it would have to be agreed on by both sides; and IDF deployment would remain the same.

Finally, the concept of unilaterally-imposed autonomy implies that Israel would, of its own volition and without negotiating the issue with Palestinian Arabs, withdraw its administrative facilities and services from specified locales and permit resident Palestinians to establish and administer their own, alternative facilities, while retaining the right to intervene or restore the status quo ante if it judged that these provisions were being abused. Proposals along these lines have been voiced in Israel from time to time — initially by the late Moshe Dayan. They reflect an assessment that the absence of a negotiating partner should not prevent Israel from taking steps that, on the one hand, would reduce day-to-day frictions and, on the other, might stimulate the emergence of a pragmatic de facto local Palestinian leadership.

In assessing the ramifications of the first two variants of autonomy — the Camp David variety, and comprehensive or deep autonomy — we have assumed that they would only come into existence as a consequence of negotiations with Palestinians. This, in turn, predicates a large measure of ongoing Palestinian collaboration in applying autonomy, which is assumed to be forthcoming as long as the Palestinians estimate that there is a good chance they will achieve independence at the conclusion of the autonomy stage.

Ramifications

The Palestinians

Unlike the status quo, Camp David autonomy holds out the prospect for a change in the political status of West Bank and Gaza Arabs. However the prospect is faint when contrasted to the Palestinians' objective of political independence. Indeed, most Palestinians perceive autonomy as a way of legitimizing perpetual Israeli control rather than ending it. They are therefore either hostile to autonomy or, at best, so indifferent that they would not consider it worth making political concessions. Nearly all Palestinians opposed Camp David autonomy when it was proposed and negotiated with Egypt. The PLO has consistently rejected autonomy, and has been supported in this stand by nearly all the Arab states (with the partial and transitory exception of Egypt). The PNC's declaration of independence in November 1988 renders it even less likely that the Palestinians would accept anything but an extremely comprehensive autonomy that could be nearly equated with statehood, and this only as an interim stage prior to guaranteed independence.

Palestinian opposition to an attempt to negotiate (or impose) autonomy would probably find expression in increased terrorism against Israelis as well as Palestinian collaborationists. It might also spill over into the international arena, where one prime target would be American citizens and institutions — assuming the US were involved in autonomy negotiations. Inside the territories, much of the terrorism aimed at torpedoing autonomy is likely to express intra-Palestinian rivalries, as collaboration by residents of the territories with the autonomy's implementation would probably intensify friction among the local population, as well as between the various Palestinian organizations. But outside the territories, terrorism aimed at undermining the autonomy agreement is likely to be orchestrated and implemented by radical elements supported by Syria.

Alternatively, it is possible to describe circumstances (widespread international and Arab consensus on the merits of autonomy, debilitation of the PLO, ruthless Israeli military and economic pressure leading to utter despair in the territories) that might induce West Bank and Gaza Arabs to agree to autonomy even though it was perceived as being aimed at perpetuating Israeli control. Even in that case, however, the agreement would only be honored until the Palestinians had recovered enough to launch a new struggle for complete independence. Besides, the likelihood that such circumstances would materialize is extremely low; even if this were to happen, it is doubtful that the Palestinians would prefer autonomy to the status quo. In any case, and barring such developments, any type of open-ended autonomy is virtually certain to be rejected by the PLO, and there is no real prospect that other Palestinians would act to defy the PLO.

From the Palestinian standpoint, then, Camp David autonomy is only conceivable if imposed unilaterally by Israel, through the withdrawal of Israeli administrative services from Arab-populated parts of the territories. Assuming this were tried, it is highly unlikely that local Palestinians would cooperate in good faith. On the contrary, the situation would probably be exploited by the PLO and local Palestinian leaders to attempt to expand the autonomy into independence, while posing an international challenge to Israel's continued authority: areas designated by Israel for unilateral autonomy would declare themselves liberated zones, hoist the Palestinian flag, announce that they constituted territory of the independent Palestinian state declared by the PNC in November 1988, and ask for international recognition. Vestiges of Israeli administration would be boycotted. Attempts by Israel to reassert control would make a mockery of its experiment in autonomy, and/or escalate Jewish-Arab friction and sully Israel's image in a way that suits Palestinian aims.

Of course, this scenario of Palestinian exploitation of autonomy for more far-reaching aims is applicable to the case of negotiated autonomy as well as imposed autonomy. Ostensibly this should encourage mainstream Palestinians to agree to negotiate even the most meager autonomy with Israel, with the objective of exploiting it for their own aims. But the risk that things could turn out otherwise is not one that Palestinians appear ready to take.

From the standpoint of Palestinian reaction, then, narrow autonomy of the variety proposed in the past by Israel, and unilaterally-imposed autonomy, offer Israel no advantages — and present a minefield of disadvantages and potential complications. Deep autonomy might be more attractive insofar as it offered Palestinians more accouterments of sovereignty, such as the symbols of statehood and greater authority for the autonomy council, as a starting point. This might also reduce the likelihood of extremist Palestinian terrorism against Israel. But the open-ended nature of this arrangement mitigates against the emergence of any radically different Palestinian approach to it.

Israeli Arabs

The attitude of Israeli Arabs toward Camp David autonomy was tested in the late 1970s, following the signing of the Camp David accords. The radical camp adopted the stand of the PLO and other Arab states and rejected the autonomy; moderate Israeli Arabs maintained a studied silence. There is no evidence to indicate a positive change in attitudes since then; on the contrary, the *intifada* has caused positions to harden. Hence, as long as the PLO and Jordan reject Israel's offer of limited autonomy, not even moderate Israeli Arabs would concur with the offer. Radical and nationalist Israeli Arab factions would probably not alter their negative position unless the Soviet Union and additional Arab states endorsed limited autonomy.

If, however, circumstances were to cause the Palestinians to embrace a limited autonomy offer, Israeli Arabs too would be accepting, since they see as their basic interest the resolution of the issue to the satisfaction of the Palestinians. In any case, the radical and extreme nationalist factions among Israeli Arabs would maintain their advocacy of a Palestinian state in the entire Land of Israel, although the onset of autonomy as a transition stage might cause them to reduce their political activity. Meanwhile the moderates would be spurred on to register parallel gains in their drive for greater civil equality. In this way greater moderation in the national sphere could be accompanied by heightened tension at the internal civil level. Certainly there is little likelihood that Palestinian autonomy would produce a cogent Israeli Arab demand for autonomy; Israeli Arabs recognize that this would be a non-starter — indeed, counterproductive — among the Jewish public.

The unilateral imposition of limited autonomy by Israeli authorities would be met by Israeli Arab unrest and opposition — in effect, an extension of the radicalization process described in analyzing the status quo.

As for deep autonomy, to the extent that it contained genuine elements of self-rule and prospects for further progress, it would have a moderating effect on radical and nationalist activity in the Israeli Arab community. At the same time, the moderates' struggle for greater civil rights could be expected to intensify, with Israeli Arabs possibly uniting all their political movements under a single organizational or party framework. This development could be mitigated were Israel to accelerate the integration of Israeli Arabs into the mainstream of society.

The Arab States

Syria is likely to oppose any option based on a Jordanian and/or Palestinian agreement that does not address its own territorial and ideological concerns and that is seen as conceding fundamental Arab positions in the Arab-Israel conflict. Hence Damascus would probably adopt a number of tactics aimed at torpedoing this option: a low-level terrorist campaign against Jordanian targets in Jordan and abroad; the creation of tension along the Israeli-Lebanese border through the use of Syria's proxies there; an escalation of tensions along the Syrian-Jordanian and Syrian-Israeli borders; and, finally, concerted military and political pressure against Palestinian factions that cooperated in the establishment of the autonomy, and vigorous support for Palestinian leaders and groups who would oppose implementation of the option.

Obviously, this attitude would apply to all variants of autonomy. But the more limited were the autonomy, the greater would be Syria's chances of success in recruiting Palestinian opposition. Syria's reaction to unilateral autonomy would also be negative, though not necessarily aggressive. Most likely, Syria would maintain a position of vigilance and try to prevent informal Jordanian-Israeli understandings from developing too far. The emergence in the territories of some sort of Israeli-Jordanian condominium might well result in a PLO-Syrian rapprochement, which would give added legitimacy to whatever reactions Syria might take. Heightened Palestinian resistance to unilateral autonomy would also serve Syrian interests.

Here it must be noted that Jordan in any event regards Camp David autonomy as a non-starter. Its reasons for rejecting the original invitation to participate in Camp David autonomy talks would presumably remain valid: the PLO must be legitimized and give its consent to an autonomy process. Besides, Jordan would continue to fear Syrian pressure. Clearly, the deeper the autonomy and the more Palestinians endorsed it, the more favorable it would appear in Jordanian eyes. On the other hand, to the extent that the autonomy were perceived as but a prelude to Palestinian independence, Jordan might fear the consequences in terms of incitement of its own Palestinian population. Nevertheless, it would have little choice but to go along with this option.

Were Israel to impose autonomy unilaterally, Jordan would not endorse such a regime, and it would continue to press for the end of Israeli occupation. Israel could nonetheless seek to win quiet Jordanian cooperation for a condominium-like arrangement, expanding on the informal Jordanian-Israeli understandings that existed in the past. This would have several advantages for Jordan. It would enhance its influence in the territories while enabling it to check, together with Israel, the more assertive varieties of Palestinian nationalism there. And such an arrangement would place Jordan in an advantageous position in anticipation of any future negotiations over the final status of the territories. However this could come about only after a major decline in the *intifada*, coupled with widespread disappointment with the PLO. Yet even in the event of a decline in the uprising and disappointment with the PLO, some Palestinians would look not to Jordan, but to militant Islamic groups for help.

Just as likely, however, is the possibility that the imposition of unilateral autonomy would lead to heightened Palestinian resistance, thereby potentially widening the conflict, to Jordan's detriment.

Egypt would be hard put not to accept Camp David autonomy, provided it were implemented in cooperation with Jordan and the Palestinians. But Egypt's recognition of the PLO's declaration of independence in November 1988 means that, at the very least Egypt, like Jordan, would press for a more comprehensive autonomy. Egypt would probably oppose unilateral autonomy on the grounds that it indicated Israel's intent to permanently control the territories. But Cairo would also continue to work for the convening of an international conference to determine the final status of the territories, and would try to encourage a joint Jordanian-Palestinian stance; meanwhile its relations with Israel might not deteriorate. However in the event of heightened Palestinian resistance to the imposition of autonomy, Egyptian-Israeli relations would deteriorate.

Libya and (non-Arab) Iran are likely to ally themselves with Syria's efforts to torpedo the implementation of a negotiated autonomy regime, whatever its nature. Libya's capacity to contribute to an Arab attempt to prevent negotiations or implementation is likely to manifest itself primarily in the realm of international terrorism. Iraq and Saudi Arabia would probably endorse an agreed autonomy, and would seek to avoid being dragged into Syrian-initiated hostilities. None of these peripheral Arab states is likely to alter its current position — whether antagonistic or moderate — in the event of Israel's imposition of unilateral autonomy, unless it resulted in increased Israeli-Palestinian violence, in which case the probability of the formation of a general Arab war coalition would increase as well.

Israel's Security

Assuming that the IDF's order of battle in the West Bank and Gaza remained unchanged following the establishment of auton-

55

omy, the security risks entailed in Camp David autonomy, deep autonomy or unilateral autonomy would be minimal. At the strategic level, two factors are likely to limit the risks. First, the autonomy option is unlikely to alter existing alignments in the Arab world. Hence, a broad Arab war coalition would probably not emerge. Secondly, as long as the mainstream Palestinian organizations assessed that the mechanism of successful autonomy would enable them to accumulate credit toward the future establishment of an independent state, their actions would be directed at ensuring stable relations between the autonomy and Israel. However if the arrangement — Camp David autonomy or comprehensive autonomy — "went sour," or alternatively, if it expired without generating movement toward a new agreed political status for the territories, then the Palestinians would likely renew their uprising. Similar consequences are likely to follow the unilateral imposition of autonomy.

At the operational level, four additional premises underlie the expectation that the risks entailed in the establishment of any type of autonomy would be minimal. For one, Israel would remain responsible for external security. Quite possibly, at least during an initial interim period, Israel would remain in charge of internal security as well — until the autonomy's self- governing authority were capable of assuming this role. Then too, Israel would evacuate and transfer to the autonomy's self- governing authority facilities and territories currently held by the IDF that are deemed not essential to its missions. This would help reduce possible friction between the IDF and the emerging autonomy. Third, Jewish settlements in the West Bank and Gaza would remain intact and Israel would continue to be responsible for the safety of the settlements, their residents, and the roads leading to them (although obviously this arrangement could create or perpetuate friction between the settlers and the local Arab population). Finally, the IDF would maintain its prepositioning facilities in the West Bank, its firing ranges in the Jordan Valley, and its exclusive control over West Bank airspace, including the right to overfly the West Bank.

Syria and the Palestinian rejectionists would have a strong incentive to prevent implementation of this option. Syria would fear that the option would isolate it and doom its claim to the Golan Heights to oblivion. The rejectionists among the Palestinians would not accept the option under any circumstances because this would require giving up the hope of ever realizing their vision of Greater Palestine.

Israel's security forces would have no real problem in suppressing the resistance of extremist Palestinian elements. Hence, the latter are likely to have little impact on the process of implementing the agreement, unless, perhaps, they succeeded in assassinating key Palestinian autonomy leaders. As for Syria, it is bound to judge that the risks involved in launching war under this option are considerable. As it is consistent with the spirit if not the letter of Camp David, the implementation of negotiated autonomy would strengthen Egyptian-Israeli ties, thus clearly diminishing any possible hope Syria had of implicating Egypt in a war against Israel. More generally, as existing alignments in the Arab world are unlikely to be affected by the establishment of autonomy, Syria would likely calculate that it might have to bear the burden of battling Israel alone. At best, Damascus might expect assistance from an Iraqi expeditionary force — an unlikely prospect in the event that Syria launched a war on its own.

Also, with autonomy established, the IDF would be freed of the burdens of the *intifada*, and thus would be better positioned to deal with a Syrian challenge. Finally, to Syria's detriment, Israel's international standing would be much improved if any variety of negotiated autonomy were implemented, thus increasing its odds of obtaining external political-military support against Syrian aggression. Under these conditions, Syria's ability to prevail militarily would be extremely limited. Nevertheless, threatened with isolation if autonomy were implemented, Syria might launch military action — designed to induce a political process — even if the operation were to fail militarily. The Soviets' position on this matter would probably be an important factor in Syria's decision to launch or refrain from such action. In the near term, Moscow is likely to continue to play a restraining role vis-a-vis the Damascus regime.

The Israeli Domestic Setting

Negotiated autonomy is, on balance, the most acceptable option to all Israelis. Neither hawks nor doves would be enthusiastic over it, but most of the public could manage with it, whatever their doubts and suspicions. For doves, it offers the advantage of detaching Israel and the IDF from responsibility for directly administering the lives of 1.5 million Palestinians. Hawks recognize in autonomy the possibility of avoiding transfer of sovereignty over any part of Greater Israel, while retaining all or most of their settlement enterprise in the territories. Broad Israeli public approval of the Camp David agreements also renders autonomy more acceptable. The Likud is officially committed to Camp David autonomy, which is considered by many to be the political legacy of Menachem Begin, hence a rallying point for a national consensus. Even a settlement based on comprehensive autonomy is perceived to fall within the Camp David framework. Labor, too, sees autonomy as a viable and legitimate option.

Reservations regarding autonomy on Israel's political extremes derive from radically different perceptions. The Far Right — Moledet, Tsomet, Tehiya, Gush Emunim, and some elements within the Likud — together with some Labor activists, view the autonomy plan as a sure prescription for the eventual establishment of a Palestinian state in the entire area of Judea, Samaria and Gaza, that would threaten the very existence of the State of Israel. In contrast, the Zionist Far Left is opposed to autonomy as a long-range alternative to an agreed territorial settlement because it considers autonomy as a prescription for continued Israeli rule over the Arab population in the territories. It would probably approve of an autonomy accepted by the Palestinians that guaranteed the future establishment of a Palestinian state, and be more accepting of deep autonomy than of Camp David autonomy.

Under conditions prevailing in late 1988, for any autonomy to be acceptable to a large portion of the Israeli public, it would have to satisfy a number of demands. Strong safeguards against a transformation of the autonomy into independent statehood would have to be built into the agreement; these should consist of American commitments, along with continued IDF and General

Security Service presence. Indeed, Israelis would insist on being able to rely on Israeli forces to come to the immediate aid of endangered Jewish settlers in the territories. Israel would not agree to rely on a Palestinian police force to defend the settlers.

In looking at the prospect of deep autonomy, to the extent that it were seen by Israelis as constituting a prelude to Palestinian independence, most would probably reject it. If, however, the autonomy agreement were to include provisions allowing for its extension over a relatively extended period of time, it might be more appealing to Israelis, insofar as they would see in the passage of time an additional safeguard and test of Palestinian intentions. Nor could deep autonomy involve any substantial reduction in Jewish settlements in the territories. The removal, say, of the small Jewish settlement in the heart of Arab Hebron, and the consolidation of small and isolated settlements, would probably be tolerable even to a portion of the settler public. Still, some settlers might resort to violence to try to prevent the application of autonomy.

Israelis, incidentally, would be more likely to accept autonomy that reflects a genuine, perceived readiness on the part of the Palestinians to abandon armed struggle and move toward a peace agreement and the eventual settlement of all outstanding problems, including the Palestine refugee question. Here they would be influenced by the declarations of Palestinian leaders themselves, as well as reactions on the Arab street, both in the territories and in Israel, and the position of the surrounding Arab states. Therefore autonomy negotiated with a lone moderate Palestinian faction would be less acceptable.

The IDF would find this option advantageous insofar as the army would be able to divest itself of its administrative functions vis-a-vis the Palestinian Arab population, and concentrate on military preparedness proper. But to the extent that the application of autonomy were not accepted by the Palestinian population — particularly in the case of unilaterally-imposed autonomy, but also in the event that a negotiated autonomy agreement began to unravel — it would involve the army in heavier anti-terrorist and riot-control duty, rendering the imposition of autonomy disadvantageous. And to the extent it were opposed by Jewish settlers and their supporters, the army would clash with them. These, in turn, would affect IDF morale and motivation.

In sum, of all the compromise settlements, negotiated autonomy appears to be the most acceptable to the Israeli public. Most of the disadvantages are tactical in nature, and might find compensation in the modalities of the autonomy agreement. But to the extent that deep autonomy were seen by Israelis as constituting a prelude to Palestinian independence, or independence in disguise, most would probably reject it. As for unilaterally-imposed autonomy, it would be judged largely along security parameters: if it were seen as a successful method of guaranteeing peace and quiet and possibly improving Arab-Jewish relations in the territories, it would be approved of; if, on the other hand, it were perceived to be a precursor to greater friction, it would be rejected by the Israeli public. However, as long as the public felt certain that unilateral autonomy could, if it failed, be reversed unilaterally, it would not oppose a government proposal along these lines.

Demography, Geography and Economy

To the extent that the autonomy agreement could be predicated as a transition stage toward some future status of greater Palestinian independence, its application (by the Camp David agreements) to all the Palestinians of Judea, Samaria and the Gaza District is highly disadvantageous to Israel from a geographic standpoint. For the post-autonomy stage could be inferred to apply to all the territory of these areas. By returning to the pre-1967 Green Line boundaries, Israel would forfeit control over catchment basins of groundwater resources located in the Samarian and Judean foothills just a few kilometers east of the Green Line, that are vital to its economy. In this sense Camp David autonomy, if carried to its logical conclusion, is geographically detrimental to Israel.

Implementation of limited autonomy without a corresponding attempt to deal with the Palestinians' growing economic and social problems would generate a degree of internal instability in the autonomy that would quickly redound on the stability of the agreement. The current rapid rate of population growth would have to be matched by employment opportunities; lack of natural resources and agricultural land would have to be balanced by large-scale investment. This implies the need for participation in an autonomy agreement by interested third parties capable of shouldering this burden.

Under limited autonomy, the borders with Israel would remain open to the movement of workers and goods. Israel would control water resources, state-owned lands, immigration and customs. The autonomy authorities would have to develop the public sector of the territories on their own; they would have to rely on the Israeli and Jordanian financial systems in raising capital for the public and private sectors. Hence they would find it difficult to develop agriculture, absorb educated workers from the Palestinian diaspora, defend infant industries (which require tariff barriers), encourage investment in new industries and develop export markets.

Under expanded autonomy, on the other hand, control of water, immigration and customs would be shared by Israel and the autonomy authorities. As a result, the autonomy would be able to secure at least partial control over its economic future. Nevertheless it would still face considerable difficulties in developing the public and industrial sectors.

The economic implications for Israel would depend somewhat on the definition of autonomy. Limited autonomy, with borders open to the free flow of goods and workers, would reduce the potential damage to the Israeli economy to a minimum. Under expanded autonomy Israel might be obliged to make costly concessions on water allocation. However the cumulative net effect of the economic implications of this option with regard to Israel would be positive. Relocation of military installations would not be so extensive as to be prohibitive. As a consequence of Israel's improved international standing, foreign debt per capita would continue to decline, and Israel's GNP would likely continue to rise, as would private consumption.

The United States

Under a Camp-David style autonomy that was arranged by agreement between Israel and Arab parties, American-Israeli relations would be enhanced. This alternative has, in principle, long been favored by successive American governments and would likely come about after a period of strong US advocacy. It appeals to an American sense of justice and fair play. Although there might be individuals on the Right who thought Israel had made too many concessions and some on the Left who continued to advocate an independent Palestinian state, sentiment in the United States would be overwhelmingly positive from all sectors of both polity and society. Aid from the United States and from other countries to assist in the implementation of the agreement would be made available. If the agreement began to deteriorate because of what was perceived in Washington as Arab obduracy, the US-Israeli relationship would be further strengthened.

The most likely conceivable case in which tension with Israel might arise under autonomy would be a situation in which problems occurred in enacting the agreement and Israel was seen to be at fault. But there are alternative scenarios in response to which Israel might take unilateral action opposed by the US administration. Perhaps the cycle of violence and oppression was continuing. Or the government in Jerusalem might conclude that the Palestinians were moving too far in the direction of political independence and were violating the autonomy agreement. Alternatively, the Israelis and the Palestinian autonomy regime could become engaged in a vehement debate over water resource disposition or migration issues. Even here, however, unless the Israelis were seen as having acted capriciously and irresponsibly, there would be a degree of sympathy for their position in the American political system, notwithstanding inevitable criticism in newspaper columns and within the executive branch.

Americans would be prejudiced in favor of any agreement reached between Israel and an Arab party, no matter how such an accord compromised individual pet theories espoused beforehand. In the past, official US spokesmen have shown an interest in solutions that look into alternative forms of national sovereignty.

Thus the United States would view comprehensive autonomy more positively than limited autonomy. Indeed, the more comprehensive conception is closer to the type of autonomy America has supported since Camp David.

Official US spokesmen have repeatedly stated their opposition to unilateral autonomy, arguing that it would contradict the spirit and the letter of the Camp David Accords. The US might support unilateral actions by Israel, but only if they were seen as conducive to the peace process. However, in the aftermath of the initiation of a US-PLO dialogue in mid-December 1988, Washington might view an Israeli attempt to impose autonomy as an effort to derail that dialogue. A hostile Arab response, including widespread unrest in the territories, would probably accentuate the negative American response.

The Soviet Union

When the autonomy idea was raised by Israel during the peace negotiations with Egypt in the late 1970s, it was vehemently rejected by the USSR for two major reasons. In the first place, since the autonomy plan fell short of giving the Palestinians full self-determination, it was interpreted by the Soviets as a manipulative attempt to perpetuate Israeli rule over the territories. On a more immediate level, the circumstances in which the idea was raised were most unfavorable from Moscow's point of view: a process of bilateral Israeli-Egyptian negotiations under American auspices, from which the USSR and its Arab allies were totally excluded.

Against this backdrop, it is highly doubtful whether the Soviets would support any autonomy plan regarding the territories — particularly one presented as a unilateral Israeli initiative. Given the widespread institutionalization of public recognition of the Palestinians' right for a state of their own, and Moscow's own recognition of the PNC's declaration of Palestinian independence in November 1988, the Soviets could hardly afford to back down from an idea that they were among the first to support. Yet if the Arab side (first and foremost, the PLO) were to accept the autonomy idea as an *interim stage* on the road to an independent

63

state, the Soviets might back such a position. Indeed, a salient theme in Soviet policy statements during the Gorbachev years has been the declared readiness to abide by any decision taken by the Palestinians regarding both the form of their representation in an international peace conference and the nature of the newly established entity.

Conclusions

Of the three options involving a negotiated solution with an Arab partner analyzed in this report (autonomy, a Palestinian state, and a Jordanian-Palestinian federation), negotiated autonomy is the most acceptable to Israelis, and the least dangerous politically and militarily; Israeli Arabs would not adopt positions detrimental to implementation of this option; it is satisfactory from a military strategic standpoint, and problems of security and counter-terrorism could be addressed more easily than under alternative options that involve territorial compromise. But its greatest immediate advantage as perceived by many Israelis (as they define this option) — the fact that it leaves open the ultimate status of the territories — is precisely its primary disadvantage for the Palestinians.

However applicable this option may or may not appear to be, it does not offer a solution to the Palestinian problem. Moreover, it is unacceptable to the Palestinians as even a minimal solution, and could backfire on Israel if imposed upon them unilaterally.

Autonomy is only feasible, and productive for Israel, with an amenable Palestinian negotiating partner. Under present circumstances the PLO would not countenance this option — in either its Camp David or its "deep" variant — unless Israel agreed in advance to end autonomy and proceed, within a fixed period of time, to the independence which the PLO has already declared. This, a considerable portion of the Israeli public fears to do. Moreover the Palestinians might find comprehensive or deep autonomy particularly objectionable insofar as it is predicated upon a more extended autonomy period, yet with no greater promise of eventual independence. Nor would the Soviet Union and most Arab states endorse anything less than an autonomy plan with a guarantee of independence after a fixed period of time.

There are two sets of circumstances that might alter this stance: First, were the Palestinians to assess that they had no realistic alternative, even in the long run. But even if the *intifada* were crushed successfully, it does not seem likely that Palestinians would prefer limited Camp David autonomy to the status quo. Secondly, were autonomy to be defined in relatively broad terms that in many ways approximated sovereignty, with some provision made for possible genuine sovereignty within a fixed period of time, the Palestinians might be more forthcoming. But this last nuance goes beyond even our definition of deep autonomy.

III. Option Three—Annexation

Definition

Annexation implies a unilateral Israeli act of Knesset to apply Israeli law to Judea, Samaria and Gaza, or parts of these territories, following the pattern of the East Jerusalem (1967) and Golan (1981) laws. In view of the presence of over 1.5 million Palestinians in these territories, Israel would have to decide upon their status: here the variations run along a continuum from the granting of full citizenship rights, at one extreme, to deportation ("transfer") at the other. Median possibilities would comprise the granting of limited civil rights, the imposition of some form of autonomy, or the imposition of a military government similar to that maintained among Israel's Arab community from 1948 to 1964.

Annexation is technically feasible; Israel requires no partners to carry it out. If it could be sustained over time, it might formalize Israel's strategic military and demographic presence throughout the Land of Israel — in effect, fulfilling the commitment to Greater Israel. It would also tie the hands of future leaders who might wish, or be forced, to negotiate a compromise peace settlement.

Israel might choose this option if the situation in the territories became unbearable due to Palestinian violence, and it assessed that the only options available were annexation or unilateral withdrawal. Israel's leaders might be motivated to carry out annexation by a perception — not necessarily anchored in reality — that the world was preoccupied by some other major event, and the superpowers and Arab world were too divided, and distracted, to react. Alternatively, an extreme right wing Israeli government that was pledged to a platform of annexation might carry it out regardless of internal or external circumstances. Finally, an Israeli government might opt for this measure if it assessed that the United States, in collaboration with the PLO, the USSR and Arab states, were about to introduce a solution that Israel could not tolerate.

Ultimately, as a consequence of annexation, demographic realities might force even those Israelis who oppose transfer in principle, to weigh it as a possible practical means of guaranteeing the ongoing existence of a Jewish state in Greater Israel. Hence the issue of transfer is discussed in this chapter, although obviously some forms of it could be contemplated within the framework of alternative options. The ramifications of unilaterally-imposed autonomy are addressed in chapter II. The problems of some form of continued military government for the West Bank and Gaza Arabs are addressed here, as are the ramifications of granting citizenship or civil rights.

The act of transfer assessed here is assumed to encompass hundreds of thousands of Palestinian Arabs. Transfer, as envisaged by its advocates, could take a number of forms. It could follow a war initiated by Syria in which the Palestinians in the territorieŝ sought to play an active role. Secondly, it could be a seemingly unprovoked act, reflecting a deliberate Israeli government decision. Third, in a non-war situation, it could involve a policy of mass expulsions in retaliation for a major challenge to Israeli authority in the territories. Fourth, Israel could seek to create such unbearable "ghetto" conditions of daily life in the territories that many inhabitants would "choose" to leave.

Finally, the advocates of transfer also suggest that it could be embodied in an agreement with Arab states to resolve the refugee problem and to eliminate the refugee camps. This sort of resettlement program is not considered as transfer. It must be dealt with separately, as a very necessary component of a peace settlement.

Ramifications

The Palestinians

Palestinians outside the territories would react to annexation with outrage. A political campaign would be launched to galvanize worldwide condemnation of Israel, and sanctions against it. In Lebanon, PLO militias might exploit the opportunity to make a concerted effort to reassert their dominance in that country and to step up attacks against Israel and Israeli targets abroad. Palestinians in the West Bank and Gaza would have a wide range of responses — from physical resistance, all the way to an attempt to embrace annexation, raise demands for full political equality within Israel, and achieve such extensive political power that they could transform Israel into a binational state as a first stage toward Palestinian dominance.

Indifference is hardly likely. Acceptance and peaceful political participation are at least theoretically possible, based on the precedent of Israeli Arabs after 1949, and the assessment of a few Palestinian intellectuals that the best way to undermine Israel is from within. Yet this stretches the limits of credibility: citizenship on a large scale would not likely be offered by an Israeli government; if it were, its acceptance would smack of capitulation, and even those few who might contemplate the possibility would be deterred by threats of others, inside and outside the territories. Thus the most likely prospect would be for more intense resistance, whether or not the annexation was accompanied by some cantonal plan (identical to "unilateral autonomy").

An attempt by Israel to implement transfer — even in the unlikely event that some neighboring state were willing to accept mass deportees — would encounter physical resistance on the part of Palestinians, and would therefore require the application of massive and continuous force. This is primarily because the Palestinians are aware of their own history. They know from the experience of those who left in 1948 and, to a lesser extent in 1967, that their departure would not be temporary and that what awaited them at the end of the road would not necessarily be more attractive. To the extent that there were any coordination of Palestinian resistance, its purpose would be to prolong the evacuation process and bring domestic Israeli and international political pressures into play before the territories had been completely cleared of Arabs. It is therefore conceivable that a transfer policy, once invoked, might fail to achieve the goal of physically removing the Palestinians.

Resistance to annexation, to say nothing of transfer, would expand the *intifada* from parameters of civil disobedience and rockthrowing, to armed attacks by Palestinians on Israeli civilian targets. Palestinian terrorism would involve cross-border penetrations encouraged by neighboring Arab states. It would be directed at moderate local Arab leaders, as well. Terrorism in the case of annexation would be dominated by the organizations: the radicals, as well as centrist members of the PLO. All self-imposed constraints related to considerations of public image and political costs would be dropped. Individual acts of terrorism would proliferate. Palestinians who had exercised restraint under the status quo in the hope of political gain, would now abandon caution. General Palestinian anger at annexation would make recruitment to terrorist organizations easier. Logistic constraints would then comprise the only factor limiting the level of terrorism in all arenas, including the international scene.

Annexation, then, implies for Israel heightened Palestinian resistance. Transfer offers Israel a strategic advantage with regard to the Palestinians, in the sense that it physically removes them. But the long term ramification of this option is that the Israeli-Palestinian conflict would be removed yet further from its communal parameters and implanted more decisively on the inter-Arab stage — thereby raising the specter of war between Israel and an Arab war coalition.

Israeli Arabs

Annexation of the administered territories conflicts with the interests of Israeli Arabs. Annexation is tantamount to perpetuation of the conflict, whereas most Israeli Arabs seek termination of the conflict through an agreed political solution.

In general, virtually all Israeli Arab factions would respond to annexation by supporting the position of the Arabs in the territories; subsequently they might push for granting them full political rights, followed perhaps by a struggle for the establishment of a Palestinian state within the boundaries of the 1947 Partition Resolution (unless the PLO had categorically abandoned this goal). Were Israel to impose upon the Palestinians some form of genuine self-rule, Israeli Arab radicals might well insist on similar rights for Israeli Arabs.

All Israeli Arab political groups would probably act to form a single Arab political lobby in the Knesset and a supreme leadership representing the different strata of Arab society, based on the infrastructure of the already existing Follow-up Committee. Alternatively, finding this ineffective, they might boycott the Knesset and elections entirely, and transfer their activity to the street or to the underground. The radical and extreme nationalist camps, who would probably gain majority influence under these circumstances, could resort to political subversion, sporadic terrorist activity, mass protest and diverse forms of civil revolt — tactics that for the most part have been tried in the past. Arab physical resistance to annexation in the territories would inspire growing emulation by Israeli Arabs, and even collaboration across the Green Line. But it is the more predominant and widespread political protest activities of Israeli Arabs which should, under these circumstances, give the most concern to Israeli authorities, as they would render Arab- Jewish relations within Israel virtually intolerable.

The unlikely event of annexation accompanied by the granting of citizenship would wed the Arabs on both sides of the Green Line in a single legal and political framework, thus creating a powerful force in Israeli political life, and one capable of dictating a radical change in the very nature of the state — from Jewish-Zionist to binational Arab-Jewish — and the Arabs' status within it. More likely, each group would have a different political status: the Israeli Arabs enjoying full political rights, the Palestinian Arabs in the territories denied them. One result would be a rise in irredentism among Israeli Arabs. The moderate bloc that seeks accommodation within the Israeli system would be extremely enfeebled (with the possible initial exception of Druze, Circassians and part of the Bedouin). The extreme nationalist bloc's view of the Palestinians on both sides of the Green Line as a single monolithic bloc, would receive new impetus. The radical camp (Communists and Progressives) would probably abandon its public support for a Palestinian state alongside Israel, and move toward the extreme nationalist position. But the extent of its reaction would depend to a considerable extent on the response of outside actors, like the PLO and Arab states, and on the overall regional circumstances in which Israel opted for annexation.

Mass deportations of Palestinians from the territories would doubtless multiply many of these general reactions to annexation.

Israeli Arabs would inevitably fear that they, too, were candidates for transfer, and this might deter many from taking extreme action. An alternative Israeli policy of forcing compulsory military or national service upon Israeli Arabs with the aim of underscoring the difference between them and the Arabs in the territories and of bolstering their loyalty, is itself liable to provoke domestic ferment. Nor is this a likely eventuality, as Israelis would by this time have good reason to suspect Israeli Arabs of a distinct lack of enthusiasm for the project.

Thus, were Israel to implement annexation, it would gain no strategic advantages, but a number of distinct disadvantages, from the Israeli Arab sector. Under these circumstances, transfer of Palestinians from the territories might become a self-fulfilling prophecy regarding Israeli Arabs as well — with extremely negative ramifications for Israel and Israeli society.

The Arab States

Israel's annexation of the West Bank and Gaza would constitute the nightmare option for most Arab governments. It would provide a unilateral "resolution" of the conflict — by establishing Greater Israel — totally unacceptable to the Arabs on the most basic level. It would drastically raise the immediate saliency of the Arab-Israel conflict in general and the Palestinian issue in particular, reversing a decade-long trend of accommodation among many of the Arab states. Almost certainly, it would put an end to Israeli-Egyptian peace. Joint Arab action to resist its implementation could be expected, particularly if annexation were accompanied by a significant transfer of Palestinians from the West Bank and Gaza. Arab resistance might well range from the encouragement of an international political coalition to bring Israel to its knees through sanctions, to the creation of a wide, possibly wall-to-wall Arab war coalition against Israel. Neighboring Arab states — Syria, Egypt and Jordan — whose borders are normally closed to terrorist passage, would likely relax their restrictions on cross-border terrorist attacks by the PLO. To the extent they did so, this would be a signal of their intention to prevent or hinder the annexation, even at the risk of Israeli retaliation, escalation and war. The PLO's longstanding feud with the more extremist Palestinian organizations backed by Syria and Libya would probably be resolved with the disappearance of any Arab hope for a political settlement.

Thus, the long-standing division of the Arab world into two distinct groups — an essentially moderate, pro-western majority and a radical, Syrian-led minority — would likely be erased. Moreover, in their common opposition to this option, the Arab states are likely to gain encouragement from both the expected crisis in US-Israeli relations and from the deep divisions that would probably appear within Israeli society as a consequence of annexation. In the realm of Israel-Arab relations, this option would clearly involve very heavy costs: the destruction of all de facto and de jure forms of accommodation between Israel and parts of the Arab world, and the initiation of a process eventually leading to war under unfavorable terms.

With or without transfer, annexation is bound to threaten seriously, perhaps even mortally, the stability of the Hashemite monarchy. Jordan would be placed under tremendous pressure by the Palestinians to serve as a center for resistance. It would be compelled to go a considerable distance toward placating Palestinian demands, thus bringing it into confrontation with Israel. In anticipation of precisely this development, Jordan would seek wide Arab support, even if it came with significant strings attached. In particular, under such circumstances Jordan would probably feel compelled to yield to diverse Syrian demands. The odds that it would be able to abstain from participation in a future Arab-Israeli war would diminish considerably.

Certainly any effort to instigate a massive transfer of Palestinians from the West to the East Bank is likely to mean war with Jordan. To date the Hashemite monarchy has succeeded in retaining its control over the East Bank even while becoming demographically a Palestinian state. However, a significant influx of forcibly deported, embittered Palestinians would not be assimilable into Hashemite Jordan. Hence Jordan would use all the means in its possession to prevent implementation of transfer. Such measures — particularly those designed physically to prevent the transfer from taking place — could themselves develop into all-out war, with wider Arab participation.

Syria could be expected to attempt to organize collective Arab resistance; its position in the Arab world would be significantly enhanced by the evidence that annexation would supply to its long-standing argument — that Israel is an aggressive, expansionist state against which all Arab capabilities should be mobilized. Given the opportune international climate resulting from annexation and the expected realignment in the Arab world, Syria may alternatively choose to launch a war on its own, on the assumption that other Arab states would later join the fighting.

Egypt would react to annexation by severing all ties with Israel, even at the risk of renewed conflict. But it would probably be constrained from engaging in immediate conflict. Egypt would avoid provoking a war with Israel by taking unilateral action in Sinai. The presence of an international peacekeeping force there – – the MFO — would facilitate this Egyptian military restraint. The force can only be removed by mutual agreement; certainly the United States would wish to avoid precipitating an Egyptian-Israeli war by agreeing to withdraw its observers.

Egypt would maintain — with its position enhanced by American support — that Israel had violated one of the basic premises upon which the Camp David accords were based, namely that the final status of the territories would be determined only through negotiations. Egypt's activism under such circumstances would also be propelled by its desire to deny Syria domination over the process of creating an all-Arab coalition against Israel.

Iraq, Saudi Arabia and the smaller GCC states, Iran and Libya are likely to contribute to an all-Arab effort against Israel were the latter to annex the West Bank and Gaza. In light of its military capacity, particular importance should be attached to Iraq's role in this context: Baghdad could be expected to demonstrate active involvement on behalf of the Arab cause, as the situation would provide it with an ideal opportunity to reassert its pan-Arab credentials in the Arab-Israel arena. It would provide military backing for Jordan, including the dispatch of troops, and possibly for Syria too, particularly if Damascus were willing to provide Baghdad with a commitment to reduce its support for Iran. Saudi

Arabia and the other GCC states could be expected to bankroll Palestinian and Arab resistance, partly as protection money. A token Gulf Arab contribution of military units could also be expected. In addition, the Saudis would seek massive western pressure on Israel to compel it to rescind the annexation decision and to cease the application of transfer. Libya is likely to support Syria's efforts — including the dispatch of arms and troops — while at the same time offering material and financial assistance to the Palestinians.

Israel's Security

The central military cost entailed in the annexation option is the reestablishment of a wall-to-wall Arab war coalition against Israel. Sooner or later, it would engage Israel in war.

The short-term likelihood of such a war would depend on the coalition's estimate of the risks and opportunities involved. This would likely comprise a number of considerations. On the one hand, Israel's unilateral move would be interpreted as a sign of activism and self-confidence. Hence its deterrent profile during the post-annexation period would be higher. On the other, the Arab coalition could draw encouragement from the weakening of Israeli deterrence generated by possible sharp domestic Israeli conflict over the annexation initiative, coupled with the suspension of Israeli-American strategic cooperation and the general erosion of US support for Israel.

The newly created Arab coalition might wish to engage Israel in war soon after annexation was implemented in order to exploit the consequent internal rift within Israel, amounting to a loss of national consensus on foreign and defense policy. Another consideration favoring a quick attack would be the desire to exploit a congenial international environment: the post-annexation international condemnation of Israel — including the possible imposition of political and economic sanctions by the United Nations — and, more important, the post-annexation rift between the United States and Israel, possibly leading the US to participate in, rather than veto, the imposition of sanctions. The Arab coalition is likely to assess that if attacked under such circumstances, Israel would not enjoy external support. The validity of the assessment would depend on the coalition's ability to make it crystal clear that its attack was induced by Israel's unilateral act of annexation and was aimed solely at undoing that act.

Alternatively, the Arabs might favor postponing the attack for purely military considerations: the need to develop joint planning and careful preparations, as well as the desire to await the possibility of achieving strategic surprise. In addition, the Arab states may wish to wait until Israel is further weakened by the cumulative effects of the various ramifications of annexation, including political isolation and the deterioration of US-Israeli relations.

From the Israeli standpoint, the specific costs and dangers entailed in annexation would depend on the context within which it were carried out. If annexation were imposed following a war launched by Arab states and won by Israel, and in which Israel was clearly perceived as being devoid of responsibility for the Arab attack, then Israel's post-annexation costs in the international arena would probably be considerably lower than under an "annexation out of the blue" scenario. Certainly in a post-war, post-annexation scenario an Arab war coalition would be dissuaded from attacking Israel not only by the less congenial international environment but also, and especially, by the fatigue and attrition that some of its members would have experienced following their defeat in the war they launched against Israel. Similarly, the aforementioned risks and costs are likely to be somewhat reduced in the event that annexation were imposed only on parts of the West Bank and Gaza.

Some of these considerations might lead the Arab war coalition to postpone its attack, thus reducing the short-term risks of war. But with time, the considerations originally dissuading the coalition from war would lose their validity. Israel's increased deterrent profile in the immediate post-annexation period would diminish as the country's domestic consensus was increasingly eroded. Concurrently, the Arabs' preparations for war, including their efforts at joint planning, would progress. Should annexation follow an Arab defeat in a war with Israel, the history of the past 40 years teaches us that the Arabs would gradually recuperate.

Meanwhile, the international environment would become increasingly hostile to annexation. Thus, even if some considerations would be conducive to avoiding another Arab-initiated war in the immediate post-annexation period, the war would not be avoided in the longer term.

Clearly, should annexation be accompanied by mass transfers of Palestinians from the West Bank and Gaza to the surrounding Arab states, then the short and the long term likelihood that the resulting Arab coalition would launch a war against Israel would increase accordingly. Arab states to which the Palestinians might be expelled would have an additional motivation to battle Israel, fearing that the expulsion would create unacceptable burdens on their own demography, society, and economy. Their assessment of the risks and opportunities entailed in such a war would lead them in the same direction: the Arab war coalition is likely to regard the post-transfer international outcry, and the even more pronounced rift between Israel and the United States, as an extremely conducive environment for a war.

The costs and outcome of such a war would depend on a number of factors. On the one hand, the disposition of IDF forces in the framework of this option would be optimal, since the IDF would be positioned on the Golan Heights and along the Jordan River, with the Sinai Peninsula serving as a buffer between the IDF and Egypt's armed forces. Further, should the Arab coalition decide to attack Israel in the immediate post-annexation and/or post-transfer period, its odds of achieving surprise would be minimal. On the other hand, this option would maximalize the size of the Arab war coalition that Israel would face: as noted earlier, annexation, particularly if accompanied by transfer, would likely lead to the emergence of a broad, or even wall-to-wall Arab war coalition. Also, annexation and transfer could create a highly unfavorable superpower reaction, thereby altering, to Israel's detriment, the balance of political, economic, and military assistance — including arms transfers — that they would be willing to provide to Israel and the Arab states respectively. Finally, the deterioration of Israel's internal cohesion and armed forces' morale in the post-annexation period would affect the IDF's motivation to fight.

For Israel then, annexation implies a high probability of all-out war with a broad Arab coalition, at a time when Israeli morale would be low, international support for Israel virtually nil, and support for the Arab cause high. Transfer would reinforce yet further these probabilities and motivations.

The Israeli Domestic Setting

Realization of this option would fulfill the dream of *Eretz Yisrael HaShlema*, or Greater Israel. As such, the option would apply the declared policies of the Israeli Far Right — Gush Emunim, Tehiya, Tsomet, Moledet — as well as many Orthodox activists in the National Religious Party, and some ultra-orthodox movements as well. The Likud, too, is favorably disposed toward annexation, but it insists that its commitment to the Camp David framework obliges it to forego this option for the time being. Theoretically, were the Likud to change its mind, it could, within the framework of a narrow rightist-religious coalition, pass an act of Knesset that applies Israeli law to the administered territories. Based on the Golan Heights precedent of 1981, one could speculate that annexation might be enacted into law within less than 24 hours, thereby allowing little or no time for the political opposition to mobilize public opinion against such a move.

Opposition to annexation is expressed by two political camps. Leftists and centrists who favor territorial compromise view annexation as a death blow to the prospect of reaching a peaceful settlement. They also contend that annexation, by including over 1.5 million additional Arabs within the confines of the State of Israel, would generate a demographic threat to its democratic and Jewish foundations. In this assessment they are joined by many adherents of the Greater Israel principle, who, while rejecting territorial compromise, also oppose annexation due to its ultimate demographic ramifications. Over the years Israeli public opinion has become increasingly sensitive to the demographic issue. Polling results from late 1987 indicate that no more than 25 percent of Israelis overall support annexation as their preferred solution, while as many as 30 percent of Israeli settlers in Judea, Samaria and Gaza reject annexation.

Certainly most of the proponents of annexation have no intention of granting Palestinian Arabs the rights of Israeli citizenship, as this would mean the end of Israel as a Jewish-Zionist state. Most advocates of annexation argue that the Palestinians could continue to hold Jordanian citizenship within the framework of autonomy under Israeli rule. Even before July 31, 1988 (when King Hussein unilaterally severed legal and administrative ties with West Bank Palestinians) this arrangement would have been dependent on Jordanian and PLO concurrence with an Israeli initiative that they totally reject. Hence some advocates of annexation (indeed, even advocates of the status quo) recommend the deportation or "transfer" of large numbers of Palestinians in order to right the demographic balance. The Moledet Party, which made this issue its primary platform plank in the November 1988 Knesset elections, received just under two percent of the Israeli popular vote. Undoubtedly some additional Israelis who voted for alternative rightist parties also favor transfer; one survey taken in June 1988 indicated that, under current conditions, as many as 45 percent of Israeli Jews viewed transfer as the preferred way to preserve the "Jewish and democratic" character of Israel. This attitude, which in some versions relates to the deportation of Israeli Arabs as well, derives in no small part from a sense of despair over the possibility that Jews and Arabs can coexist inside Greater Israel.

Any attempt to carry out a mass transfer of Arabs — in whatever form, under whatever name, and at whatever pace — would send shock waves throughout Israeli society. Large portions of the Jewish population would refuse to cooperate in the execution of deportations; some might oppose it by force. Left of center political leaders, including the Labor Party, might call upon IDF troops to refuse to obey relevant orders. This in turn could persuade the government to establish special forces to carry out the transfer. The transfer itself could conceivably be met by the creation of an underground manned by extreme leftists.

The IDF, incidentally, would ostensibly benefit from annexation in the sense that, at least by Israeli law, it would cease to be an occupying army. In reality, though, it would still be called upon to carry out the "police" duty of quelling violent Palestinian protest inside (Greater) Israel. Indeed, at a minimum annexation could oblige Israel to delineate areas in the territories in which it imposed a military government, similar to that invoked inside Israeli Arab regions until 1964 — but in far more negative circumstances. Thus the justification that many Israelis currently apply to the IDF's policing activities — that they are a function of a temporary situation that can only be changed by a political settlement — would no longer pertain. Moreover those policing activities would become increasingly difficult, since Palestinian violent resistance to annexation would presumably exceed the level experienced during 1988.

Two separate circumstances would ease problems of army morale and motivation: if annexation and/or transfer were to be seen as inevitable consequences of an Arab-Israel war fought against an Arab invader in the West Bank; and/or if these acts were carried out by a broad-based Israeli government. Neither of these circumstances seems likely.

There appear, then, to be no strategic advantages for Israelis in annexation, unless one starts with the doubtful proposition that there are no alternative options, and even the status quo has become untenable. Opposition to annexation from within Israel would be paralleled, and nourished, by opposition on the part of world Jewry and the international community. The government would alienate itself from at least half its own population, and from its natural allies abroad. An attempt to carry out transfer would multiply this effect several fold.

Demography, Geography and Economy

Annexation would turn Israel into a binational state, with the numerical balance between the two ethnic communities gradually shifting in favor of the Arabs. Even if we rely on official Israeli population figures (which probably underestimate Palestinian population growth), the non-Jewish population of Israel, following annexation, would form 40 percent of the total by 1991. Extrapolating current Arab and Jewish birth rates, non-Jews would outnumber the Jewish population early in the 21st century. In order to preserve a Jewish majority after annexation (and without transfer), massive Jewish immigration to Israel would be required. An influx of 700,000 Jewish immigrants would be needed by the year 2000 merely to preserve the Jews' 60 percent proportion of the immediate post-annexation population. Were Israel to seek, after annexation, to restore the current proportion of about 80 percent Jews within the population of the State of Israel, then some eight million Jews (virtually the entire Diaspora) would have to immigrate to Israel within the next ten years.

But further large-scale immigration of Jews to Israel is doubtful. Hence only large-scale transfer of Palestinian Arabs could ensure a comfortable Jewish majority in Greater Israel. For the Jews to remain numerically predominant for the next 40-50 years, at least half the Arab inhabitants of Judea, Samaria and Gaza, or some 750,000 people, would have to be deported before the year 2000.

One possible byproduct of annexation without massive transfer could be the expansion of the areas in Greater Israel inhabited by Arabs, and the amalgamation of the economies of Israel and the territories. Assuming the inhabitants of the annexed territories were able to move and reside throughout the country, large numbers of residents of crowded refugee camps in the Gaza Strip would probably move to Arab towns and villages in the Galilee and the coastal plain, or settle in slum areas in Jewish urban centers. Greater Israel's finite water resources might also have to be shared equitably with Arabs in the territories, while the act of annexation would rule out, for political reasons, any chance of acquiring water from Egypt, if only for the requirements of the Arab population.

From the economic standpoint, annexation means amalgamation of the economies of Israel and the territories. Annexation would also almost certainly close Jordan and other Arab states to goods and workers from the territories. Low quality labor-intensive industrial products from the territories could compete favorably with those produced in Israel, to the detriment of Israel's economy, while such agricultural industries of the territories as olive oil production would suffer from the closure of export markets. These effects would further add to the economic burden upon Israel presented by the annexed territories. Israel would also have to provide residents of the territories with public service infrastructure. Public sector consumption in the territories is currently equivalent to some two percent of that in Israel, while the population of the territories is equivalent to over 30 percent of Israel's; integration of the two economies would generate pressures upon Israel to correct this imbalance.

Were Israel, somehow, to overcome these seemingly insurmountable demographic dilemmas created by annexation without large-scale transfer; were it to survive the political, economic, social and perhaps military consequences of annexation; and were its Jewish population to expand; then it would enjoy the advantage of ensuring, through economic development and expansion of the Israeli economic dynamic, extensive areas of potential Jewish settlement in Judea and Samaria, thereby reducing inevitable demographic pressures on the coastal strip.

Were Israel to expel large numbers of Palestinians in order to avoid the demographic and economic consequences of annexation, it would suffer substantial economic damage from a different direction, due to its dependency on international trade: its trade agreements with the EEC and the United States would be canceled, and American aid would almost certainly be reduced drastically. Were annexation/transfer to generate an Israel-Arab war of the scope, say, of the Yom Kippur War of 1973, the harm to Israel's economy would approach five billion dollars, together with a direct reduction in GNP by some 10 percent over one or two years.

The United States

There are many issues that might cause tensions between Israel and the United States, but all pale by comparison with an Israeli annexation of the West Bank and Gaza, particularly if accompanied by massive transfers of the Arab population. The American response would be extremely negative, and the likely reactions severe. Protests would be reinforced and stimulated by the United States' European and Japanese allies. With the exception of a few "Israel right or wrong" stalwarts in the Orthodox Jewish movement, among American conservatives and in the Christian right,

Israel would confront a disillusioned Jewish community, an indignant Congress and a furious administration. Particularly if the media were able to supply "visuals," a precipitous drop in the public opinion polls could be anticipated.

Were Israel to implement annexation, the US reaction would be harsh. The act would be seen to compromise Israel's reputation as a democratic country and one that honors its agreements (in this case, Camp David). Insidious comparisons to South Africa would be ubiquitous. The administration would likely declare that it did not recognize Israel's actions. It would probably make the strongest American statement ever in support of Palestinian political rights as part of any future agreement, adding that any realistic and fair solution must involve the creation of a Palestinian entity. The US would likely consider the possibility of joining in international moves designed to force Israel to reverse its decision. At the least it would probably not veto UN initiatives to apply sanctions. Whatever the annexation contingency (after a war, in response to some extreme Palestinian measure or act), it would at a minimum entail very severe costs to Israel's relations with the United States.

An Israeli government that initiated some kind of policy of annexation would likely have anticipated a negative impact on its relations with Washington. It would probably try to "soften the blow" by organizing its own version of autonomy. If the Arabs responded with terrorism rather than diplomacy, many Americans, especially Jews, might begin to accept arguments that there were justifications for Israeli actions. If, after a year or two, the Jerusalem government seemed to have quieted critics at home and abroad and brought a measure of tranquility to the annexed territories, there would be some stabilization of the American-Israeli relationship, although annexation would still have constituted a severe blow.

One other case deserves special mention. Were Israel to annex and, as a result, the Arabs to go to war (no transfer involved), the United States would want to use the crisis to initiate a peace process and to reverse annexation. Sympathy for Israel, even if it suffered heavy losses, would be low, and there would be a strongly held attitude that the Israelis had precipitated the war and should be punished. Nevertheless the United States would still not countenance a threat to Israel's existence.

As this analysis implies, the extent of specific American sanctions against Israel would vary with the circumstances of annexation. The "best case" scenario — in the event of annexation with a successful autonomy plan, or in the unlikely instance whereby Israel granted full citizenship rights to the Arab residents of the territories — might not be much worse than the damage caused by a deteriorating status quo; it presages a drop in US financial aid, a gradual cooling of Israel's strategic relationship with American Jewry and the US government, growing American collaboration over Middle East issues with the USSR, and possible sanctions against Israel.

The "worst case" would be that entailed by annexation accompanied by transfer. The specific actions that could emerge from this contingency would include the following:

1. A reduction in aid of significant proportions: possibly the entire economic aid allocation of 1.2 billion dollars, and 25 to 50 percent of military aid.

2. A fundamental change in the diplomatic stance of the United States at the UN — in both the General Assembly and the Security Council. There would be a greater willingness to vote against Israel, or at least to abstain, including on a vote regarding a package of economic sanctions.

3. Strategic cooperation would cool immediately. At the very least there would be symbolic reductions, such as cancellation of meetings, exercises and port visits. But the cuts might well include concrete elements of the strategic cooperation program. Highly "visible" arms shipments, like F-16 aircraft, would be suspended. At the same time the US would act cautiously lest it signal the Arabs that Washington would acquiesce in an attack on Israel.

4. With even a minimum of Soviet reasonableness, the United States would likely begin to coordinate moves, perhaps leading to joint Soviet-American proposals and diplomatic efforts directed not only at canceling annexation, but at moving toward imposition of a comprehensive settlement.

Certainly US collaboration with Western Europe and Japan for this purpose would be vigorous.

5. The effectiveness of the pro-Israel community would be significantly reduced. For example, AIPAC would be severely inhibited in its ability to block arms sales to pro-western Arab states.

6. Jewish contributions to Israel would drop significantly, as would Jewish tourism, particularly if annexation generated violence in the territories and resistance within Israeli society.

This description of reactions assumes that the annexation and mass expulsions would occur simultaneously and be completed in a short time. The longer the period in which the transfers of population were being implemented and the greater the television coverage (which Israel could not prevent on the "other side"), the more Israel would be condemned. Israel's possible claim that Arabs were "choosing" to leave would make little positive impression. If the expulsions indeed dragged on, the US might well support a token UN force designed to stop them. Conceivably American troops might participate. Certainly the US might well try to use the threat of such action as a means of causing Israel to stop expelling Palestinians. Any administration would conclude that it must take some precipitous action to preserve relations with Arabs, as a humanitarian gesture, and in order to save the Hashemite dynasty from eventual overthrow by deported Palestinian masses (if they were being deported to Jordan).

The impact of the annexation and deportations would of course vary with the particular conditions. If regional conditions were confused, and Israel were not perceived as the sole cause of Arab departures, then more Americans might excuse Israeli policy. For example, if transfers were carried out in the course of or immediately following a war initiated by the Arabs and fought in the West Bank, and the deportees were shown to have tried to hinder Israeli troop movements, there might be a degree of understanding for Israel in Congress and the Jewish community.

But even in the best possible light, the visual impact of Arabs leaving the territories would be very negative. Any ultimate "normalization" would leave a qualitatively different relationship than before, at a much lower level and without the pre-existing substantive intimacy. There still would not be a complete break, but economic aid would be minimal, and military assistance would be severely reduced. US criticism of Israel would be overt and widespread. Strategic cooperation would be suspended. American Jewish identification with Israel would be weaker. US diplomatic intimacy with, and arms sales to, Arab governments would be greater. Coordination with the Europeans, the Palestinians, and possibly the Soviets, would be increased.

But even this lower level of relations would be preserved only if the post-annexation, post-transfer situation stabilized. In general, for many Americans this option would represent the Israel of Arab propaganda suddenly come to life.

The Soviet Union

Israeli annexation of the territories is the worst possible scenario from the Soviet point of view. True, on the face of it, such a move appears to entail short term advantages for Moscow, as it is likely to drive a wedge between the United States and its Arab allies due to the latter's disappointment with US failure to prevent the annexation. But in contrast with Soviet passivity in the face of Israel's annexation of the Golan Heights in 1981, in this case it is doubtful whether Moscow could afford to be complacent in the event of an Israeli annexation of the West Bank and the Gaza Strip. For it considers the Palestinian question to be the heart of the Arab-Israel conflict.

Given the turmoil in world public opinion that would probably follow the Israeli action, the Soviets might find themselves caught between the hammer and the anvil. On the one hand, they would be fully aware that if there were any power capable of forcing Israel to reverse its decision, it would be the United States and not Moscow. This, in the long run, could boost the US position in the Middle East, and might even lead to the USSR's worst nightmare — Pax Americana. On the other hand, an American failure to reverse the Israeli decision would mean the perpetuation of the Arab-

Israel conflict, and this too, under present circumstances, would hamper Soviet interests.

Hence the Israeli move would introduce an element of considerable tension into Moscow's relations with its local allies. If hitherto the USSR deemed the merits of rehabilitating relations with Israel to exceed the liabilities of such a development, this would no longer be the case: the costs of such a move would now increase dramatically, whereas its major potential gain, namely, injecting "realism" into the Israeli decisionmaking process, would almost completely disappear.

Concretely, the Soviets are likely to respond to an Israeli annexation of the territories by decisively strengthening their identification with the Arab cause, even to the point of abandoning for some time their notorious caution. This might include, to begin with, curtailment of the evolving rapprochement with Israel. It would be followed by far greater responsiveness to Syria's military requests and, ultimately, possible acquiescence in (if not encouragement of) a limited Syrian military move against Israel, particularly in circumstances in which US-Israeli relations had deteriorated as a consequence of the annexation and its aftermath. By way of embarking on this new path, Moscow could imply a more "permissive" interpretation of the military clauses in the Soviet-Syrian Friendship and Cooperation Treaty of October 1980; yet it is highly doubtful whether the USSR would be more forthcoming regarding the long-pending Syrian request to upgrade this treaty into a defense pact.

On the diplomatic front, the USSR would attempt to mobilize international opposition to the Israeli move. Its first priority would probably be a joint superpower initiative to force Israel to cancel annexation, followed by a UN Security Council resolution on sanctions against Israel, and possibly including Soviet participation in an international intervention force. In its anxiety to appear as the foremost defender of the Arab cause, the USSR might try to implicate the United States in the Israeli move, or at least to create the general impression that it was Soviet support, rather than US pressures on Israel, that ultimately would break the new political stalemate. Yet as far as the United States was concerned, the USSR could be expected to seek to keep the overall structure of

Soviet-American relations intact, if not to encourage actual bilateral coordination.

Annexation, then, would place the USSR squarely into confrontation with Israel — not militarily, but as an ally of those Arab states that would seek to oppose the Israeli move by military means, or as a partner in a superpower effort to roll back the Israeli move.

Conclusion

This option threatens to end the trend of Arab accommodation with Israel evinced over the past decade, and to begin a spiral toward war, possibly with Soviet support for Arab belligerents. It presages a violent Palestinian reaction involving escalating terrorism. It would cause the United States to condemn Israel harshly, cancel the "strategic relationship" and apply extreme sanctions, and to enhance political contacts with the PLO. It might well bring the US and USSR together in dialogue over ways to compel Israel to reverse its decision.

Thus the pressure from the superpowers and the Arab states would focus initially on the demand that Israel revoke its unilateral annexation. Failing this, the Arab states would concentrate increasingly on the prospect of employing force. The entire process would generate a crisis within Israeli society and the IDF, with the Israeli Left possibly reacting with violence. It would produce far greater radicalism among Israeli Arabs. It would place upon Israel a demographic and economic burden of the territories and their population. American Jewry would be increasingly alienated as a strategic ally. Economic damage to Israel in terms of reduced aid and trade and tourism sanctions would be extensive; a war, were it to be generated by annexation, could be extremely costly in human lives and economic resources.

The expulsion of large numbers of Palestinian Arabs from the territories ("transfer") would be a likely derivative of annexation, as even the unlikely immigration to Israel of as many as 700,000 Jews in ten years could not produce a comfortable Jewish majority within Greater Israel. Transfer would exacerbate all of the aforementioned negative ramifications of annexation. Conceivably it might even be opposed physically by a multinational force dispatched to the Arab side of Israel's border crossing points. Alternatively, Jordanian military opposition alone might prevent the transfer. Certainly an Israeli attempt at mass transfer would spell a drastic deterioration in the Israeli-American relationship of recent years, which is based essentially on the perception of shared values of democratic government and social justice.

On the international plane, too, the momentum of the reaction to annexation of the West Bank and Gaza might jeopardize previous world acquiescence in Israel's earlier annexations of East Jerusalem and the Golan Heights. Further, even if international pressure eventually caused Israel to reverse its annexation decision, the overall atmosphere might by that time have deteriorated to the extent that Israel could not return to the status quo ante in its international relations, including its ties with the United States.

A gradual or partial approach toward annexation would do little to mitigate these developments. On the contrary, by allowing time for a reaction to build up, it might exacerbate the option's negative consequences. Nor would an attempt to impose autonomy within the framework of annexation assuage opposition. If annexation in and of itself would be difficult to enforce upon the Palestinian Arabs, then they would certainly refuse to collaborate with imposed autonomy under these circumstances, thereby rendering it either meaningless or a source of additional friction. Transfer carried out by means of deliberate non-violent economic and social disincentives — creating an oppressive ghetto atmosphere, refusing to permit the return of those who depart for studies or employment, etc. — might arouse somewhat less opposition; but by the same token, it would be less effective quantitatively. Indeed, the Palestinians' highly developed ideology of "steadfastness" (*sumud*) might render it marginal. Yet Israeli reliance on more repressive means would attract greater condemnation and sanctions.

The negative ramifications of annexation might be mitigated somewhat, particularly in the short term, were it to be carried out following an unprovoked Arab war against Israel. Many characteristics of the war would determine the degree to which Israeli society, the United States and the Arab world found annexation tolerable. Certainly large-scale transfer — particularly insofar as the transfer of hundreds of thousands of Palestinians under wartime conditions would entail reliance on considerable brutality — would constitute a source of extreme hostility toward Israel. Then too, annexation carried out within the framework of a war not clearly instigated by the Arabs would offer no mitigating circumstances.

Annexation that follows a war that was fought in the West Bank against an Arab invader possibly assisted by a local Palestinian fifth column, would likely be perceived by the world as more justified than annexation of the West Bank and Gaza following a war with Syria on the Golan. Still, it is hard to envisage circumstances under which any Arab-Israeli war would be the road to improving Israel's strategic position regarding the Palestinian conflict. The damage wreaked upon Israel by the war might well neutralize even the short-term benefits of an annexation that escapes disastrous world criticism; the demographic and democratic problems would remain; and the Palestinian issue would certainly be institutionalized even further as the principal Arab grudge against Israel.

This, then, is a highly destructive option for Israel.

IV. Option Four—A Palestinian State

Definition

An independent Palestinian state would be established in most of the territory of Judea, Samaria and Gaza, following negotiations between Israel and the PLO. The agreement between the two would specify that the Palestinian refugee problem would be resolved — within the framework of negotiated agreements — by settling most of them in Arab countries, including the new state of Palestine. The agreement would also cancel the Palestinian "right of return." In addition it might delineate specific stages for the phased establishment of the state.

Security provisions for Israel would include demilitarization of the territories (with regard to significant Arab forces of any sort), alterations to the 1967 borders, the deployment of limited Israeli forces, the implementation of security arrangements, and possibly an international observer force.

Jewish settlements located within the IDF deployment zones would be retained, at least as long as these zones existed. Some additional settlements would presumably be included in territories near the 1967 border that would be annexed to Israel. The remainder would probably have to be evacuated, although conceivably agreement could be reached for them to function under Palestinian sovereignty, while retaining special links to Israel, if their inhabitants so desired.

The border between the Palestinian state and Israel would be open to two-way passage of the two countries' citizenry. On issues that involved both states, such as the disposition of water resources, customs and economic issues, they would collaborate. State lands in the territories would be subject to Palestinian sovereignty, with the exception of those included within Israeli security zones.

Ramifications

The Palestinians

Of all the options on the Israeli agenda, an independent Palestinian state comes closest to satisfying the variety of aspirations and needs of the different Palestinian constituencies. It provides the end of Israeli rule for West Bank and Gaza residents; normalcy for all Palestinians (a flag, citizenship, a national airline, etc.); opportunities for political achievement by intellectuals and activists; and an asylum (of first or last resort) for Palestinians wishing to escape intolerable conditions elsewhere. Of all the options we have considered, this comes closest to meeting the Palestinians' requirements. It most closely approximates the conditions of the November 1988 PNC declaration of independence.

What it does not provide is the "satisfaction" of destroying Israel and liberating all of Palestine. Nor does it offer the possibility of physical "return" for the 1948 refugees — neither to Israel nor, for many in Arab countries, even to the new Palestinian state. In this sense, it is impossible to know how acceptable a settlement might be until it is proposed and negotiated. Certainly, Palestinian attitudes would be affected by the concessions they know they would have to make — particularly those resulting from Israeli security demands. However it is likely that most West Bank and Gaza Arabs, except for radical Muslims and radical leftists, would favor such an idea. Similarly, the positions adopted by the PLO in late 1988 make clear that the organizations that apparently represent the bulk of the Palestinian diaspora (Fatah and its allied movements within the PLO, and the Palestine Communist Party) as well as non-aligned individuals, would accept a West Bank/Gaza state.

Yet even for these Palestinians, the content of the concessions called for by this option is problematic. Any contractual limitation on the movement of Palestinians to the new state would be totally unacceptable; even a formal renunciation of the "right of return" to Israel would be very difficult. Moreover, it is unlikely that territorial deviations from the 1949 armistice demarcation lines would be acceptable, apart from very minor rectifications (and even those might require at least symbolic reciprocity). From the Palestinian perspective, some local forces would be necessary for symbolic and internal security needs, although substantial limitations on size, equipment and deployment would be feasible. Israeli observers and unobtrusive intelligence installations could also probably be tolerated. But any other Israeli military presence, except as a limited transitional arrangement whose duration is specified in advance, would probably be resisted. And even if such forces were accepted, they would subsequently constitute a provocative insult to Palestinian national sensitivities and a focus of anti-Israel incitement.

The same is true of Jewish settlements in the territories. Palestinian negotiators would be extremely reluctant to endorse the continued presence inside their state of such settlements; were they made a *sine qua non* for withdrawal, Palestinian leaders might acquiesce, but settlements thereafter would be a source of rancor and friction, and would become a particularly attractive target for Palestinian rejectionists seeking to derail the solution.

While the outcome of such negotiations is largely a matter of speculation, the more critical question is whether, from the Palestinian standpoint, a Palestinian state of this nature, once established, would form the basis for a stable post-settlement system of peaceful relations — or a prod to renewed instability and conflict. The latter might happen because of the conscious intentions of Palestinians. Alternatively, the state might be structurally unable to abide by its commitments — due to domestic economic weakness, popular political pressure, or because restrictions on Palestinian freedom of movement or decision made the agreement intolerable.

Insofar as intentions are concerned, the preference of most Palestinians would almost certainly remain fulfillment of the "strategy of stages," i.e., the ultimate elimination of Israel and the liberation of all of Palestine. Even those leaders who endorsed a settlement, particularly those whose personal roots were in pre-1967 Israel, would not be emotionally reconciled to peace with Israel. However, while irredentism constitutes a predilection, it does not inevitably lead to hostile foreign policy, much less war.

93

What would determine whether or not irredentism was translated into active hostility would be the overall relations of forces, both domestic and regional.

The ideological ultras who oppose any compromise solution — rejectionist factions and the Islamic fundamentalists — would be hard to satisfy. They would likely employ terrorism against both Israel (abroad) and Palestinian moderates in the hope of deterring or discrediting them, and thereby torpedoing any agreement along these lines. Were the agreement nevertheless to be implemented, they would seek to undermine it by launching terrorist attacks from Palestinian territory against Israelis, in the hope of provoking retaliation by Israeli forces, and escalation. In these efforts they would be supported, probably unobtrusively, by Syria and Libya. But they themselves are aware of the debilitating impact upon their ideology of a formal political settlement and the creation of a state, with all its vested interests; that is precisely why they so resolutely oppose any talk of compromise within the more pragmatic PLO mainstream.

A second force that would likely remain actively irredentist are the 1948 refugees, especially those living in marginal circumstances in camps outside the borders of the new state (Lebanon, and to a lesser extent Jordan and Syria). But the new Palestinian state is perceived as part of a comprehensive solution of the Palestinian problem — including the liquidation of UNRWA and the refugee camps, some emigration and resettlement, and rehabilitation and conferment of citizenship or legal residence status on refugees elsewhere. Hence what remained of this group would likely not be strong enough to drag the new state into war or to overthrow a government that probably would be dominated by Fatah, intent on abiding by the agreement with Israel and enjoying, at least on this issue, the support of most of its residents.

The expectation that the government and population of the new state would not embark on a confrontationist posture is grounded in a number of assumptions. For one, the satisfaction, albeit partial, of important Palestinian needs (i.e., sovereignty and the symbols of sovereignty) would reduce the collective motivation to resume the conflict. Secondly, Palestinians would likely be inhibited from trying to do so by the effective demilitarization of their state, by fear of losing their independence in a war, and by fear of painful lower-level Israeli economic and military sanctions. Third, with the exception of Syria, it would be difficult for Palestinians to mobilize effective Arab support for a renewed conflict with Israel after Arab states and Palestinians had legitimized peace with it.

The second question concerns the possibility of structural breakdown of Palestinian authority. Widespread frustration with the quality of life in the Palestinian state might be displaced onto Israel, with Jewish settlements inside the new state providing a particularly inviting target for dissidents, and this would create irresistible pressures to "heat up" the situation as an alternative to dealing with insoluble domestic problems. The domestic political issues that normally preclude governmental stability or stable foreign relations in third world countries are egregious economic inequalities, huge social and cultural gaps between center and periphery or between modernized and traditional sectors, and primordial ethnic or religious cleavages. While some of these problems might threaten domestic stability in a Palestinian state, none would exist to such an extent that domestic instability would be inevitable.

As far as economic sources of instability are concerned, the central question is whether the state would be able to satisfy some subjectively defined level of economic demands, both by local residents and by those moving to the new state in the future. There is no intrinsic reason why the state could not do this, but it would definitely need to mobilize additional resources. Palestinians in relatively comfortable personal circumstances — in Israel, the Gulf states, Europe and the western hemisphere — would probably be content to identify emotionally with an independent Palestinian state. Since any immigrants permitted into the new state would likely be relatively less prosperous Palestinians, i.e., camp dwellers from Lebanon, Syria, and perhaps Jordan, the new state would not only have to preserve access to the Israeli labor market, it would also have to secure new sources of investment capital — several billion dollars over the first few years and a continuing flow of funds at a lower level thereafter — to finance housing stock, education, social services and job creation. Its ability to do so would depend on the willingness and ability of

Arab and other states, as well as international organizations, to provide this large-scale economic assistance, with its stabilizing effect.

The availability of international financial support would, in turn, depend at least in part on the foreign policy and international orientation of the Palestinian state. As long as the largest potential donors continue to be western states or pro-western Arab oil producers interested in regional stability, the Palestinian state would likely favor a pro-western alignment and non-belligerent behavior in the region.

It remains possible, of course, that in some longer-term, the domestic and regional factors upon which this projection is based could change in very dramatic ways. For example, Palestinian and other Arab moderates could collectively adopt a radical stance; or the military balance might shift strongly to Israel's disadvantage; or other elements of Israel's deterrent might weaken. If, by that time, Palestinian irredentism had not diminished as a result of the experience of peaceful relations with Israel and the passing from the scene of the 1949 generation of refugees, then it is likely that the Palestinian state would embark on an aggressive course vis-a-vis Israel, including military actions.

Israeli Arabs

Of all the options examined, this is the most desirable for Israeli Arabs, because it comes closest to resolving the Palestinian problem. An independent Palestinian state would undoubtedly imbue Israeli Arabs with a sense of national pride and identification similar to that felt by Diaspora Jewry toward Israel. At the same time, implementation of this option would create a new situation in which part of the Palestinian people sees its political aspiration — political expression for their longings as a people — realized, while another portion, the Israeli Arabs, continues to live as a minority in a state whose raison d'etre is to give expression to the national aspirations of the Jewish people (which, in the Arab conception, is accomplished at the expense of the Palestinians).

Thus the central challenge that Palestinian statehood would pose for Israeli Arabs would concern the question of their ultimate identity: Would the new situation set in motion irredentist trends, leading to demands by Israeli Arabs for their cooption into the Palestinian state? Or would it ease their return to their pre-1967 status of acceptance of their minority status within a Jewish state? The most significant factors that might affect the outcome are sentiment within the Palestinian state itself — irredentist, or conciliatory — Israel's overall strength and vitality, and Israel's concomitant efforts to integrate Israeli Arabs more fully into the mainstream of national life. Israeli Arabs would observe the new state closely, drawing constant comparisons between their own situation and that in the Palestinian state with regard to political influence and social and economic achievements. Concurrently, a resolution of the Palestinian problem would rekindle the debate in Israel over the rights and obligations of Israel's Arabs, including military service. The challenge for Israeli government policy would be to ensure that Israeli Arabs did not see life in the Jewish state as an ongoing traumatic experience, but rather as an acceptable alternative to jeopardizing all they had achieved in a futile attempt to attain an independent political existence.

If Israel fails in this challenge, irredentist tendencies are liable to develop among radical elements. These would not be significant unless the new Palestinian state itself encouraged them as part of the PLO's "strategy of stages," designed to bring about the demise of the State of Israel by gradually weakening its foundations while expanding Palestinian sovereignty wherever possible. In this case, irredentist incitement might become problematic in areas like the Galilee, the Triangle and perhaps even the northern Negev. Israeli Arab moderates and radicals would be split, with the radicals blurring the distinction in their demands between the struggle for equal civil rights and a campaign for autonomous rights. Arab-Jewish tensions would grow.

Assuming that Israel met this challenge successfully, the Palestinian state option would create an opening for the full integration of the Israeli Arabs into Israeli society, to the point where they themselves would evince a readiness to fulfill national obligations such as military service. Under these circumstances a new era could develop in relations between the Israeli Arabs and the state. Their full integration could have a ripple effect and impact indirectly in various spheres. New employment channels that would be opened to Israeli Arabs would enhance their contribution to the Israeli economy.

Still, there is no guarantee that the granting of greater rights would in itself be sufficient to uproot irredentist inclinations. Even if the proportion of radical and nationalist elements in the Arab sector were to decline, they would not disappear from the political map overnight. Hence parallel to its conciliation policy, the government would in any case have no choice but to implement policies that have the effect of deterring radical and extreme nationalist activity. This would be made easier under this option, because Israel would enjoy complete legitimacy after the resolution of the Palestinian problem, while the moderate camp would have been strengthened, thus reducing the radicals to a minority.

In this sense, the advent of a Palestinian state would be advantageous for Israel in terms of the Israeli Arab community, only if it were accompanied by a parallel policy of greater integration of Arabs into Israeli society, together with adequate deterrents against radical incitement, while the Palestinian state itself successfully curtailed irredentist tendencies. This would ensure more harmonious Jewish-Arab relations. It would be disadvantageous if the Palestinian state sought aggressively to spread irredentist incitement, or if Israel failed to counter the effects of Palestinian statehood by encouraging greater social and economic integration.

The Arab States

This option does not spell a change in existing alignments in the Arab world. Most Arab states would back the creation of an independent Palestinian state, which they have in any case already recognized. Arab-Israeli relations would in general be enhanced as a result of the settlement of the most salient source of conflict between the two sides. But while diminishing the probability of an Arab war coalition forming against Israel, this option might well increase the possibility of war with Syria, which would seek to sabotage an Israeli-Palestinian settlement both before and during its implementation.

Jordan would prefer a federation or confederation in which it exercised a degree of influence over the West Bank and Gaza — to a completely independent Palestinian state. Conceivably, Jordan could seek to sabotage an Israeli-PLO negotiating process, either alone or with Syria. However it is more likely that Jordan would seek a middle road between Syria and the PLO, taking a low profile during the implementation stage and attempting to establish close relations with the new state once it came into being, in the hope of influencing its political and economic course, while adopting measures designed to insulate itself from negative currents emanating from the new state that might destabilize the Hashemite Kingdom. In this sense, Jordan might seek to establish a confederation with the new state, and the Palestinians are likely to be receptive. In addition, Jordan might actually seek to cooperate in maintaining the security arrangements laid down in an Israeli-Palestinian agreement, even if it were not a party to them, through direct negotiations with Israel.

Syria would be unhappy with an Israeli-PLO settlement, since it would run contrary to basic tenets of Syrian foreign policy that reject any partial or separate settlements, negate the notion of a resolution of the Palestinian issue without an all-Arab consensus on the matter, and reject any settlement of the Arab-Israel conflict at least until the Arabs have achieved a favorable military balance. The establishment of an independent Palestinian state that is not subservient to Syrian influence also contradicts the Syrian desire to be the dominant regional actor in the Levant. Most immediately unsettling for Syria would be its assessment that prospects for a return of the Golan Heights had been further diminished.

In its opposition to a separate Israeli-PLO agreement, Syria is likely to employ diverse means — including support for terrorist attacks against Israel from Lebanon and support for radical elements within the new Palestinian state. Indeed, Syria might opt for a military thrust in the Golan as the only effective means for preventing the agreement's implementation. Yet concern about a probable negative Soviet reaction, and fear of isolation in an Arab world that was largely supportive of the creation of a Palestinian state, might severely constrain Syria. Nor is it inconceivable that a future Syrian regime would, in this situation, claim its right to negotiate a similar settlement of the Golan Heights issue.

Egypt would be content with the creation of an independent Palestinian state and would regard implementation of this option as validation of the position it has held since the peace process was launched. Accordingly, Egypt is likely to seek to play the role of the benevolent "big brother" to the new state.

Saudi Arabia and Iraq are likely to support the creation of an independent Palestinian state, assuming the settlement bears the PLO's and Arafat's seal of approval. Riyadh's role under such conditions would be to grant generous financial aid to the new state, and to persuade its fellow GCC members to follow suit. This would be critical, as from the Israeli standpoint this option would require extensive inter-Arab cooperation in solving the Palestinian refugee problem. This is a particularly complex issue. Even if we leave aside political considerations, it is unlikely under existing demographic conditions that any of Israel's immediate neighbors would undertake to admit large numbers of Palestinians. Egypt is extremely overpopulated already, while Jordan is fast becoming so. Virtually all of Lebanon's ethnic factions seek to reduce that country's Palestinian population. Syria has the capacity, in the Jezirah region, to absorb large numbers of immigrants; but here the political motive would clearly prevail against such a prospect. Only Iraq might have both the geographic capacity, and the motivation, to absorb relocated Palestinian refugees.

Indeed, Iraq is likely to go along with its Arab allies in supporting an Israeli-Palestinian settlement. Conversely, Iran and Libya are likely to oppose it, allying themselves with Syria.

Thus from a broad inter-Arab standpoint, this option offers Israel the advantage of garnering maximum Arab support for its implementation and ongoing stability. The traditional axiom that a Palestinian state would inexorably serve as a platform for an all-Arab (and Soviet) thrust against Israel would no longer be valid, insofar as most Arab states and the USSR would support the peace settlement. However, much would depend on future developments. A Palestinian state not committed to the settlement and involved in steadily rising tensions with Israel would likely become the focus of inter-Arab rivalries and have a strongly destabilizing impact on Arab-Israeli relations. An Arab world not prepared to support the settlement could bring about its collapse.

Israel's Security

A clear advantage of this option is that, relative to the others considered, it comes closest to meeting the Palestinians' national aspirations. A complete resolution of the Israeli-Palestinian dispute would diminish the intensity of the Arab-Israeli conflict significantly.

In assessing the implications of the establishment of an independent Palestinian state on Israel's security a number of difficult questions must be posed. For one, assuming that the Palestinian state leadership would desire to maintain peaceful relations with Israel, what is the likelihood that it would be capable of constraining Palestinian elements from within the state and from the outside who sought to circumvent Israeli-Palestinian relations through terrorism? Secondly, assuming that at some future point the Palestinian state leadership wished to improve upon its achievement of sovereignty, and to attempt to implement the "strategy of stages" in order to assert Palestinian control over Greater Palestine, what dangers might this entail for Israel? Here the question must focus not only on the prospective state's military capacity to damage Israel on its own, but also on the likelihood and associated risks that the future state would serve as a catalyst for attack on Israel by a broader Arab coalition.

The first question is not easy to answer. The capacity of the new Palestinian leadership to enforce peaceful relations with Israel would depend on the extent to which it succeeded in maintaining effective internal security. This, in turn, would depend on the prospective Palestinian government's capacity to enjoy a monopoly of force -- including the deployment of an effective internal security service — following the establishment of state independence, and on its will and determination to enforce its priorities and policies internally. Currently, the Palestinian leadership is not equipped with such a mechanism, although the PLO and its component organizations have developed a rudimentary security apparatus. Under the best of circumstances it would take 2-3 years until such an agency could begin to function effectively in situ. Until such time, Israel's security services would have to retain responsibility for internal security in the West Bank and Gaza.

The second question relates to the possibility that the Palestinian leadership, following the achievement of statehood, would later itself wish to implement the strategy of stages, and seek to undermine the Jewish state. In this context, it must be noted that the balance of military power between Israel and the prospective Palestinian state would be so one-sided that such a state — even if it so desired — could not alone constitute a serious threat to Israel's security and survival. Indeed, Israel is not likely to face serious military difficulties should it decide to reassert its control over the territory of the newly created state, although an operation of this nature would probably generate both internal and external political complications. In any case, mainstream forces within the future state would presumably argue against any measure that might propel Israel to overturn the Palestinians' historical achievement.

We have already noted that the establishment of a Palestinian state would strengthen existing divisions within the Arab world. Syria is likely to oppose the state's very existence, while Egypt, Iraq, and Saudi Arabia are likely to be supportive, and Jordan is likely to acquiesce while acting to ensure that the new state does not threaten the Hashemite Kingdom. In this sense, the danger that Israel might again be faced with a wall-to-wall Arab war coalition — inspired, in this instance, by the Palestinian state — would be diminished. The possibility remains, however, that in the longer term Palestinians aiming to fulfill the strategy of stages, but sensitive to their state's weakness, would attempt to achieve their objective by again catalyzing a conflict between Israel and the surrounding Arab states.

Should Arab states wish to threaten Israel again, the added danger entailed in the establishment of a Palestinian state would depend on the precise security arrangements implemented following the IDF's withdrawal from the West Bank and Gaza. There are a number of reasons why such arrangements would then be of critical importance to Israel's security.

First, the IDF suffers from a dramatic quantitative asymmetry in

102

comparison with the standing military forces of the surrounding Arab states. While Israel's armed forces remain numerically inferior even when fully mobilized, the asymmetry in the latter case is less pronounced, and is partly addressed by Israel's qualitative edge. Hence the IDF must enjoy adequate early warning in order never to be confronted by a serious Arab military threat except when fully mobilized.

Secondly, Israel would be extremely vulnerable following a withdrawal from the West Bank and Gaza, given that a vast majority of its Jewish population and most of its industrial capacity are located in a 9 to 13 mile-wide strip along the Mediterranean coast, from Haifa in the north to Rehovoth at the center, and in the narrow corridor leading to Jerusalem. And lastly, the mountains of Judea and Samaria enjoy superior elevation over Israel's coastal strip, providing considerable advantage to the military force that achieves control over this area first. Topographically inferior and lacking strategic depth, the coastal plain does not afford adequate defense against modern conventional forces. This remains the case regardless of the introduction of ballistic missiles and nonconventional weapons to the arena.

Under such circumstances, critical importance must be attached to security arrangements that give Israel the ability to conduct defense-in-depth should a serious threat to its survival develop. Without security arrangements allowing effective defense-in-depth, the Arab states might perceive Israel's vulnerability as too tempting to ignore.

Conversely, adequate Israeli security arrangements would virtually guarantee that any war initiated by the Arab states from the east would be conducted at the eastern edge of the West Bank, and even in Jordan. This is likely to prove a deterrent against Palestinian inclinations to catalyze such a process, since the invading Arab armies and the IDF would conduct extremely lethal large-scale warfare in the midst of Palestinian civilian population centers, possibly leading to the annexation of the territory and the expulsion of its residents if the IDF emerged victorious.

The security arrangements implemented once the Palestinian state was established would have to meet three criteria: first, that Israel be provided with timely early warning and an adequate capacity to conduct defense-in-depth in the West Bank or even to transfer the war to Jordan; secondly, that such security arrangements would continue to apply as long as the aforementioned threats remain; and finally, that security arrangements that generate a high degree of friction between the IDF and the Arab population of the West Bank and Gaza be avoided. Should friction occur, the basic relationship between Israel and the prospective Palestinian state would be endangered, thus resulting in a self-fulfilling threat.

With these considerations in mind, and assuming the establishment of a Palestinian state without any extensive transition stages, the following security arrangements should be concluded:

> — the demilitarization of the Palestinian state from either indigenous or foreign military forces, except for internal security forces equipped with small arms and armored cars but lacking tanks, artillery, naval forces, and combat aircraft;
> — the ongoing deployment of IDF forces and facilities required for early warning and intelligence, and for delaying the invasion of foreign forces into the West Bank until IDF reserves could be mobilized and deployed. In this context, it should be noted that any facilities placed on territory that is not under Israeli sovereignty would necessarily be of a transitory nature;
> — the freedom of movement by IDF forces to and from such facilities and installations, along agreed axes and itineraries;
> — Israel's right of hot pursuit into Palestinian territory when required to ensure Israel's security against terrorism;
> — maintenance of the Israel Air Force's air control over the West Bank and Gaza;
> — a Jordanian undertaking not to permit the entry of additional Arab armies into Jordanian territory without prior agreement with Israel (which would be forthcoming only if Jordan required reinforcements to defend against an Arab or Iranian threat), and to impose agreed measures of force limitation on its territory near the Jordan River border;

— the participation of Israeli observers in the prevention of arms smuggling into the Palestinian state. These observers would be included in mixed supervisory forces deployed at the points of entry into Palestine along the Jordan River, the port of Gaza, the surface corridor linking the Sinai to Gaza, and the Palestinian state's civilian airport.

In order to enhance the stability of post-independence Israeli-Palestinian relations, the following additional understandings would have to be reached between the two states:

— that some of the aforementioned security arrangements would be lifted following a long interim period during which Palestinian compliance could be verified, and after peace agreements that permitted the resettlement of the Palestinian refugees had been concluded between Israel and the remaining Arab states, and the resettlement process was well underway.

— that IDF forces required to perform the aforementioned missions be kept to a bare minimum;

— that international observer teams supervise the borders of the new Palestinian state in order to insure that the latter's sovereignty is not violated or abused by Israel, and vice versa.

In the event that not all of the aforementioned security arrangements were applied, and assuming they were both circumscribed and supplemented by the above considerations as well as international guarantees, Israel would have to further minimize those risks entailed in the establishment of Palestinian independence that derive from two internal Israeli considerations. For one, Israel would have to provide its intelligence community — whose coverage, almost by definition, can never be foolproof — with all necessary means for the rapid assessment of developing strategic and operational military threats. Then too, the Israeli political leadership would have to be educated and socialized to the fact that once such intelligence is received and assessed, immediate decisions would have to be made in order that swift preemptive military action be taken. Only if the means and the willingness to react to developing threats in a timely and effective fashion were acquired, would Israel be able to withstand the irreducible risks and uncertainties involved in implementing Palestinian state independence.

The Israeli Domestic Setting

Under present circumstances it seems highly unlikely that a Knesset majority would approve this option. Were it to do so, it would be virtually impossible to implement such a settlement. Both major political parties, and a large majority of Israelis, reject the establishment of a Palestinian state in Judea, Samaria and Gaza.

Still, a radical change in the political environment relative to such a settlement cannot be ruled out. Such a change could be sudden and drastic, or gradual. Possible catalyzers include a clear and sustained move toward genuine political moderation among the PLO leadership; the emergence of an alternative Palestinian leadership in the territories; an Israeli setback in a war with Arab states or a loss of control over the *intifada*; or strong American pressure upon Israel. Further, it is not inconceivable that the Labor Party and other actors on the Center and Left of the Israeli political spectrum would, on the basis of a reassessment, conclude that the "Jordanian option" is no longer a viable solution due to King Hussein's reticence, and that their hopes for a settlement based on territorial compromise must be pinned on the Palestinian mainstream.

Certainly the Likud, all factions to its political right, and most of the religious public are resolute in their opposition to the Palestinian state option. The Likud would oppose vehemently any compromise territorial solution, even with Jordan — certainly with the PLO.

Here a number of Israeli public perceptions appear relevant. Since 1967 the Israeli public has been conditioned to look upon Jordan as Israel's partner in solving the Palestinian issue; Jordan is perceived as a responsible state that shares many of Israel's interests in controlling Palestinian irredentism. The PLO, in contrast, is perceived at the very least as lacking in political maturity, hopelessly divided against itself, and incapable of compromise; at worst it is, for many Israelis, the incarnation of evil. The fact that a rather large percentage of Israelis is prepared, under a variety of circumstances, to dialogue with the PLO, should not necessarily be construed as reflecting a broad readiness to deliver most of the territory to it (indeed, the most far-reaching border adjustments currently acceptable to the majority of Israelis are those implied by the Allon Plan — which is not acceptable to Palestinians); many Israelis, including some extreme rightists, take the pragmatic view that Israel should seek to talk with its enemies, if only to know them better and perhaps disarm them in a political sense.

Because this option is so far-reaching, and because its implementation entails the most grave challenges to the delicate fabric of Israeli society and to the very unity and integrity of the nation, it is difficult to conceive of any Israeli government attempting to implement it without prior approval by some sort of national referendum. Since the Labor Party has pledged to hold a referendum on any solution involving territorial compromise, this (or new Knesset elections) would almost certainly be the case regarding an agreement to establish a Palestinian state. The ensuing national debate would be divisive to an extreme, and would leave heavy scars on the Israeli body politic. Further, rejection by the Israeli public of such an agreement reached by its own government would present Israel to the world — including the United States and world Jewry, two key strategic allies — as having rejected peace, and it would risk losing their sympathy and support. This could bear heavy consequences for Israel's national morale. A new Arab-Israeli war might find virtually half the Israeli public feeling that they were taking part in a struggle forced upon them by the obstinacy of their fellow Israelis.

On the other hand, majority approval of a Palestinian state settlement would guarantee a bitter reaction by at least a portion of the Israeli Right, who would wage a fierce struggle to prevent its implementation. Few if any of the Israeli settlers in the territories would agree to continue to live inside the Palestinian state, even if this were politically possible. For the most part, their ideology is religious-national. They view the settlement movement as a way of expanding the borders of the State of Israel to encompass the Land of Israel. No specific settlement location is more or less holy than any other. In this sense, Elon Moreh and Shiloh in Samaria are, for them, neither more nor less significant than Tel Aviv and Petach Tiqva; they would not remain in Elon Moreh, once it were located within a Palestinian state, merely because of its religious significance. Hence the most dedicated of the settlers would likely refuse to live in an Arab state (Palestine), while those without ideological motivations would certainly have little reason to remain. Besides, there is a grave problem of security. It would be reasonable to assess that a residual Israeli presence inside the new Palestinian state would be seen by responsible Israelis and Palestinians alike as provocative, if not a downright danger to stability.

The forced evacuation of Yamit in the northern Sinai in 1982 might be seen as a preview, on a small scale, of the difficulties involved in removing Israeli settlers forcibly from their homes in Judea, Samaria and Gaza. Such an operation would present far more complex logistic and emotional challenges to IDF units sent to do the job. Based on the Yamit precedent, it is virtually certain that rightist politicians and activists would lobby and pressure soldiers and commanders to refuse to carry out orders. On the other hand, the fact that there had been a referendum and that, consequently, implementation of this option indeed reflected the will of the Israeli people, should act to neutralize violent opposition. No doubt this would be the nature of the government's appeal to the people: that what was at stake was not the agreement or the principle of withdrawal, but rather the rule of law and the very democratic nature of the state. Still, many settlers and supporters of the Greater Land of Israel ideology would oppose the move by force. For them, the evacuation of Jewish towns and villages from the heart of the Land of Israel is inconceivable. This might lead to bloodshed amongst Jews. In self-justification, some settlers would claim that only a referendum among Jews worldwide could decide the fate of Eretz Yisrael; indeed, that it is not within the authority of this generation of the Jewish people to concede control over its age-old heritage.

A forcible evacuation of settlers to make room for a Palestinian state would render a large portion of the Israeli public angry and, in their frustration and disappointment, perhaps even prepared to abandon the Zionist dream. These deep feelings of frustration, betrayal and despair could be turned against Israel itself. A minority, we have noted, would oppose evacuation by force. Further, some extreme rightists might seek to oppose the entire political program of a Palestinian state settlement by resort to terrorism. Israel's experience with right-wing terrorism in the territories in the early 1980s suggests that, under even more extreme pressures, the phenomenon could be worse. Not only Arab targets, but moderate Israeli politicians and even the IDF could be singled out by a Jewish underground opposed to this solution.

Against this backdrop of destructive ramifications inside Israel of a Palestinian state settlement, it must be born in mind that most Israelis, including many rightists, are sensitive to international pressure. They appreciate that Israel cannot remain viable and vital if it has to oppose the rest of the world over a long period of time. Should such pressure be applied, it is conceivable that a large majority of Israelis might come to see a Palestinian state as less risky than prolonged Israeli isolation and sharply reduced support from abroad.

Demography, Geography and Economy

The creation of a small, landlocked state in parts of Judea and Samaria, with a highly overcrowded adjunct in the Gaza Strip, would bring into being a political entity burdened with grave geographic, demographic and economic problems, some of which would be shared by Israel. For one, as pointed out with regard to autonomy, the location of the border would be critical for ensuring Israeli access to water resources and room for minimal development. These demands would have to be reconciled with the Palestinian need to ensure water reserves, as well as adequate communications between Samaria and Judea, and, via Israel, with Gaza. Then too, due to its own lack of resources, at least in the early stages the new state would be heavily dependent geographically and economically on at least one of its neighbors — Jordan and/or Israel. While Jordan provides a natural ethnic affinity, Israel's ports of Haifa and Ashdod (or Gaza, reached via Israel) are far closer and more accessible to the West Bank than Aqaba, Jordan's only port, or Lebanese ports.

Paradoxically Gaza, which would impose upon the new state its most immediate and serious demographic burden, is also more amenable to programs for accelerated development. Its geographic location would enable it to receive water supplies from Egypt, to intensify its agriculture and develop industry, and to export to European markets. But everything would depend on a massive project to reduce Gaza's refugee population.

Current geographic and demographic factors, then, would render the new state heavily dependent on Israel — at least initially. This may be advantageous in encouraging overall cooperation, but harmful in terms of the frictions generated. Were the Palestinian state to decide on economic separation from Israel, it would require immediate aid of around 1.5-2 billion dollars per annum for several years, merely in order to avoid a sharp drop in standard of living. Alternatively, it would be desirable for the new state, at least in the early stages, to permit the continued movement of workers and goods between itself and Israel. It could then gradually establish tariff barriers to protect infant industries that would absorb workers employed in Israel, and diversify its trade in order further to reduce dependence on Israel.

The extensive infrastructure investment required to create a minimal basis for the provision of sources of livelihood for the majority of the working force would approach 2-2.5 billion dollars for basic industries as well as electricity, roads, and a port in Gaza. Additional investment would be required in housing, particularly if the new state were to absorb refugees. The success of the industrialization process would, however, require more than economic aid. To absorb industrial technologies and maintain large economic enterprises, the new state would require a labor force that is presently either unavailable, or underemployed, as well as export markets that do not currently exist. For the Palestinian state to place this economic burden upon its Arab neighbors would require considerable goodwill on their part — hence, their benevolent attitude toward the new solution.

At the same time, successful implementation of a Palestinian state solution would benefit the Israeli economy, since Israel would be better situated geopolitically than before to attract investment, trade and tourism. The Palestinian input to Israel's economy is small. Even a total severance of economic ties by the Palestinian state would lower the Israeli GNP by only 1-2 percent over a period of three to four years. Israel would, however, require some 2 to 4 billion dollars in order to relocate IDF forces and training installations, and another one billion were it to perceive a need to fence and seal the new border. It would require another 3 to 5 billion dollars for relocating, say, 20,000 Israeli settler families. Thus if the Palestinian statebuilding process were accompanied by separation from Israel's economy, and Israel received no additional foreign aid, the Israeli economy would be hard hit. It would suffer an immediate drop of 3-4 percent in GNP; private consumption per capita would also be reduced for about four years; and foreign debt would rise by 2-3 percent per annum.

The United States

The United States has traditionally opposed an independent Palestinian state. President Bush has explicitly opposed this solution. Although Washington continued to insist that its position on this issue had not changed despite the initiation of the US-PLO dialogue in December 1988, the US move at least raises some questions regarding Washington's commitment to rejection of a Palestinian state option. Clearly the US has played an active role in moderating the PLO's stated objectives. But the limits of this moderation, from the PLO's standpoint, appear to be the organization's acceptance of a two-state solution for the Israeli-Palestinian conflict. Yet by agreeing to talk to the PLO the United States apparently did not alter its fundamental conception of the outcome of negotiations — some kind of solution involving self-government by the Palestinians of the West Bank and Gaza, in association with Jordan.

Therefore three possible alternative results may emerge from the US-PLO talks: 1) A PLO willingness to begin a prolonged peace process that starts with serious contacts between Israelis and residents of the West Bank and Gaza and ends with a Jordanian-

Palestinian federation. 2) American acceptance of a two-state solution, i.e., a Palestinian state alongside Israel. 3) A breakdown of the dialogue. Whatever the results in the short term, America's willingness to conduct a dialogue with the PLO suggests at a minimum that Washington's opposition to Palestinian statehood may be less than absolute.

For most American officials the favored solution continues to be a Palestinian-Jordanian federation, rather than an independent Palestinian state. Yet many in Washington increasingly argue that the feasibility of their preferred solution has diminished considerably. Therefore, should the positions adopted by Arafat in late 1988 — recognition of Israel, renouncement of terrorism, and acceptance of UN Security Council resolutions 242 and 338 as the basis for negotiation with Israel — be matched by effective PLO moves to end terrorism against Israel, Washington would be impressed. If the talks led to positive results (e.g., abrogation of the PLO covenant; dramatic alteration of the PLO's conceptions of the procedures and substance of a settlement), then the US would likely urge the government in Jerusalem to talk with the PLO. There would be tensions in the relationship if Israel refused to talk.

Certainly, if Israel became a prime mover toward a Palestinian state solution, and if the PLO and Israel reached an agreement, the United States would acquiesce. Nevertheless, there would be concerns. Even if Israel agreed to a PLO state, some Americans, including members of the executive and legislative branches and Jewish community leaders, would be asking whether the settlement would be stable, whether the PLO state might not become a base for Soviet activities in the region, and whether it would represent a threat to Jordan.

However, whatever doubts American officials might have during negotiations and at the time an agreement was reached, US-Israeli relations would be enhanced, at least in the flush of excitement surrounding a successful Palestinian-Israeli deal. Such elements of the relationship as economic aid, strategic cooperation, Israel's image, and military assistance would all be facilitated and improved. Israel would be seen to have taken serious risks for peace, and the government's courage and willingness to sacrifice would be universally praised. But admiration would not prevent misgivings, which inevitable Arab and Israeli opposition to the agreements would intensify. When probable difficulties arose, the United States might not side diplomatically with Israel if it were perceived to be the recalcitrant party, and differences between the two governments could well emerge.

The Soviet Union

After an initial period of skepticism following the October 1973 War, the USSR has gradually come to include the idea of an independent Palestinian state as an integral component of its peace plan (the other two elements being Israel's withdrawal from the territories occupied in 1967, and international guarantees for the security and inviolability of the frontiers of all Middle Eastern states and their right to independent existence and development). Explicit in this program is Soviet recognition of Israel's right to a secure existence, and total rejection of the maximalist Palestinian demand for the establishment of a democratic, secular Palestinian state in all of mandatory Palestine. Thus the Soviets have repeatedly emphasized that they envisage the Palestinian state as coexisting alongside Israel rather than replacing it.

What the Soviets have left somewhat vague, however, is the question of the Israeli-Palestinian border: should the Palestinian state be confined to the West Bank and Gaza Strip, or should it include territories granted to the Arabs by the UN General Assembly decision of 29 November 1947. On the one hand, the standard Soviet position recognizes only the 1947 partition lines as the borders of Israel, and official atlases still illustrate this fact. On the other hand, as early as the late 1960s the Soviets implied their willingness to recognize the 1949 demarcation lines as Israel's legitimate boundaries within the framework of a comprehensive settlement. This willingness was apparently relayed to the US in 1970, during the two-power talks on the Rogers initiative. It was reiterated on numerous occasions during the 1970s and the 1980s by official statements and in the mass media and, above all, it is reflected in the fact that Security Council Resolution 242 is viewed by the Soviets as the basis for an Arab-Israeli peace.

In this sense, the Soviet attitude toward alterations in the 1967 borders in Israel's favor must be presumed as negative. However Moscow would probably not seek to derail the peace process if the Palestinians accepted such revised borders.

In any case, despite the Soviets' keen awareness of the constraints on the viability of a Palestinian state in the West Bank and Gaza (indeed, perhaps because of these very problems and the consequent potential dependence of that state on Soviet security guarantees and economic aid), Moscow would consider such a state the only realistic entity that the Palestinians could aspire to — whether on its own, or in confederation with Jordan. Hence, by way of reducing possible Palestinian apprehensions of Israel, Moscow could be expected to invest considerable efforts to ensure the most solid international guarantees for the agreement, including its participation in an international supervisory force under the auspices of the United Nations.

In the longer run, the USSR is likely to be a major contender for influence in the newly-established Palestinian state and to invest abundant political and economic resources to this end. The general thrust of influence, though, would be in the direction of moderation, namely, to temper Palestinian irredentism so as to maintain the Israeli-Palestinian arrangement.

Thus, on the one hand, Israel would benefit from constructive Soviet support for a Palestinian state solution, in the sense that this could moderate PLO, and perhaps even Syrian, attitudes. On the other, the Soviets would back Palestinian objections to border rectifications, and would seek to exercise dominant influence in the new state. Soviet dominance over the Palestinian state would not be welcomed by Israel.

Conclusions

This option offers Israel the possibility of resolving the Palestinian issue, but at considerable risk. An Israeli government decision to negotiate the establishment of a Palestinian state with the PLO would encounter widespread opposition, some of it violent, among Israelis. The results could also be highly divisive within the IDF, particularly if it had to counter Jewish terrorism, and insofar as it would be required to evacuate settlers by force (most settlers would leave peacefully, but if the evacuation were to encompass, say, 20,000 settler families, then several thousand settlers might attempt to resist evacuation forcefully).

Under the conditions prevailing in late 1988 it seemed unlikely that any Israeli government would attempt to implement this option unless more public support became evident. This could be generated if the PLO's move toward moderation in late 1988 — comprising an explicit and authoritative recognition of Israel, renouncement of terrorism, and acceptance of 242 and 338 as the basis for a negotiated settlement — were enhanced by a practical termination of all PLO terrorism, by annulment of the clauses in the Palestinian National Covenant that reject Israel's right to exist, and by frequent repetition of the PLO's commitment that the future Palestinian state would coexist peacefully alongside the State of Israel. Moreover, following the initiation of the US-PLO dialogue in late 1988, it is no longer inconceivable that American pressure would be applied upon Israel to accede to this option. Under these circumstances many Israelis might view the establishment of a Palestinian state as less risky than prolonged Israeli isolation and sharply reduced support from abroad.

In the short term, most Palestinians would support this solution, as it satisfies their national aspirations in a way hitherto unknown, while seeking to minimize the implied infringements on their sovereignty, such as the essential demilitarization of the prospective state. Yet extremist Palestinians would probably opt immediately for "armed struggle."

In the long term, it might be difficult for the Palestinian mainstream to avoid or prevent developments leading to deterioration: irredentism, terrorism (both internally and against Israel), and friction with the remaining Israeli military presence. There is a particular danger that an influx of refugees to the new state would jeopardize both security and long-term stability. A second possibility for negative developments envisages a scenario whereby the Palestinian government commences a calculated attempt to implement the "strategy of stages" by subverting the Israeli Arab population from a base in Judea, Samaria and Gaza.

115

But it can also be argued strongly that in the long term the PLO would develop an interest in conciliation, hence stability, along with the capacity to maintain it.

With the exception of Syria, most of the surrounding Arab states would give their blessing to this solution, and it could act to catalyze Israel's relations with additional Arab states. Syria, however, could both sponsor terrorism and ensure that a resolution of the refugee issue did not reach either its own or Lebanon's camps, thereby hindering a successful settlement. Jordan might be negatively affected by radicalization of its Palestinian population as a consequence of the establishment of the new state. Certainly, successful implementation of this option would depend on an understanding with most of the Arab states on their participation in resolving the Palestinian refugee issue. As for superpower attitudes, the US would be accepting, and the USSR supportive.

This solution, were it implemented, would require extensive security arrangements for Israel that would inevitably be perceived as infringements upon Palestinian sovereignty. These should include alterations in the 1967 border (rendered advisable also by geographic and water considerations), essential demilitarization of the Palestinian state, and the placement of early warning, air defense and minimal defense forces. Adequate supervision over internal security affairs in the Palestinian state — to prevent terrorism and subversion against Israel — would be vital for Israeli security, and would have to be carefully detailed in advance. In this conjunction, there may indeed be a gap — in terms of extent and duration — between Israeli security requirements and the Palestinians' readiness to accept the restrictions on their state sovereignty entailed by these requirements.

Heavy financial aid would also be required by the Palestinian state to enhance its stability. Satisfactory solutions for the resettling of Palestinian refugees would have to be found in order to neutralize the potential danger they pose to Israel's long-term security. These security modalities might be critical in convincing a highly skeptical Israeli population.

In view of the security risks it poses, this option is less desirable for Israel than options II (autonomy) and VI (a Jordanian-

Palestinian federation, assuming that Hashemite rule could be maintained over the long term). But it is potentially acceptable to the Palestinians — whereas the other options are not. And it does go farther toward solving the essential conflict than any other option we have analyzed.

In this context, under all the scenarios that affect Israel's long-term security interest a distinction must be made between Palestinian intentions, which may be either benevolent or malevolent, and Palestinian capabilities of disrupting the peace settlement, which would be highly limited under the conditions of the agreement and in view of Israel's deterrent capacity. There is a critical need for a significant transition period during which Palestinian intentions and capabilities could be tested, and confidence-building measures implemented. Thus it would seem advisable that, in any event, a Palestinian state solution be preceded by extensive autonomy, with the movement toward sovereignty gradual, negotiated, and supported by genuine achievements in stabilizing the situation, eliminating irredentism, preventing terrorism, and solving the Palestinians' own potentially troublesome demographic and economic problems. The transition period should also be accompanied by a settlement with Jordan that would reinforce the security provisions of the Israeli-Palestinian settlement by providing Jordanian guarantees for Israel's security similar to those embodied in the Israel-Egypt peace treaty. General Arab support, in the form of peace treaties between Israel and additional Arab states, as well as international guarantees and a genuine resettlement plan for Palestinian refugees, would also be necessary.

V. Option Five — Unilateral Withdrawal From Gaza

Definition

Israel withdraws its forces from the Gaza Strip unilaterally, without prior negotiation or agreement with any Arab party, including Palestinians. The withdrawal would involve a complete severance of ties. To prevent terrorist infiltration from Gaza and ensure Israel's security, the border would be electronically fenced and mined. To deter introduction of arms for a Palestinian army, Israel would patrol the sea off the Strip.

Jewish settlements in the Qatif area of the Strip would remain; other settlements in the Strip (that contain only a few dozen families) would be dismantled. The Qatif settlements would be retained for several reasons: they constitute a fairly homogeneous Jewish region, with no Arab settlements interspersed among them; they are accessed directly from Israeli territory; and they constitute a security barrier of sorts between Gaza and Egypt. For these reasons, too, their dismantlement would be a controversial act in terms of Israeli public opinion.

There are two variations to this option regarding the extent to which Arab laborers from the Strip should be permitted to enter Israel: total prohibition of entry, and limited entry. The rationale for a prohibition of Arab entry rests on a key Israeli consideration. From a security standpoint, the moment the IDF and the Israeli General Security Service abandon their responsibility for developments inside the Strip, it would require an inordinate effort to ensure that the 50,000 or so Arab workers who enter Israel daily from the Strip were not armed for terrorist activity. By way of comparison, Israeli security authorities can process some 3,000 travellers a day, mostly Palestinians, at the Jordan River bridges; they enter from Jordan, which shares Israel's interest in preventing infiltration of terrorists.

The rationale for permitting limited entry would be to enable Gazans to continue to support themselves economically, while retaining a "stick" (the threat of closing the border completely) that might ensure better relations. Israel could perhaps permit some Gazans to remain in the country for fixed periods of work. It could possibly reduce the number of Gazan workers to a minimum of low-risk (from a security standpoint) persons prior to closing the border, or, alternatively, close the border crossing completely, then slowly allow a graduated increase.

Additional variations include the possibility of prenegotiating withdrawal with Egypt and/or the UN, and phased unilateral implementation by Israel that "keeps the Palestinians guessing" and retains an Israeli capacity to "roll back" the withdrawal if its initial phases backfire.

The inhabitants of the Gaza Strip would be free to choose whatever political framework they wished, including a Palestinian state led by the PLO, with all the accouterments of statehood. Gazans would have the right to come and go via the sea and air and — if Egypt agreed — by land as well.

All the measures invoked for inhibiting the introduction of arms to the Strip would be designed primarily to prevent a genuine heavy military buildup there. Clearly, terrorists and light arms could be infiltrated — by means of commercial air flights, for example.

Israel's objective in adopting this option would be to divest itself of a small section of territory in which over half the inhabitants are refugees, and the rate of population increase is so high that it will reach about one million by the year 2000. This option would allow Israel to cut itself off from responsibility for seemingly unsolvable population problems that could only grow worse with the passage of time, at the price of the emergence of a minuscule Palestinian state. But this clearly is, at best, a partial option: it does not aspire to solve those fundamental aspects of the Palestinian problem that center geographically in Judea and Samaria.

An Israeli government might opt for this strategy out of the conviction that the Gazan population explosion rendered it impossible not to act, and the sooner the better; and on the assumption that it had no option to negotiate an alternative acceptable solution with either Jordan or the PLO.

Ramifications

The Palestinians

Unilateral Israeli withdrawal from Gaza would provide two advantages for Palestinians: removal of the Israeli presence from Gaza itself, and the creation of an independent Palestinian mini-state, both of which would be secured without any Palestinian concessions to Israel in return. Indeed, the Palestinians' unilateral declaration of independence of November 1988 would now receive explicit confirmation in the form of territorial sovereignty.

The direct beneficiaries of removal of the Israeli presence would be Gaza Strip residents, although it would be a rather dubious benefit in view of the price they might pay: immediate and extreme immiseration due to the possible closing of the Israeli labor market. Unless economic interaction with Israel, including access to its labor market, were permitted (which would exacerbate Israel's security problems) the main occupation of unemployed Gazans, especially youth, would be to attempt to smuggle in weapons and use them against Israel.

The aftermath inside the Strip would probably be an intense power struggle between secular nationalists (reinforced by PLO elements arriving from abroad) and Islamic fundamentalists, who are much stronger there than in the West Bank. Whatever the outcome, the mini-state in Gaza would inspire ongoing conflict with Israel. No other Palestinians would derive any immediate benefit from it.

Gazan authorities would be hard put to contain violence directed at Israel. While they certainly would be concerned about violent Israeli reprisals, and would be unenthusiastic about reoccupation, it is not clear to what degree the general population would be deterred by the latter threat: conditions in Gaza would probably get so bad that some Gazans might even look back on the Israeli occupation with a measure of nostalgia.

Among Palestinians elsewhere, the main consequence of Israeli withdrawal from Gaza would be the perception that Israel had been forced to leave because it could not cope with the problems of

121

staying. In other words, this would be a victory for *sumud* (steadfastness) and *intifada*. West Bankers would view unilateral withdrawal from Gaza as a precedent and a model to be emulated. At the same time, the perception of an Israeli aim of withdrawing from Gaza in order to facilitate permanent retention of the West Bank, would further increase the sense of urgency among West Bankers about their own efforts. This would likely be translated into a more intense *intifada*. The PLO, too, would be encouraged to believe that unrequited concessions could be extorted from Israel by means of an intensified uprising in the West Bank. Hence it would probably seek to limit the resort to terrorism (as distinct from a popular uprising) that this option would likely inspire among the more radical Palestinian organizations in the West Bank.

Were the PLO to succeed in stabilizing its authority inside the Gaza Strip itself, an alternative pattern suggests itself. The Gazan mini-state might seek to set an example and a precedent for peaceful coexistence between Palestine and Israel, in the hope that this would inspire international and domestic pressure upon Israel's government to withdraw from the West Bank, too. Certainly the "rules of the game" would change, insofar as Israel would, for the first time, have to deal with a Palestinian state that possesses territory of its own.

All told, from the standpoint of Palestinian reactions, unilateral withdrawal from Gaza appears to be highly detrimental to Israeli interests.

Israeli Arabs

The advent of national sovereignty under a PLO regime in a portion of Palestine, without any prior commitment to coexistence with Israel, would augment radical tendencies among Israeli Arabs. In the atmosphere of uncertainty produced by the unilateral Israeli move, Israeli Arabs would most likely assess that the real Israeli intention was to annex the West Bank — thereby increasing their own anxiety.

On the other hand, the Israeli withdrawal from Gaza would in many ways be perceived as a peripheral issue not departing greatly from the status quo. While they would welcome the withdrawal in principle, Israeli Arabs see the focus of the problem as the West Bank and the PLO, neither of which would necessarily be directly involved in contacts with Israel concerning the withdrawal from Gaza. Moreover, most Israeli Arabs' family ties are in the West Bank rather than Gaza. The radicals, seeing withdrawal as a sign of Israeli weakness, would step up their drive to reactivate the 1947 Partition Resolution boundaries and/or to dilute the Zionist character of Israel, but this phenomenon would be limited and, from the Israeli standpoint, controllable.

Were withdrawal to include a complete cutting off of movement of laborers from Gaza, Israeli Arabs would enjoy a modest economic windfall. The enhanced Israeli demand for manpower would generate an improvement in the employment picture in the Arab sector, where unemployment stood at 10 percent in 1987.

All told, then, unilateral Israeli withdrawal from Gaza would lend impetus to the radicalization process among Israeli Arabs in the ideological sphere — impelling them, for example, to demand the 1947 UN Partition Plan boundaries. In the political realm, the radicals would gain support, as would the cause of establishing a single massive Arab political party.

The Arab States

Israel's unilateral withdrawal from the Gaza Strip would create confusion, suspicion and uncertainty among the Arab states. Inter-Arab alignments would not be affected by the withdrawal itself. However, given the considerable likelihood that the implementation of this option would lead to increased violence on the West Bank and would generate an embittered, militant Palestinian mini-state in Gaza, the consequences of this option in the inter-Arab and Arab-Israeli spheres are likely to be similar to those expected for the first option we considered, the status quo. However, in this case the ramifications of developments in Gaza are likely to have a more direct effect on Israel's relations with Egypt. In addition, most Arab states and non-state actors are likely to regard Israel's unilateral withdrawal from Gaza more as a defeat for the Jewish state than as a Machiavellian maneuver to annex the West Bank. Hence implementation of this option is likely to redound negatively upon the way in which the Arab states view Israel, resulting in diminished Israeli deterrence.

Jordan is likely to regard the creation of a Palestinian state in Gaza as a threat to whatever remains of its own influence and aspirations in the West Bank, in that West Bank Palestinians would envisage their own future in terms of Palestinian sovereignty too. However, Jordan would seek to establish links with the new entity with a view to preventing it from developing radical tendencies that might radiate into the West Bank and even beyond, to the East Bank.

Similarly, implementation of this option may present Egypt's relations with Israel with new sources of stress. Egypt's proximity to Gaza — and its historical attitude toward the Strip — are key factors in this regard. Since 1949 Egypt has refused to accept direct and full responsibility for administering the lives of Gazan Palestinians. It is highly unlikely that Cairo would agree voluntarily to undertake such responsibilities under a scenario of Israeli withdrawal.

In order to prevent a crisis in Egyptian-Israeli relations, Cairo would have to help interdict the transportation of arms and equipment from Egyptian territory into Gaza. On the other hand, until the Israeli-Palestinian conflict is settled, Egypt might wish to avoid the task of protecting Israel from arms smuggling. Yet once such smuggling occurs, and the weapons are used for terrorist acts against Israel, the latter is bound to register its complaints with the Cairo authorities. Hence, the anticipation of tensions in Egyptian-Israeli relations following the implementation of this option.

On the other hand Egypt would probably seek to be involved in constraining the growth of Islamic fundamentalism. In this realm, its interests in the Strip are likely to coincide with Israel's concerns. In this sense Egypt could be expected to spearhead efforts to mobilize Arab and international economic assistance for the Gazans. Concurrently, Egypt would continue to press for additional Israeli concessions on the Palestinian issue.

Syria is likely to hail an Israeli withdrawal from Gaza as a victory for the *intifada*, and encourage the Palestinians to redouble their struggle. Rhetoric aside, this option neither poses a major threat to Syrian interests nor provides it with significant opportunities. Hence Syria could be expected to avoid any major effort to prevent the option's implementation. At the same time, to the extent that Israel's deterrence of Syria becomes an increasingly central issue for war avoidance, diminished Israeli deterrence, due to the perception that Israel had withdrawn from Gaza unilaterally under pressure, could spell negative consequences.

Saudi Arabia could be expected to provide financial support to the new Palestinian city-state, as would Iraq and the smaller GCC states. Iran and Libya are likely to follow Syria's lead and be indifferent to the option's implementation.

Israel's Security

The unilateral evacuation of the Gaza Strip would not alter Israel's military-strategic setting. Hence, the implications of this option for Israel's defense are unlikely to be materially different than those associated with the continuation of the status quo — with one important qualification: Israeli deterrence is likely to suffer as a consequence of the general perception that Israel withdrew from Gaza due to cumulative Palestinian pressures, and without extracting any concessions from the Palestinians. As such, this may redound negatively upon Israel's deterrent standing by encouraging other Arabs, particularly in Damascus and the West Bank, to attempt to compel Israel to capitulate in a similar fashion.

In addition, Israel's unilateral withdrawal may create particular security risks inside the Gaza Strip itself. Their extent would depend on developments in the Strip following Israel's withdrawal. Three possibilities should be mentioned: first, the deterioration of life in Gaza into total chaos, including a civil war between followers of the PLO and Muslim fundamentalists; secondly, the transformation of Gaza into a single large refugee camp, run by UNRWA; and finally, the creation of a PLO mini-state which would consider itself the precursor of a similar entity in the West Bank.

These risks suggest a number of potentially dangerous developments for Israel. A chaotic internal situation in the Strip is particularly likely if access to Israel is closed, and Gaza residents are no longer able to maintain their present sources of employment and income. The frustration of the Strip's Palestinian population might then find an outlet in acts of terrorism against Israel. Then too, it would be difficult to isolate the Strip from external supplies of lethal weaponry. In light of the location of Rafah, a town divided between the Strip and Egypt's Sinai region, it would be nearly impossible to prevent arms smuggling from Egypt to the Strip. Smuggling via air and sea, using the port of Gaza and a civilian airfield that the Gazans would probably construct, would be even more difficult to prevent. Further, Israel's unilateral withdrawal from Gaza is likely to encourage the Palestinians of the West Bank to intensify their violent struggle, in the hope of inducing Israel to withdraw from that region as well.

Effective deterrence against terrorism from Gaza would be nearly impossible to establish given the chaotic situation likely to develop there. Israel's experience with Lebanon has demonstrated that deterrence cannot be established where there is no central government that enjoys a monopoly of force. Certainly Egypt might find it difficult to ignore post-withdrawal deterioration in the Gaza Strip. The resultant tensions between Cairo and Jerusalem on this issue could invade other realms of the bilateral Egyptian-Israeli relationship.

Ultimately, a total deterioration of conditions in the Strip could compel Israel to reoccupy it. By that time it is likely to be literally swamped with light and medium arms — making the reoccupation costly.

While these risks are considerable, they might be mitigated if, as a consequence of the power struggle likely to develop following Israel's withdrawal from Gaza, the PLO should emerge victorious and establish central authority there. Under these circumstances the organization might wish to establish its credibility as a responsible party willing to establish relations of peaceful coexistence with Israel. In other words, Gaza under the PLO might wish to have its management of life in the Strip viewed as a confidence-building measure toward the possible establishment of a similar entity in the West Bank, with the hope that the two regions would then merge into an independent Palestinian state.

Should this become the PLO's priority, and assuming that it indeed succeeds in establishing central authority in Gaza, the risks of terrorism and insurgency from the Strip would diminish significantly. But the conflict would continue, most likely in the form of an intensified *intifada* in the West Bank.

The Israeli Domestic Setting

Public opinion in Israel would tend to view this option as an Israeli admission of failure: having failed to rule, and having been overwhelmed by the physical, human and economic burden involved in maintaining its presence in the territories, Israel would be abandoning the Gaza Strip with absolutely nothing to show in return. The cardinal principle of withdrawing only in return for an agreed, and beneficial settlement — a principle fully endorsed by Israel's ally, the United States — would be violated. Israel would be confronted with a Palestinian mini-state in Gaza of its own making, and with a potential dynamic over which it had absolutely no control.

Further, this option could actually unite Israeli hawks and doves in opposition. The hawks would object to Israeli withdrawal from any part of the Land of Israel — even a relatively insignificant sector like Gaza. They would also fear the ramifications for Judea and Samaria of the precedent of permitting such a withdrawal. However since the withdrawal would require a minimal removal of settlements — the Qatif area settlements would remain as a barricade between the Strip and Egypt — it would not generate significant friction between the Israeli Right and the government or the IDF.

Israeli doves would likely oppose this option too, but for converse reasons. They would fear lest withdrawal from Gaza serve as a convenient way of deflecting pressures upon Israel to solve the Palestinian problem, thereby affording the opportunity to perpetuate the Israeli presence in Judea and Samaria.

Perhaps the most telling reason for popular opposition to this option would be the fear that Palestinian terrorism would quickly spill over from the Strip — however "hermetically" Israel sealed it off — into the Israeli southern coastal region and northern Negev.

Comparisons with the tension between northern Israel and Lebanon during the pre-1982 period would be inevitable. Were Gazan laborers allowed into Israel and terrorism to occur, the Israeli public's reaction would be to demand either a total "sealing" of the Strip, or its reoccupation.

These reservations would be balanced to some extent in Israeli public and political thinking by recognition that Gaza, Khan Yunis and Rafah do not hold the same significance for Israeli culture and history as do key locations in the West Bank, like Hebron and Shiloh, which are seen as the "cradle of Jewish civilization." Moreover in recent years public awareness of the Palestinian demographic threat has increased; the Gaza Strip is perceived as the ultimate expression of this problem. Even some rightists who support the Greater Land of Israel movement might be moved to view withdrawal from Gaza as a minimal concession necessary to stem the demographic tide. Hence Israeli public opposition to a withdrawal would likely lack the emotional fire that would be directed at any sort of territorial compromise in the West Bank, and IDF morale and motivation would not be affected. Were the public to be made to feel reassured concerning the security risks involved, it might be generally accepting. Here the advantage for an Israeli government would be that, compared to other options that require withdrawal, "Gaza first" could be accomplished with reduced public objections.

Geography, Demography and Economy

The severance of the Gaza Strip from Israel by a closed boundary would return Gaza from an economic point of view to its pre-1967 condition — but with a population 65 percent larger. As over 60 percent of the Gazan work force is employed directly in Israel or indirectly by Israelis, severance could ultimately reduce Gaza's GNP (taking into account a multiplier effect) by about 75 percent (it would reduce Israel's GNP by only one percent). The Gaza Strip would require half a billion dollars annually merely to compensate it for this drop in income.

In the longer term, Gazans could actually support themselves only if most of the Strip's refugee population (roughly half its

650,000 people) were resettled elsewhere, and if local water resources — which are fast being depleted through excessive pumping — were supplemented by water piped in from the Nile in Egypt. The first measure, resettlement, would require a radical departure from the policies of the past 40 years on the part of Palestinian and other Arab leaders, who have hitherto insisted that the only resettlement possible is in Israel. The second would require either a benevolent attitude on Egypt's part, or an Egyptian decision to attain overriding influence in the Gazan mini-state by making it dependent on Egyptian water supplies. In addition, a modern harbor could be built at the city of Gaza to handle agricultural exports. Here the European states, to which Gazan agricultural exports are already directed, could play an instrumental financial role. In any event, under the best of circumstances it would take at least a decade to implement programs like these; meanwhile the Gaza population would be destitute.

Here it bears emphasis that optimistic assessments concerning Gaza's economic prospects that are based on analogies with prosperous city-states like Hong Kong and Singapore, are unconvincing. Gaza has no natural economic hinterland, cannot offer a skilled, educated or disciplined work force, and would be too fraught with tension to attract foreign investment or reliable suppliers of raw materials. From an economic standpoint it might, for some time, remain little more than an UNWRA protectorate.

These acute geographic disadvantages would inevitably generate massive human suffering and unrest that could only redound to Israel's detriment. They point to the need for an Israeli withdrawal to be coordinated with the Arab world rather than executed unilaterally, and for Israel to avoid a complete cutoff of the Strip and its working population.

Lastly, unilateral withdrawal from Gaza would generate minimal damage to the Israeli economy: no more than a one percent drop in GNP over 2-3 years.

The United States

Of the six options considered in this study, the American reaction is most difficult to predict in this case, because it has been discussed less than the others in both policy circles and in the press and media.

In assessing the American response two factors are critical. First, what else would be happening in the Arab-Israeli relationship? Did the announcement of a withdrawal from Gaza occur in a period of tension vis-a-vis the territories? Did Israel appear to be desperately seeking a means of diverting mounting international pressure, of using this device as a means of avoiding difficult decisions? Or did Israel seem to be acting to shake up a completely stalled peace process in the apparent hope of demonstrating flexibility and encouraging negotiations? The perceived intentions of the Israeli government would have a major impact on the reaction in the United States.

Secondly, the declared timetable would play a major role. If Israel announced suddenly that it was withdrawing from Gaza within a very short period (days, weeks), the response, in all probability, would be negative. There would likely be an international humanitarian uproar, accompanied by criticism that Israel had acted irresponsibly, and that it was callous toward the indigenous Arab population. The negative response would be intensified if it began to appear that the United States would be obliged to pay the bill for Israel's abdication of responsibilities.

The administration would immediately be concerned about a possible impact on the Egyptian-Israeli peace treaty. Especially if the decision had not been discussed with the administration in advance, Washington would be suspicious that this move was a prelude to Israeli annexation of the West Bank, Israel having delayed the demographic time bomb for 20 years. In any case, the US is bound to protest that, as a unilateral measure, Israel's withdrawal from Gaza contradicts the Camp David framework stipulation that the final status of the territories be determined by negotiations. Against this backdrop the US might be moved to enter discussions with the PLO on ways to avoid the political and security repercussions of a sudden Israeli withdrawal.

However, the negative American reaction would not be far-reaching. Americans are instinctively sympathetic to initiatives. As long as Israel could avoid the appearance of a ruse intended to cover West Bank annexation, understanding would exist for the Israeli move, even if many in the administration perceived it as poorly conceived. There would be enough support in the Congress, the Jewish community and the media to create at least an acceptable rationalization for the Israeli action.

On the other hand, if Israel announced in advance (nine months to a year) that it intended to leave the Gaza Strip at a certain date, there would likely be greater support in the United States. The Israelis would appear more responsible and serious. There would be time to deal with the ramifications and the implications of this step. The administration would want to deal with Egypt and possibly the PLO on the details, to organize an international consortium that would raise capital to cover at least the fundamental human needs of the new mini-state, to gain at a minimum some kind of financial coverage for those Palestinians who would be losing their jobs in Israel, and to cater to the political organization of the new entity. If Israel provided advance notice in this spirit, there would be a greater likelihood that the US would see this as a genuine effort to ameliorate the atmosphere even though it had been motivated by Israeli demographic and political necessities on the ground, rather than by a genuine display of interest in helping to resolve the conflict.

Even under the best of conditions, from the American perspective there would be a major problem with this option: why stop with Gaza? What about the West Bank? If the PLO acted responsibly and peacefully and prevented hostile acts toward Israel from Gaza, pressures would increase on Jerusalem to initiate negotiations for a further settlement. The United States might well publicly favor a PLO state.

On the other hand, if tensions and terrorism increased in the Gaza Strip, no matter what their source, there might be a host of negative consequences: the worsening of Egyptian-Israeli relations; intensified West Bank violence; perhaps ultimately an Israeli reoccupation of Gaza. The complexity of the situation would yield uncertainty and it would not be surprising for the

131

administration to be divided and therefore inconsistent in its interpretations of events and in its actions. A frustrated America would try to prevent further deterioration and initiate a new peace process. American-Israeli relations would probably resemble a roller coaster, alternating between intimacy and hostility.

Thus, of all the options considered here, the unilateral withdrawal from Gaza is likely to be greeted with inconsistency and confusion in Washington. There might be disagreement with Israel; there would not be sanctions. Israeli-American relations would likely enter a volatile phase, but within the framework of the "special relationship" that has characterized the two governments' dealings in the past.

The Soviet Union

In the best case, a unilateral Israeli withdrawal from the Gaza Strip is likely to be perceived by the Soviets as a preliminary modest step on the road to a comprehensive settlement; in the worst case, the USSR would view this move as an attempt to evade a real solution to the Israeli-Palestinian problem. In any case, Israel could expect Soviet emphasis on the need for a prompt follow-up in terms of a more comprehensive solution.

Conclusions

This option would encounter limited Israeli domestic opposition, and its implementation would place manageable burdens on Israeli security forces. It offers Israel the advantage of divesting itself of control over 650,000 Palestinian Arabs (one million by the year 2000). And it could render less costly the possible annexation by Israel of the West Bank.

The option would appear relatively harmless in terms of Arab reactions, with the possible exception of a deterioration in Egyptian-Israeli relations. The American reaction could be confusion, or the generation of new pressures upon Israel for additional withdrawals, depending upon circumstances; the overall international reaction would be negative.

Further, this option entails grave risks. Of all the options analyzed here, this scenario projects the greatest degree of uncertainty regarding the consequences for Israel. It would create a Palestinian mini-state that owes Israel nothing through negotiations or agreement, and might radically alter the international "rules of the game" under which Israel has sought to delegitimize the notion of a Palestinian state.

Further, Israel would risk being perceived by the Arab states, the Palestinians, and Israeli Arabs as retreating due to weakness: this would encourage Palestinian militancy and terrorism, with an escalatory effect within the Arab world. Moreover, at best (from the Israeli standpoint), unilateral withdrawal would generate a Palestinian entity that sought, while maintaining quiet in Gaza, to achieve political expansion by promoting unrest in the West Bank; at worst, it would produce a mini-Lebanon, a source of friction with Egypt, and a base for terrorism. Certainly, Gaza after Israeli withdrawal would require extreme economic first-aid measures to prevent total destitution that would breed even greater radicalization.

Modifications to the notion of a sudden and total severance of ties might make the option less damaging. Israel could try to develop security arrangements that enabled at least limited passage by Gazans working in Israel. This might ensure some contribution to economic stability, and form an incentive to maintain good relations. And gradual implementation — in terms of functions and territories abandoned — might be contemplated, in order to ensure greater Israeli control over the process. In this way Israel might enhance its own freedom of maneuver.

Overall, this appears to be a very risky option. The balance of risks and benefits spells considerable danger for Israel, with few possible associated advantages beyond the obvious attraction of relinquishing control over 650,000 indigent Palestinians.

VI. Option Six — A Jordanian–Palestinian Federation

Definition

The establishment of a Jordanian-Palestinian federal entity would be negotiated by Israel with Jordan and Palestinians. It would comprise the Hashemite Kingdom as currently constituted (i.e., the East Bank) and most of the territory of Judea, Samaria and the Gaza District. Overall rule would be Jordanian, including responsibility for defense, internal security and foreign affairs. Beyond these parameters, there would be a large measure of Palestinian self-rule in the territories.

As in option IV (a Palestinian state) above, the peace treaty would comprise provisions for the resettlement of the 1948 Arab refugees. Security provisions would include an IDF presence in the early stages, with Jordanian internal security forces eventually playing a more active role, as security improves and trust increases. Additional military security arrangements for the long term would, as in option IV, include a large measure of demilitarization of the territories, border adjustments, and an international supervisory force.

Supervision of the Jordan River crossings would be carried out jointly by Israel and Jordan. As for Jewish settlements, some would be located in territory annexed to Israel. Others located in Israeli security zones would be retained at least as long as these zones existed. Settlements located inside the new federation would probably have to be evacuated, although conceivably they could be permitted to remain, under Jordanian sovereignty, with agreed links to Israel, if they so desired.

The border between Israel and the federation would be open to passage of citizens from both sides. Collaboration in the disposition of water resources would follow the pattern outlined in option IV above. State lands would fall under the jurisdiction of the federation, with the exception of those located inside specified IDF security zones and Jewish settlements that chose to remain.

Israel might find this option attractive, as it provides for a political settlement that does not involve the creation of an additional, potentially irredentist state. The transfer of essential elements of control over the territories to Jordanian rule assumes that Jordan is more trustworthy and anxious to live at peace with Israel than is the PLO, and that mistrust of the Palestinians is a common denominator uniting Jordan and Israel. Hence the arrangement would presumably generate minimal existential strategic conflicts between Jordan and Israel over the territory of the Land of Israel.

But the option of Jordanian rule over most of Judea, Samaria and the Gaza Strip, as a result of negotiations with Israel, would appear not to be feasible unless a genuine upheaval were to alter the regional environment. This would require Jordan to attain a far more influential status among the Arabs of the territories and among those moderate Arab states that currently favor a PLO-centered solution. The prerequisites for such changes comprise significant diminution of the PLO's status, the complete collapse of the *intifada*, and the reversal of the Palestinians' declaration of statehood of November 1988. These developments appeared particularly unlikely in the aftermath of the launching of the US-PLO dialogue in December 1988.

Here a brief word is in order regarding the use of the terms federation and confederation. The former refers to a single state composed of more than one political entity, and in which overall rule is centered in a single sovereign. The latter refers to a union between two sovereign entities that agree to recognize a single, essentially titular head-of-state, while retaining their essential political independence.

The notion of a Jordanian-Palestinian federation or confederation is current in Israeli, Palestinian, Jordanian and American thinking. Some versions even predicate a tripartite confederation, including Israel as well. To the extent that a Jordanian-Palestinian entity is perceived in Israel as a viable option, Israelis generally assume a predominant role for Jordan within the entity, i.e., a Jordanian dominated federation, with central authority in Amman, rather than a confederation comprising two sovereign states. The latter notion corresponds more closely with that mentioned in public statements by PLO and Jordanian leaders.

136

The PLO appears to see the confederal formula as a way both of mitigating Israeli and western suspicions of its intentions, and of assuring its eventual influence in Jordan, without conceding its independence. Thus it consistently presents confederation as a status to be adopted voluntarily *after* it achieves independence. As for Jordan, there is reason to assume the existence of a gap between King Hussein's seeming adherence to this sort of genuine confederation, and his real intention of achieving sufficient dominance within such an entity to ensure the neutralization of any Palestinian threat to his kingdom. Hussein appears to view confederation as a formula for subordinating the Palestinian entity to his rule, without seeming to neutralize its independent status during negotiations and thereafter.

Here we shall analyze the option as it appears on the overt Israeli political agenda, and as it may still exist on King Hussein's covert agenda — to the extent he still sees himself as a principal player in the process — i.e., a Jordanian-dominant federation. The confederal variety in not analyzed separately here, although insofar as it is a variant on the option of an independent Palestinian state it is addressed in chapter IV.

Here we must also take note that a third variant of the "Jordanian option" — absolute Jordanian sovereignty over the territories — has been broached in the past. This would be conditional upon Israel's agreeing to give up all of Judea, Samaria, the Gaza Strip and East Jerusalem, thereby satisfying a long-standing Jordanian condition for a bilateral settlement. The validity of this longstanding proposal of King Hussein's has never been put to the test. Certainly it was rendered doubtful by the events of the second half of 1988: Hussein's renunciation of responsibility for the West Bank in July, and the PNC declaration of independence in November. In any case, this option is not on the Israeli political agenda, and is not dealt with here. Still, from the Israeli standpoint the federation option is essentially a "Jordanian option." Israel would deliver control over territories and population to Jordan; and federation would constitute the Jordanian-Palestinian formula for ruling over those territories.

Ramifications

The Palestinians

Jordanian rule in the territories would get Israel "off the backs" of West Bank and Gaza Palestinians, and they might welcome such a development with varying degrees of enthusiasm. Another advantage for the Palestinians would be that the end to Israeli occupation would be achieved without the PLO having to make far-reaching concessions. But this option would do little to satisfy Palestinian aspirations for independent statehood. It would also be regarded by the Palestinians as representing a strategic retreat, after the November 1988 PNC declaration of independence had won broad international recognition. Therefore there would probably not be sufficient incentive for the PLO to endorse the option of a Jordanian-Palestinian federation unless it saw it as a temporary arrangement, i.e., because there was a prior agreement that Jordan would subsequently withdraw from the territories, or because the PLO was confident that Jordan could be forced to do so.

Thus most Palestinians could be expected to oppose such an option, and might use force against Jordan, as well as against fellow Palestinian "collaborators" who supported Jordan. Their opposition would be attenuated only if the inter-Arab constellation permitted the emasculation of the PLO at the same time that the *intifada* was decisively repressed. Yet the first of these conditions appears to be extremely unlikely. And even in this case, while dispirited Palestinians might at first pose no obstacle to Jordanian rule, after an initial period of confusion they could be expected to resume the struggle for their national aspirations within the context of Jordanian politics, seeking either secession or takeover of the entire country. The means they might adopt could include terrorism against Jordan (and/or against Israel, in the hope of provoking Jordanian-Israeli friction), and subversion. PLO mainstreamers and rejectionists would unite in a common cause, benefiting from Syrian support, and exploiting the international arena as well.

It is difficult to assess their prospects for succeeding. The social-cultural proximity between Palestinians and Jordanians might make Palestinian resistance to Jordan less determined than that against Israel. Moreover, the nature of the Jordanian regime, and the fact that disturbances could be presented to the world as an internal Jordanian affair, would permit Jordan to adopt measures that Israel denies itself in repressing unrest. A strong and vital Hashemite regime might survive and reduce the saliency of the Palestinian issue. Thus, with regard to the Palestinians, the advantage for Israel of the Jordanian option is a function of the success of the Hashemites in reducing the Palestinian threat to Israel's security.

Hence the possibility of an eventual Palestinian takeover of Jordan cannot be ignored. One of the reasons attributed to Hussein for explicitly renouncing any claim to the territories in 1988 was his fear that the *intifada* would spread to the Palestinians on the East Bank; the reinstitution of Jordanian rule in the West Bank and, even more, the addition of the Gaza Strip would increase the specific weight of the Palestinians within the Jordanian polity. Palestinians now living peacefully under Jordanian rule on the East Bank would probably be content to continue doing so if Palestinian national aspirations were satisfied elsewhere. This assumption could not be made with the same degree of confidence were Jordanian rulers to take actions that were interpreted as a betrayal, in league with the Zionists, of the Palestinian cause, even if that "conspiracy" resulted in the "liberation" of all the territories lost in 1967.

It should be recalled that Palestinians were very active in anti-Hashemite parties in the 1950s, and they narrowly failed to supplant Hashemite rule in the late 1960s. Their political consciousness is even higher now. It is not difficult to imagine circumstances in which the Palestinian threat to Jordan of the 1950s and 1960s would be revived, with greater intensity, after a political settlement based on the restoration of Jordanian rule. In such circumstances the end result of the Jordanian option might well be a Palestinian state on the West Bank — one established through secession, and without any treaty obligations toward Israel — or even a Palestinian successor state, created through revolution, on both Banks.

Israeli Arabs

The majority of Israeli Arabs reject the Jordanian option. Nevertheless, assuming the option were implemented in a situation of pronounced PLO weakness combined with massive Jordanian and Israeli influence, the Israeli Arabs would have little basis on which to oppose it, and in the course of time might be compelled to accept it. The Israeli Arab radical camp would probably continue to espouse the ideology of the PLO and/or the Rejection Front organizations, and some extremist nationalist elements might be involved in terrorist activity, but this would not significantly impact on the overall picture.

For Israel this is the most desirable option in terms of relations with the country's Arab minority. True, unlike option IV — a Palestinian state — it would not bring immediate calm; that would be contingent on a certain normalization in the region. However this option is free of the risks that are inherent in Option IV, in the sense that the absence of an independent Palestinian state would mean that the potential for particularist Palestinian pride would not be realized. Under these circumstances a government policy designed to facilitate integration of the Israeli Arabs into the state could be implemented. This would strengthen the moderate camp at the expense of the radicals and the extreme nationalists. Still, while there would be a greater disposition to identify with the state to the point of fulfilling national obligations, it would nevertheless be accompanied by an escalation of the struggle for equality of rights.

From the Israeli Arab standpoint, Israel would bear the onus of making this option a success. This becomes a particularly critical point when we speculate upon the effects on Israeli Arabs of a possible Palestinian takeover of the Jordanian-dominated federation projected by this option. Assuming this shift does not occur in the short term, then by the time it does, the integration of Israel's Arabs could be far enough advanced to confine irredentist trends to a manageable nationalist minority.

The Arab States

This is the only option on the Israeli agenda that calls for the transfer of territory to a neighboring Arab state. Hence the reactions and attitudes of that state, Jordan, are of primary importance in analyzing the overall Arab reaction. Five features of this option pose problems for Jordan: the territorial concessions it would have to make; the security arrangements that call for a continued IDF presence on the ground; Palestinian willingness to accept Jordanian domination; Arab legitimacy for Jordan's right to negotiate on the Palestinians' behalf; and the absence of any reference to the pursuit of a comprehensive settlement that would address Syrian demands as well.

Jordan has always held fast to the Arab interpretation of UN Security Council Resolution 242 as calling for the withdrawal of Israeli forces from all of the areas conquered in 1967, except for minor, agreed and reciprocal border rectifications. Security arrangements of the type that exist in Sinai would have posed few problems for Jordan, but the arrangements suggested under the terms of this option are far more problematic.

Nonetheless, these do not necessarily pose insurmountable hurdles. Jordan has hinted that it could accept less than full Israeli withdrawal from the territories after a settlement, if it had Arab and Palestinian backing in the framework of an international conference for peace in the Middle East. In this sense the federation option must appear to have been freely chosen by the Palestinians themselves. In the aftermath of the PLO's late 1988 declaration of independence, this appears extremely unlikely.

Jordan has formally committed itself to Damascus not to pursue any separate or partial settlements of the Arab-Israeli conflict. One of the attractions of an international conference for Jordan is that it establishes a mechanism for addressing Syrian demands. In the final analysis, assuming all other conditions were met, Jordanian assent to this option would not be conditional on a settlement of Syria's demands on the Golan Heights. However, some kind of fig leaf for the Syrians in the initial stages of agreement and implementation would be highly desirable for Jordan.

Jordan's chances for converting this option into a durable settlement must be assessed in view of two factors: the Palestinians, and the Arab world. Over the longer term, reunification of the "Jordanian-Palestinian family" (to which both the PLO and Jordan pay homage) would pose a considerable challenge to Hashemite dominance. The population of the federation (Jordan might insist on calling it a confederation to create the illusion of Jordanian-Palestinian equality) would be around 80 percent Palestinian. The likely attempt, after a period of recovery, by important segments of the Palestinian national movement to undermine Jordanian control does not presage an automatic Hashemite collapse. Unlike the situations in Iraq, Syria and Lebanon, there are no ethnic or religious cleavages that might amplify conflicts between Jordanians and Palestinians. Nor are democracy and "majority rule" overriding political principles in the region: the regimes of Jordan's Arab neighbors to the north and east — Syria and Iraq — have long been both autocratic and dominated by minorities.

Assuming that no tangible progress is made in addressing Syrian demands, Jordan would need considerable backing to neutralize Syria and Palestinian radicals: from its Arab allies, from Israel, and from the US and Western Europe. The greater the level of Palestinian acceptance, the easier it would be for Jordan's Arab allies to endorse such a settlement. In the absence of Palestinian consent, the allies would probably sit on the fence and refrain from endorsing it. Indeed, in view of the extensive international backing received by the PNC's November 1988 declaration of Palestinian independence, the Arab states are hardly likely to endorse a Jordanian-centered solution.

Damascus, in any case, would make every effort to torpedo implementation of this option. Syria's rejectionist stance, on both the declarative and the operative level, would be similar to the one discussed in our analysis of the fourth option — the creation of an independent Palestinian state. The principal distinction between Syria's reactions to the two options is that in this case Damascus' preventive and punitive measures would be directed primarily against Jordan. Indeed, were the PLO too to oppose the option, this would open the way for a Syrian-PLO rapprochement and joint

142

action aimed at undermining the option's implementation. Such measures could include attacks against Jordanian targets abroad; activation of Syrian-based Jordanian opposition movements for the purposes of propaganda and sabotage; collaboration against Palestinian elements that might support the option's implementation; cancellation of bilateral agreements, such as that guiding the distribution of the Yarmuk waters; and finally, the threat and application of military force.

The degree of Egypt's support for this option would be determined by the extent to which it won the Palestinians' approval. Should the PLO leadership oppose the option, leading to a crisis in PLO-Jordanian relations, Egypt would be extremely hesitant about lending its support. Despite Egypt's recurring criticism of the PLO's leadership, it regards the organization as the symbol of Palestinian nationalism; cutting the PLO loose completely would risk widespread internal and regional criticism. On the other hand, Egypt would not wish to see other parties, i.e., Syria and/or Iraq, try to upset the settlement by threatening or attacking Jordan.

As in the Palestinian state option, inter-Arab cooperation beyond the immediate Arab confrontation states would be vital in providing for the resettlement of Palestinian refugees. This constitutes a key criterion for the success of any compromise settlement. Saudi Arabia and Iraq would support this option to the degree that it won the PLO's consent. On the other hand, any settlement likely to spell further conflict between Jordan and the Palestinians would displease the Saudis, inducing them to adopt a low profile. Conversely, Libya and Iran are likely to oppose the option, allying themselves with Syria.

Israel's Security

As in the case of a Palestinian state (option IV), IDF withdrawal from the West Bank and Gaza would constitute a central determinant of the risks involved in this option. On the one hand, its implications for Israel's defense are essentially similar to those attributed to option IV. Hence Israel would have to insist that, following IDF redeployment, the same security arrangements, as well as the added understandings stipulated in the discussion of option IV, be applied to this option as well.

On the other hand, a number of differences between the two options would affect the extent of the risks entailed. Perhaps most significantly, implementation of this option is likely to be opposed by both Syria and the PLO — or radical Palestinian factions — and might lead to a renewal of Syrian-PLO strategic cooperation. This would likely manifest itself first and foremost against Jordan and Israel, in an effort to torpedo this option. A Syrian-Palestinian strategy of this nature is likely to be applied gradually, escalating from Syrian state-sponsored terrorism to direct military confrontation. Indeed, Syrian-Palestinian activity could combine an effort to raise the level of violence in the West Bank with direct military pressure applied along the Syrian-Jordanian border.

Within this context, if lower levels of activity fail to torpedo the new Jordanian-Palestinian federation, Syria might escalate its efforts into direct military confrontation with Israel. Here it would be motivated by fear lest the successful implementation of this option render the Golan Heights problem the only remaining unresolved issue of the Arab-Israel conflict — one on which Israel might never yield, thereby forcing Syria to concede the Heights de facto to Israel. On the other hand, should Jordan's agreement with Israel be supported by Egypt, Saudi Arabia, and Iraq, Syria would have to risk confronting Israel alone. Syria's willingness to assume such a risk would likely depend on its capacity to achieve a degree of strategic parity with Israel, at least to an extent that is assessed as sufficient to protect it from a devastating Israeli counterblow.

Concurrently, and again assuming their opposition to the option, the Palestinians are likely to seek to build up the potential to derail implementation. This would likely include a renewal of the uprising in the West Bank and Gaza, and heightened terrorism in all arenas against Israeli and Jordanian targets. Here Jordanian repressive measures are likely to be more effective than those Israel could conceivably invoke.

A second major risk involved in the Jordanian federation option is that, following its implementation, Jordan's present regime could face insurgencies from two political directions. First, a Palestinian revolution would be aimed at establishing Palestinian state independence in both the East and the West Bank. Were it to succeed, the state's new Palestinian regime would then have to decide whether it would continue to adhere to the stipulations of the Jordanian-Israeli accord that brought about Israel's withdrawal and the federation's establishment. Israel, for its part, might decide to reoccupy the West Bank preemptively, either in order to save the Hashemite regime, or to renegotiate its security arrangements with the new Palestinian regime.

In a second insurgency scenario, Jordan could experience a coup conducted by Hashemite extremists seeking to separate the East Bank from the West Bank in order to avert the negative demographic ramifications entailed in the federation option for the stability of the Hashemite Kingdom. Such a development might also propel Israel to weigh the possibility of preemptively occupying the West Bank in order to prevent the establishment of a Palestinian state that was not bound by security agreements with Israel.

Conversely, there are a number of reasons to assess that Israel's security interests would be better met through the federation option than by the establishment of an independent Palestinian state. For one, Jordan's past record provides strong indications that it would successfully maintain internal security in the West Bank and Gaza following Israel's withdrawal. Then too, since the West Bank would comprise only a small part of the Jordanian-Palestinian federation, it would be easier for Jordan to accept and comply with complete demilitarization of the area, as well as with the other security arrangements detailed in our analysis of the implications of Palestinian statehood. These would include an undertaking not to permit the entry of additional Arab armies into the Jordanian East Bank without prior agreement by Israel, and agreed measures for demilitarizing a strip of Jordanian territory immediately east of the Jordan River. Further, given the record of Jordanian-Israeli relations during the past 20 years, it would be easier for Israel to consent to the temporary introduction of Jordanian forces into the West Bank and Gaza should this be required by the internal situation in these territories. And with appropriate economic aid, Jordan could take responsibility for the resettlement of a large number of refugees from Gaza and the West Bank.

Finally, the most important difference between the two options lies in the implications for Palestinian irredentism. It is certainly conceivable that, following the establishment of an independent Palestinian state, its leaders might seek to fulfil the dream of Greater Palestine by implementing the "strategy of stages." But Jordan — once having reasserted control over the West Bank, given its collective memory of the consequences of its own past participation in wars with Israel, and in view of the absence of a Hashemite irredentist motive and the complementarity of Jordanian and Israeli strategic interests — is far less likely to attempt to liberate by force the entire land of Palestine (even though it could not formally renounce, in the Palestinians' name, their "right of return" to Israeli territory). Nor, under these circumstances, would Jordan be as likely as the Palestinians to join or facilitate an Arab war effort against the Jewish state waged from Israel's east.

Thus there are a number of reasons to judge that this option involves fewer security risks for Israel than those entailed in the establishment of an independent Palestinian state. Yet by the same token, the establishment of a Jordanian-Palestinian federation dominated by the Hashemite regime is unlikely to be regarded by the Palestinians as meeting their quest for national self-determination. Hence they are unlikely to accept this option as a solution to their problem and an end to the Israeli-Palestinian dispute. As such, they can be expected to continue to play a destabilizing role in the region, probably to a much greater degree than could be expected if the fourth option — Palestinian self-determination within an independent state — were implemented.

The Israeli Domestic Setting

This option is more acceptable to Israelis than a pure Palestinian state option. It would not require that a large part of the Israeli public overcome its emotional reservations about negotiating directly with the PLO as principal partner. Nor would it negate the political wisdom — whatever its objective accuracy — cultivated in Israel over two decades since 1967, according to which there is no room for an additional Arab state between the

Mediterranean and the Arabian Desert. Moreover, King Hussein is not perceived as an enemy; indeed, he is respected in Israel for his success in preventing terrorism from Jordan against Israel since 1970. Israeli public opinion would display a high degree of confidence in agreements reached with Hussein. The IDF would welcome the prospect of being freed of responsibility for security and administration in the Palestinian sector, while coordinating with the Jordanian military essential aspects of Israel's security. For the Israeli public, these are the main advantages of this option.

On the other hand this option, too, delivers up most of the territories to Arab sovereignty. Here, as in Option IV, Jewish settlers would not wish to remain inside the new entity, even if they were allowed to. Hence, for many Israelis, there would be no essential difference between the end-result of this option and that of the Palestinian state option. Indeed, opponents of the Jordanian option argue that ultimately it would pave the way for a Palestinian option, as the Hashemite Dynasty would not long survive as the ruler of a federation in which Palestinians (from both the West and East Bank) constitute around 80 percent of the population. This thesis received support from Hussein himself when he cut his kingdom off from the West Bank in July 1988, and then recognized the PLO's declaration of Palestinian independence in November 1988. Many Israelis saw this as an admission on the King's part that he was better off without the West Bank Palestinians.

The extremely divisive consequences for Israeli society of any attempt to implement a Palestinian state solution, or of a referendum that approved it, were described with regard to Option IV. The situation would be very nearly as acute were the same territorial concessions to be made in favor of a Jordanian-Palestinian federation. Forcible evacuation of settlers would again place the IDF under extreme pressures of morale and motivation, and in open confrontation with right-wing Israelis who, like anyone else in Israel, are themselves present among the ranks of the army. In this case, too, extreme right-wing Jewish elements could be expected to invoke terrorism, and possibly attempt to assassinate Israeli leaders.

Geography, Demography and Economy

From a geographical standpoint this option offers the most reasonable solution for the territories. They would merge again with Jordan, which has a reasonably well-organized administration and infrastructure and some natural resources, and could provide marketing outlets for Palestinian produce. Good neighborly relations with Israel would allow some movement of labor across the new boundary, but Jordan would wish to develop sources of livelihood for the majority of Palestinians presently employed in Israel. This would be a daunting task, in view of Jordan's current economic difficulties. Nevertheless, the Jordanian financial system would be well situated to raise funds for industrial development in the West Bank and Gaza, and Amman could provide assistance in education, joint development of water resources, development of tourist sites and cooperation in the export of winter vegetables to Europe. The Gaza Strip would present the main economic burden for the federation, both because of the lack of territorial continuity that might ensure its integration, and due to the immediate necessity to alleviate population overcrowding and infuse economic aid. Considerable international and inter-Arab support would be required to make this possible.

As in option IV, a Palestinian state, Israel would require some 2 to 4 billion dollars for relocating IDF installations and training facilities and another billion for closing off the new border and fortifying it against infiltration, if Israel so desired. A sum of 3 to 5 billion dollars would be required for relocating some 20,000 settler families.

Finally, the economic integration of the Jordanian-Palestinian federation with Israel — perhaps within the framework of a tripartite confederation — would be beneficial for all parties: Israel could provide employment during the transition stage, while the federation would afford Israel a commercial gateway to the Arab world.

The United States

Although it is becoming more difficult to maintain, a form of this option has clearly been the preferred solution of all post-1967 administrations. In the past, had Israel and Jordan reached an agreement under the American scenario, Israel and the involved Arab parties would have received praise and support, encouragement and practical military and financial backing. The United States would have helped them withstand any regional opponents. In particular, US-Israeli relations would have reached new levels of intimacy and collaboration, assuming the agreements were implemented as planned. If this option appeared likely, the United States would have been prepared to move very strongly to facilitate its consummation. Certainly, there would have been strong diplomatic activity in attempting to bring the parties together or to facilitate their agreement, as well as a willingness to contribute financially to the settlement. More likely than in any other case, US troops or observers would have been offered in a peacekeeping role.

In the event that this settlement came about as a consequence of an Israeli-Jordanian agreement aimed at squelching growing Palestinian power — either the Palestinians of the territories or the PLO or both — the US, Israel and Jordan would have been in fundamental alliance against the Palestinians, who would likely have been backed by the USSR and Arab radicals. Here the United States would have acted to make certain that its "partners" remained close. It would have done so by constant vigilance, by financial inducements and by an intimate involvement in the implementation process. If, however, a significant Palestinian grouping had endorsed a federation, then the chief American concern would have been to maintain the settlement process.

While this option remains America's preference, there are increasing indications that many in Washington may no longer regard it as feasible. For the administration, the stillborn Peres-Hussein agreement of April 1987, the *intifada*, and the Hashemite King's subsequent withdrawal from responsibility for negotiating on the Palestinians' behalf, were milestones in the decline of the option's relevance. The November 1988 PNC declaration of Palestinian independent statehood, and the broad inter-Arab and international support which this statement received, have further contributed to Washington's perception that a Jordanian-Palestinian federation, under Jordan's domination, may be more difficult to achieve than had previously been supposed. Indeed, the Reagan administration decision, on December 15, 1988 to open a dialogue with the PLO rendered the Jordan option even less conceivable. Clearly, in deciding upon such a dialogue, there were officials in the administration who understood that eventually this would necessarily involve a discussion of Palestinian statehood. At the very least, the American move implies a willingness to consider a dominant Palestinian role in any prospective settlement. Under such circumstances, Washington may regard an Israeli effort to revive a Jordanian option as a belated, irrelevant and counterproductive effort to derail a peace process in which the PLO has already been granted a central role.

Yet even if PLO-American conversations proceeded positively (and certainly if they did not), no US government could ignore a deal between two states — Israel and Jordan — so closely associated with Washington. The prospect of an arrangement between Amman and Jerusalem would give an administration pause even if Washington were proceeding in the Palestinian direction. The net result of the new US-PLO dialogue, then, is that for any Jordanian-Israeli contacts to gain American support, they would have to lead to rapid gains in order to convince the US that they had a serious prospect of success. Were the US to be convinced, however, it would likely revert to its previous preference for the Jordanian option.

Moreover, it is possible that the US will become disillusioned with the PLO as a consequence of its dialogue with the organization. In this case the Jordan option might be revived. Thus, from the American perspective, a form of option VI still exists: as a past preference, a present possibility, and a future contingency.

The Soviet Union

In discussing Soviet perceptions, it must be noted that Moscow has consistently referred to the notion of a confederation rather than a federation. Throughout the 1970s and the early 1980s Moscow's attitude toward King Hussein's plan for a Jordanian-Palestinian confederation remained highly ambiguous, twisting sharply in accordance with the political vicissitudes in the region. Whenever the Soviets deemed the confederation plan to entail a viable risk of bringing the PLO under the influence of pro-western Arab states like Egypt and Saudi Arabia, it hurried to discredit the idea as a "US-inspired plan." On the other hand, the relatively mild tone of the USSR's criticism of the plan has revealed a clear unwillingness to dismiss the idea altogether. Furthermore, with the enhancement of Soviet-Jordanian relations from the mid-1970s onwards and their culmination in regular arms procurement ties, however limited, Moscow has become extremely reluctant to alienate Jordan by rejecting its role in a future Israeli-Palestinian arrangement. Above all, Soviet reluctance to close the door to the confederation idea has been reinforced by the assessment that a Jordanian-Palestinian option would be far more acceptable to Israel than a purely Palestinian solution.

It seems clear that Moscow would welcome a genuine Jordanian-Palestinian confederation in which Palestine maintained its essential independence. But it would be anxious lest the confederation be transformed into a cover for Jordanian hegemony over the West Bank, i.e., lest the confederation be the kind of Jordanian-centered federation implied by this option as Jordan and Israel understand it. This has been reflected in the persistent emphasis of Soviet commentary on the differences between the Soviet and the Jordanian perceptions of this plan. Whereas King Hussein views the confederation as a vehicle for ensuring Jordan's continued control over the affairs of the West Bank, the Soviets envisage this arrangement as an equal partnership between the Palestinians and the Jordanians, to be preceded by the establishment of an independent Palestinian state in the West Bank and Gaza.

Hence the Soviets would not welcome an option for a Jordan-dominated federation, and might exercise little restraining influence on Syria or extremist Palestinians that oppose it. The Soviet reaction might be mitigated if some superpower understanding were reached that gave the Soviets a desirable role in the solution, or if overall Soviet-American strategic collaboration were enhanced.

Conclusions

Assuming complete implementation of security arrangements, there is no significant structural difference between this option and option IV, a Palestinian state, for Israel's defense. The essential difference between the two derives from the extent of Israel's confidence in the intentions, motivation and capacity to fulfill the agreement, of its Arab cosignatory.

Here Jordan has a clear edge over the PLO. Under this federative option, demilitarization arrangements could be better reached and maintained. Jordan's commitment to a peace treaty with Israel, along with inter-Arab support, would ensure a reduced threat to Israel: Jordan would effectively be removed from the Arab war coalition, and Israel's security could not be threatened from the east without Jordan's concurrence. Jordan could also better prevent terrorism and Palestinian irredentism.

This is why more Israelis would accept this option. It means a renewal of Israel's long-standing community of interest with Jordan, both in its implementation phase and afterwards. Still, many Israelis would oppose the requisite withdrawal from the West Bank and Gaza; indeed, some would resort to violence.

While this option could act positively to catalyze relations between Israel and the Arab world, it would probably do so less effectively than option IV, a Palestinian state. Syria in particular, in league with at least some Palestinians, would act to obstruct the agreement, and would refuse to resettle Palestinian refugees. It might be backed in this stance by the USSR. Certainly the support of most of the other Arab states, and their participation in resolving the refugee issue, would be a prerequisite for making this option a success. In view of broad inter-Arab recognition of the PNC's declaration of Palestinian independence in November 1988, this support does not seem likely.

Economically and demographically, this option would meet basic requirements of the Palestinian Arabs, in that the Jordanian connection ensures their access to markets and domiciles beyond

152

the restricted confines of the West Bank and Gaza. Israeli Arabs, too, would have little difficulty accommodating to it.

While this option still remains the United States' preference, there is also a growing American willingness to consider a more serious Palestinian role in any settlement. As for the Soviet Union, it would definitely not support a federation option in which Jordan is granted a dominant role. However the role assigned to Moscow itself in implementing the option might also affect the extent of its support.

But as Israelis, and perhaps King Hussein too, understand this option, most Palestinians reject it. Indeed, under present circumstances, the PLO could be expected to resort to terrorism to prevent it. Instead, the PLO insists on a Jordanian-Palestinian entity that in effect constitutes a confederation between two equal sovereign states. Taken to its logical conclusion, the option in this latter form would approximate Option IV, a Palestinian state. This prospect was reinforced by the PNC's unilateral declaration of independence in November 1988; in effect, for the PLO to accept a role in a federation with Jordan would constitute a retreat from the Algiers declaration.

To the extent that the Jordanian component of this option is weakened, or that an eventual Palestinian takeover is projected, the option presents Israel with a measure of uncertainty in the face of unpredictable developments. It could eventually confront a Palestinian successor state that encompassed both Banks of the Jordan, yet was devoid of treaty obligations toward it. Certainly, as long as the PLO and Palestinians in general reject this option, the *intifada* rages and the PLO is not decimated, the option cannot be considered feasible.

Nor does the option remain on the Jordanian agenda. Nevertheless, as long as there is a Hashemite Kingdom, it will, for reasons of self-preservation, never be able to divest itself entirely of a desire to negotiate a Palestinian solution with Israel. Yet if and when the issue ever reemerges as a viable possibility, its many advantages for Israel make it desirable only to the extent that one could assume the continuation of Hashemite dominance over the long term. In this sense it would have to be weighed carefully against the dangers of a more distant contingency in which, as a consequence of implementation of this option, Palestinians achieved dominance on both Banks of the Jordan, yet without any parallel commitment to coexist with Israel.

VII. General Conclusions

The preceding chapters have examined in some detail the strategic ramifications for Israel of a variety of options for dealing with the West Bank and Gaza. These are the main options for a solution that are presently on Israel's political agenda.

The status quo bodes ill for Israel. Israeli society is already showing signs of deterioration under this reality, and the only reasonable prognosis is for worse to come. The Arab world might not tolerate the status quo indefinitely. At the same time, Israel's relations with the United States and its Jewish community may become increasingly strained. While reasonable compromise options appear to be either unfeasible or too risky for Israel; while its legitimate fears of the alternatives appear to be paralyzing Israel's capacity for bold initiative; while Israel may indeed "muddle through" for some time to come — it is equally possible that the foundations of Israel's society and its deterrence will begin to crumble, thus raising the specter of war. This is not a risk that either Israel or the Arab Middle East should wish to take.

Unilateral measures — annexation, or withdrawal from the Gaza Strip — are also potentially detrimental to Israel. Withdrawing without prior agreement with an Arab partner also risks damaging Israel's deterrent image. Moreover Israel would probably be creating, single-handedly, a hostile Palestinian mini-state that owes it nothing, and enjoys inter-Arab support while it seeks to subvert Israel. Annexation, even partial, would, by violating the Camp David agreements, jeopardize Egypt's treaty obligations with Israel, and would seriously threaten the very foundations of the Israeli-American alliance. It would pit Israeli against Israeli, demoralize large segments of the population, and drive a wedge between American Jewry and Israel. Were this act to be accompanied by mass deportation of Palestinians ("transfer"), acute internal strife might ensue, and the IDF — today a unifying factor in Israeli society — might be torn from within.

Nor are the compromise solutions on the agenda likely to be implemented. A "Jordanian solution" — a Jordanian-Palestinian federation dominated by the Hashemite Kingdom and in which responsibility for security rests in Amman — offers considerable strategic advantages for Israel. But it appears not to be feasible from the Jordanian standpoint, neither at present nor in the foreseeable future, principally because it is unacceptable to the Palestinians. The limited autonomy that Israel has offered within the Camp David framework is unacceptable to Palestinians; so is a more comprehensive version, unless a prior commitment is made by Israel to eventual Palestinian independence. Under present circumstances, were autonomy to be imposed unilaterally upon the Arab inhabitants of Judea, Samaria and Gaza, or negotiated with non-PLO Palestinians (in the highly unlikely event that Palestinians willing to negotiate autonomy could be found), it would encounter a combination of boycott and an escalation of tensions.

A Palestinian state is virtually the only choice of Palestinians. However, under existing circumstances most Israelis would regard this option as unacceptable, and it is highly unlikely than an Israeli government would contemplate its negotiation and implementation. Negotiations with Palestinians over statehood would elicit widespread opposition, some of it violent, among those Israelis who consider any Palestinian state option as an existential threat to the State of Israel. Actual implementation, requiring the forced evacuation of settlements, would result in further divisiveness among the public and within the IDF. Certainly without extensive transition stages to test Palestinian intentions, and confidence-building measures to improve the regional environment, Palestinian statehood is potentially extremely risky from a security standpoint, and is as dangerous for the fabric of Israeli society as is annexation.

The central conclusion of this study is that under existing conditions and in their present form, none of the options currently on Israel's agenda seems to offer a reasonable avenue for dealing with the West Bank and Gaza. The unilateral options (annexation, withdrawal from Gaza) are feasible, but could prove disastrous. The negotiated compromise options (autonomy, Palestinian state, Jordanian-Palestinian federation) bear some promise of mitigating the conflict, but are totally unacceptable to one or both sides. Under these circumstances — and barring the emergence of a

156

major new leadership initiative, superpower intervention or some cataclysmic event — Israel must, in the immediate term, cope with the status quo and seek ways to ameliorate it. Otherwise the status quo is liable to degenerate into a situation that produces international, regional and local pressures on Israel to accept a Palestinian state solution under disadvantageous conditions.

Looking beyond the status quo, however, our analysis of the six options points to the desperate need, and the possibility, for creative thinking on the Palestinian issue both in Israel and among the Palestinians. Both sides must develop new and more promising courses of action for solving the Israeli-Palestinian conflict. In so doing, many of the beneficial aspects that we have found in the six options could be given expression, and the harmful aspects avoided. A new option would also have to reflect the constant components, such as massive international and inter-Arab participation in refugee resettlement and economic development, without which no settlement seems likely or worthwhile.

The Jaffee Center study group has developed such a proposal for a Palestinian-Israeli peace process — one that, it believes, should be on the Israeli agenda. JCSS has done so on a completely independent basis — without the sponsorship, counsel or participation of any of the American research team, persons and institutions involved in this report. The Jaffee Center's ideas on the peace process are embodied in the companion booklet to this volume, *Israel, the West Bank and Gaza: Toward a Solution*.

The American and Israeli teams wish to encourage additional individuals and groups within both Arab and Israeli society to develop creative alternatives that may be placed on the public agenda.

APPENDICES

Appendix 1

Military-Strategic Background: War Dangers, Security Arrangements, and the Arab-Israel Military Balance, 1982-1987-1992

The political settlement in each of the six options considered by the study group report does not entirely remove the serious security threat facing Israel. A move toward a settlement, from the Israeli side at least, would be undertaken in the hope of ending the security threat so that henceforth Israel could look forward to a normal existence. However, even if this is the aspiration, the mere signing of a political agreement would not herald the termination of the conflict. Rather, under the most hopeful circumstances, it would signal the onset of a new and positive process in which all the clauses and commitments of the accord are applied in practice.

If and when a political settlement is achieved, the results of the process would still be essentially unpredictable. Hence Israel could not enjoy the luxury of neglecting its military readiness to defend its very existence in the face of a possible Arab war coalition. Indeed, until irrefutable proof were forthcoming that true "peace and quiet" had been attained, the new IDF deployment called for under the peace arrangements could well precipitate an actual worsening of the conditions in which Israel might have to fight a war.

Naturally, all this also has clear implications for the investment of Israel's national resources in security. Not only would specific outlays be necessitated by a military redeployment, but no cuts in security spending could be anticipated in the future either. The only possible cuts — if a period of relative quiet ensued — would be a reduction in yearly reserve duty, and perhaps, at a later stage, in the duration of national military service.

161

Theoretically, the situation could look different if the peace settlement were to include unambiguous clauses obligating Israel and all the Arab confrontation states drastically to reduce the order of battle of their regular and reserved armed forces, scrap weapons systems (a dramatic cutback in warplanes, tanks, artillery, etc.), and slash defense budgets — all this accompanied, of course, by the creation of effective supervisory mechanisms to oversee implementation by both sides. Yet this is highly unlikely in the near future.

Security Arrangements

Before discussing security arrangements, a few basic data must be supplied concerning the Arab-Israel balance of forces and the regional geographical picture.

Israel is a small country whose Jewish population stands at 3,650,000; it has an area of about 27,000 sq. km. (including the West Bank and Gaza) and of only 20,000 sq. km. within the boundaries of the Green Line (the pre-1967 border). The IDF's military capability in facing a major threat is dependent on mobilization of reserves: regular forces number about 130,000 troops, the reserves about 310,000.

A broad Arab war coalition (Syria, Jordan, Egypt and assorted Arab expeditionary forces) creates a force ratio of 7.5:1 in the Arabs' favor in regular forces (920:130 thousand), while in a state of full mobilization on both sides the ratio improves somewhat from Israel's standpoint to 3.6:1 (1,582:440 thousand).

Comparative quantitative Arab-Israel military balance tables for the years 1982-1987-1992 are presented at the close of this appendix. The figures projected for 1992 in particular reflect the Arabs' growing resource advantage. For example, Arab Eastern front armor will increase by a factor of over 25 percent between 1987 and 1992, while Israel's will remain stationary.

Israel tries to compensate for this negative quantitative military balance through innovation and improvisation on a number of parallel planes:

— First, optimal exploitation of the national manpower potential through extended compulsory service (for women as well as men) and yearly reserve duty until the age of 55.

— Secondly, organization, regular maneuvers and readiness procedures for IDF reserves, enabling them to be called up and deployed at short notice, almost at the level of regular units.

— Third, the fine tuning of an intelligence system designed to provide early warning of a military threat, as well as the information needed to achieve optimal results on the battlefield.

— Fourth, an emphasis on the quality of weaponry and weapons systems — both those acquired from external sources and those provided through Israel's own independent R&D efforts to develop weaponry and to enhance the performance of existing systems and adapt them to the local arena on the basis of Israel's rich combat experience.

— Fifth, a defense policy that emphasizes rigid priorities within the defense system, with the objective of investing maximum resources in elements that provide a direct contribution to a decisive military victory.

— And finally, on a more abstract plane, the cultivation of original thinking, flexibility and improvisation; the personal leadership example of commanders at all ranks that is expressed by the slogan "follow me;" and emphasis on the importance of the greatest possible national consensus on issues of security and war.

We shall begin by examining two extreme situations of agreed security arrangements in the West Bank and Gaza Strip. One is the optimal situation for Israel, in which the arrangements afford it the ability to deter, thwart, block and intervene in a manner virtually identical to the situation today, when the IDF operates in the territories without restrictions or external constraint of any kind. The other is the optimal situation for the Arab side, in which there is no Israeli military presence in the territories that possesses an operational capability.

In both cases, the delineators of security arrangements would be identical where the Arab side was concerned:

(1) Demilitarization of the West Bank and Gaza from all indigenous and foreign Arab forces. A gendarmerie would be

permitted to deal with internal security. It would bear small arms, and be equipped with armored cars, light aircraft and light helicopters for liaison purposes. No tanks, artillery, anti-tank or anti-aircraft weapons would be permitted.

(2) The Arab political entity in the territories would have no air force, and the airspace above Judea, Samaria and Gaza would remain under Israeli control and responsibility.

(3) The new political entity would have no navy. In the Port of Gaza, which would probably be developed as the entity's commercial harbor, a small coast guard could be maintained, primarily to combat smuggling and infiltration by sea.

(4) No ground fortifications of any kind (fencing, mines, trenches, etc.) would be emplaced.

(5) It would be most desirable for the agreement to include a Jordanian undertaking not to permit the entry of any foreign forces to the territory of the East Bank. This would greatly enhance Israel's strategic depth disposition. There is a better chance of reaching understanding on this point in an agreement obtained according to Option VI, with Jordan responsible for conducting negotiations on behalf of the Arab side.

The difference between the aforementioned two situations would reside in the nature of the *IDF*'s presence in the evacuated areas following the political settlement. In the first case, with an optimal presence that was determined exclusively according to IDF considerations, even after the implementation stage these forces would remain in place for a very lengthy period either stipulated in advance (say, 20-25 years), or predicated on the basis of agreed need. The parameters of the IDF presence would comprise:

(1) IDF deployment along the axes ascending from the Jordan Valley to the mountain ridge. These forces would be deployed in a manner enabling them to block the axes if necessary during an emergency, but without intervening in or interrupting routine civilian Arab traffic in normal times. The force would also maintain a surface-to-air missile system; this is of the utmost importance for defending against an air threat from the east.

(2) Early-warning and intelligence facilities along the moun-

tain ridge, to be maintained as long as no effective alternative solutions (air-anchored or airborne) exist.

(3) Full IDF control of and responsibility for the airspace above the West Bank and Gaza, with the aim of maintaining Israeli freedom of the skies for intelligence, early-warning and training purposes.

(4) Israeli freedom of movement along agreed axes to and from the military facilities and units on the ground.

(5) Participation of IDF representatives (perhaps along with a third, neutral party) in the supervisory mechanism: on the Jordan bridges, at civilian airfields in the West Bank and Gaza, at the checkpoints between Sinai and the Gaza Strip, and of course at the two points of entry to the corridor linking the West Bank with Gaza via Israel. The tasks of the supervisory apparatus would be to prevent the infiltration of forces and weapons and to check out complaints concerning violations of this kind.

These arrangements, at least in part, would remain in force until the total disappearance of terrorism aimed at sabotaging the agreement, until an advance stage were reached in the process of dismantling the refugee camps in Judea, Samaria and the Gaza Strip and in the surrounding Arab states and permanently resettling the refugees, and until the resolution of the Israeli-Syrian conflict.

In the second post-transition stage situation that we have predicated, no Israeli military presence would remain on the ground. In this case, it is assumed that a joint observer and supervisory apparatus would be formed to ensure non-violation of the aforementioned conditions, both by deployment at the permanent checkpoints (see (5) above) and through authorization to carry out on-site inspections should suspicions arise that the demilitarization clause was being breached.

The sole exception must be Israeli control of the airspace above the West Bank and Gaza, both for air force training flights (a problem that has no solution within the boundaries of "little" Israel) and for early warning and intelligence flights needed to prevent the collapse of the agreement. In this context it must be emphasized that airborne or air-anchored intelligence facilities cannot provide a complete substitute for current aerial coverage capability.

The clear advantage inherent in these minimal security arrangements lies in the maximum opportunity they offer the Arab side to evince good will in maintaining the agreement. No one would be able to claim that inordinate Israeli security demands had undermined the negotiations or that security arrangements had torpedoed the actual process of implementation. However we would be remiss not to point out the dangers inherent in such a situation.

First, in the event that the Arab side did not evince a desire for peace with Israel, the incomplete nature of the security arrangements would induce, initially, violation of the demilitarization agreement, and later — if appropriate countermeasures were not taken — an attack fraught with danger for Israel. Secondly, assuming that a major calculation in the Arabs' decision involved weighing the risks of an attack against the prospects of success, the deployment described above significantly enhances those prospects while greatly reducing the risks that the Arab side would be assuming in a war situation. Thus:

(1) The temptation would be great for Arab ground forces, employing armor and artillery, to seize Judea and Samaria, completing the first stage in a single night's movement from the Jordan bridges to the Israeli border. To thwart possible IDF intervention, this move would commence with a vertical envelopment operation: the landing of helicopter-borne forces in key areas on the slopes of the mountain ridge and along the main axes linking the West Bank with Israel.

(2) There would be a temptation to create faits accomplis by carrying out "minor" violations over a long period. Materiel — small arms and anti-tank and anti-aircraft weaponry — would be smuggled in for the Arab-style "Haganah" that would be established, and camouflaged ground obstacles might be erected to impede advancing IDF forces.

(3) Even if an intelligence warning were received in time, enabling the IDF to seize the evacuated area ahead of (or parallel to) the Arab forces, the fighting that would develop after Arab forces had infiltrated and dug in would be far

more lethal than in the conditions of full security arrangements. Israel's relative disadvantage would derive from the location of all IDF POMCUSes (emergency depots) outside the area, from the need to advance along axes manned by a hostile population equipped with effective anti-tank and anti-aircraft weapons, and from the highly reduced efficacy of Israeli attack helicopters — the most important element in the blocking and containment stage of the fighting, as long as warplanes are occupied with the air battle.

(4) Another major factor is the considerable difficulty entailed in an Israeli political decision to move forces into the area and execute a "preemptive takeover" based solely on intelligence early warning. On the Arab side, all advance military activity would be carried out in the Arabs' own territory; indeed, even a demilitarization violation, while constituting a breach of the agreement, would still be viewed by the international community as an operation by an Arab force inside sovereign Arab territory. In contrast, the Israeli reaction would be tantamount to an overt decision to go to war.

The overriding question for Israel is whether a war is liable to endanger the country's very survival. It is this question that, unfortunately, has reflected the asymmetry between the two sides since the outset of the Arab-Israel conflict. There is no way to ensure that in every conceivable situation of conventional warfare Israel would always emerge victorious. An understanding of this bitter truth underlines the significance of the opening conditions of a war and of the security arrangements in any constellation.

Our analysis of the different options has revealed extreme situations in which no chance of a political agreement appears to exist unless Israel completely withdraws its forces from the West Bank and Gaza (excepting, possibly, a small observer force). One may argue that Israel could accept this condition out of faith in the good intentions of the other side, presumably with the support of international guarantees (including, perhaps, an undertaking to provide intelligence early warning from international observer force sources). These were, after all, the conditions under which Israel existed prior to June 1967, and these were the starting lines from which it emerged triumphant in the Six-Day War.

Yet the threat to Israel that we are discussing is liable to be very different from that of 1967. Since then the balance of forces — quantitative and particularly qualitative — between the IDF and the Arab forces that could deploy in the West Bank has changed dramatically to Israel's detriment. The main point, however, lies elsewhere: in June 1967 the IDF had ample time to mobilize its reserves, organize and deploy them, and even to upgrade their operational capability during the three weeks that preceded the outbreak of hostilities. Moreover, the 1967 war opened at Israel's initiative, with a stunning surprise attack on Arab forces.

In its new deployment of forces, based on political agreements, Israel would have to take into consideration a worst-case scenario: an Arab attack on Israel beginning with a surprise seizure of parts of Judea and Samaria *before* the IDF could mobilize and deploy. A military threat under these conditions would create extraordinarily difficult problems for Israel and the IDF. In the "best" case an Israeli response would entail hard fighting from and within Israel's vital areas (the metropolitan Tel Aviv area and Jerusalem). In the worst case Israel's ability to cope and achieve a decisive victory in conventional warfare would be called into question.

Of course it is also conceivable that the outcome of negotiations on an agreement calling for the transfer of responsibility (options IV and VI) would be an IDF presence smaller than the optimum required to effectively block and contain Arab forces that have launched a surprise thrust from the east. No useful purpose would be served here by an analysis of possible variants in terms of deployment of smaller Israeli forces. The extreme case would be a token force that could not possibly contain onrushing Arab forces, but would serve as a "tripwire" to scuttle the Arabs' chance of effecting a surprise and creating a fait accompli inside their own sovereign territory without firing a shot. A mechanism of this sort would enable Israel and the IDF to enter a war without getting bogged down in the wearying process of analysis of incoming intelligence, followed by protracted Cabinet discussions prior to a decision to go into action. The very existence of such a mechanism, which precludes the element of surprise, could act as a deterrent factor in the Arab perception.

An additional compromise possibility is the removal from the territories of all IDF units with the exception of air and intelligence early warning facilities on the mountain ridge. We may assume that this possibility would go the maximum distance toward meeting Arab demands, as it would involve removing from the area all forces whose presence infringes on the concept of Arab sovereignty, and all forces that are situated in prominent places, occupy large tracts, and constitute a potential for friction and provocation during implementation of the peace agreement.

Acquiescence in these arrangements would signal Arab understanding of the supreme importance Israel attaches to intelligence and early warning, and would allay fears of an Arab military surprise following the IDF's withdrawal. These facilities (of which there would be five or six at most) would be situated in inconspicuous and unprovocative sites and would occupy minimal physical space.

We have noted that good early warning intelligence coverage would reduce the chances of an Arab military move aimed at seizing Judea and Samaria by surprise. In this way the deterrent effect against embarking on such an adventure would be enhanced, and the IDF would be better situated to deploy against the Arab move immediately upon receiving alert information.

At the same time, a solution along these lines does not provide an unequivocal answer, for a number of reasons:

(a) Antecedent to such a move, the Arab side would have no difficulty harassing the small forces manning these intelligence facilities. Moreover, the Arabs, with the aid of electronic jamming devices, would undoubtedly be able to neutralize these facilities at the critical moment when they were required to supply real-time, reliable information.

(b) Even if early warning intelligence is received and is correctly evaluated, it is difficult to envision an Israeli government deciding to violate the agreement and retake Judea and Samaria solely on the basis of secret intelligence information. Naturally, Israel would be able to call up reserves and deploy in its own territory. But as long as the Arab side had not actually violated the agreement, it would require just one instance of Israeli preemptive reentry into the West Bank, while Arab forces had not crossed the Jordan River (whether because they were deterred from doing so or because they sought to embarrass Israel), for Israel to bear the brunt of heavy political fallout.

(c) Since the Arab side would surely make every effort to deceive Israel by concealing its preparations and early moves, it would be optimistic to assume that it had no chance of effecting a surprise move of this kind prior to an Israeli intelligence warning that would provide the impetus for a military response.

Another type of security arrangement that the Arab side might find acceptable consists of guarantees for intervention by a third, neutral party to prevent violation of the agreement. Indeed, the Arab side might even agree to the deployment of forces of this third party in vital areas to be evacuated by the IDF, with their mission defined as deterring and physically blocking forces trying to infiltrate from east of the Jordan.

Ignoring the political feasibility of such an arrangement, it would be subject to a number of key constraints:

(a) As regards guarantees, it is highly improbable that this third force, *if not stationed in the area from the outset*, would be able to obtain early warning sufficiently in advance to enable it to arrive from its extra-regional bases and deploy on the ground for containment, within the short time the Arab side would need to create a fait accompli. To send, say, an American or multinational third force into action in order to retake control of the area *after* Arab forces had seized it and deployed, would entail an extraordinarily difficult, and unlikely, political decision.

(b) A foreign force deployed in advance in the vital areas designated by the IDF could theoretically fulfill this task with the same effectiveness. However, the problems that would arise in this connection are of a different order. For one, with the passage of time the presence of the force would generate focal points of friction and detract from the image of Arab sovereignty. Local incidents could be expected, generating pressure to eliminate the foreign presence. Secondly, it is most unlikely that a force of this kind would have advance orders and authority at the battalion and company commander levels to open fire automatically. On the other hand, if the decision to respond with fire rested with a political echelon in Washington, at the UN, or elsewhere, the time constraints would once again work against effective employment of the force. Lastly, would not the passage of time bring Arab pressure, or even an ultimatum, for the evacuation of the force from the area, thus confronting Israel with a new political reality?

(c) A variation of this solution is also possible: a "mixed" force, perhaps the IDF together with a foreign contingent, or even a triple Arab-Israeli-foreign force with the agreement formulated in such a way that Israel would not be obligated to withdraw its forces even if the other contingents were pulled out. Obviously, this solution returns us to the first possibility of an IDF presence on the ground, with the "sweetener" for the Arab side being the integration of Israeli forces with others.

Two additional comments on defense arrangements are in order. In each of the aforementioned situations, the Arab side would probably insist on the principle of mutuality in security arrangements and demand a supervisory mechanism to oversee the activity of IDF forces in key border regions. This could be a mixed Israeli-Arab apparatus or one also incorporating a neutral supervisory element.

Then too, irrespective of the security arrangements themselves, Israel and the IDF would be exposed in a new and very worrisome manner to intelligence and early-warning coverage by the Arab side from the West Bank. The resultant information would serve not only the intelligence needs of the new Arab government, but would almost certainly find its way to other Arab countries (Syria, Iraq, Egypt) that may currently lack convenient intelligence access to Israeli territory.

The introduction of surface-to-surface missiles into the arena sometimes gives rise to the question whether the concepts of strategic depth and security arrangements remain meaningful in this new era. The answer is an unequivocal yes. Early-warning stations and the deployment of surface-to-air missile batteries can provide the time needed to sound an air-raid alert and warn the population to take shelter from a missile attack. They might even allow enemy missiles to be intercepted in mid-flight. The main point, however, lies elsewhere: as long as such missiles are armed with conventional warheads, they may cause painful losses and damage, but they cannot conquer territory and decide the outcome of a war. That mission will continue to be in the hands of conventional land forces. Hence the Arabs' very knowledge that a missile strike would not bring in its wake an immediate military walkover, along with the fear of the inevitable fierce Israeli retaliation, could deter them from firing missiles altogether.

Finally, we must address the question of whether a new "green line" would emerge in the form of a closed and controlled border between Israel and the new sovereign Arab territory. Such a border would not, of course, prevent Arab movement between the West Bank and Gaza. Nor would it be allowed to hinder the movement of Israeli forces, if so agreed, to and from IDF facilities and units inside the West Bank. The cardinal consideration here would be economic: would the "customs border" between Israel and adjacent Arab territory be situated along the Jordan River (i.e., along the border between the new Arab entity and East Bank Jordan), or on the new "green line" border between Israel and the Arab entity? In practical terms, would movement of goods and workers between Israel and the West Bank/Gaza be controlled or uncontrolled? Control of this kind is possible only if the border is closed along its entire length. Militarily, beyond the changes in the border line itself as agreed by the sides, a "green line" of this kind would be useful in helping to prevent and thwart terrorist infiltration into Israel, though it would be of marginal importance in terms of deployment for war.

Responsibility for Internal Security

Internal security — preventing or thwarting low-level aggression against Israel or Israeli targets, and protecting the Arab regime to be established in the area evacuated by Israel — constitutes the most problematic and critical sphere in terms of the prospects for maintaining an agreement as envisaged in options II (autonomy), IV (Palestinian state) and VI (Jordanian-Palestinian federation). Our point of departure is the assumption that the agreement might not meet even the minimal expectations of many Palestinians. It requires no great feat of the imagination to envisage some Palestinians resorting to terrorism to undermine the accord.

Today Israel bears responsibility for internal security in the West Bank and Gaza. This comprises both preventing smuggling of arms and explosives into the territories, and thwarting attempts to organize terrorist cells there. For 21 years Israel has dealt with this mission in an optimal manner, although there was never a hope of reaching a situation of "zero terrorism." In the circumstances anticipated under a compromise settlement, it is not certain whether the Arab regime established in the territories would possess the will, the determination or the ability to deal as efficiently with subversion. Nor is a political decision in principle sufficient for this purpose: it is essential that all operational echelons share both in recognizing the necessity for anti-terrorist activity and in implementing it in practice.

The psychological element must also be considered. If a "successful" terrorist attack, no matter how painful, is perpetrated against Israel while Israel bears responsibility for thwarting it, then Israel has no one to blame but itself. This would not be the case if that same attack were executed after an Israeli withdrawal, and an Arab regime had been responsible for thwarting it. Even if that government did all in its power to prevent the attack, there would always be parties in Israel who would feel that the government there had deliberately "turned a blind eye."

Nevertheless, three reasons militate in favor of an agreement transferring responsibility for internal security to the Arab side. The first is the political aspect: it is extremely difficult to see an Arab party agreeing to a settlement intended to resolve the conflict with Israel, that mandates the continuation of Israeli intelligence, prevention and detention activities inside the territory of the new Arab political entity. The second consideration is a practical one. Once having transferred governmental-administrative responsibility to Arab hands, it would be virtually impossible for Israel to retain responsibility for internal security. And thirdly — a psychological consideration — internal security could serve as a primary and immediate test of the Arab partner's sincerity and credibility regarding the settlement.

At all events, the Arab regime would certainly require time to organize and establish its internal security apparatus to meet this task. A rough estimate would put this period at one to three years at least: possibly one year for Jordan (option VI), but two or three years for a Palestinian administration (option IV). Since terrorism and subversion have the potential to undermine the entire peace settlement, Israel would have to retain responsibility for this vital task until the new Arab entity could establish an effective agency for internal security. The timing and nature of the transfer of responsibility would be effected by mutual agreement. An arbitrary timetable might be laid down from the outset, or the issue could be left open and flexible, with implementation contingent on the readiness and willingness of the Arab side to undertake the task. The transfer of responsibility could also be effected in stages, with a gradual transfer of control over prisons and detention facilities, over the judicial system dedicated to dealing with terrorists and subversives, and finally over the intelligence, prevention and detention apparatus. It could of course be argued that it would be in the Arab interest to demand this responsibility as soon as possible, but by so doing the Arab entity would risk the evolution of conditions that would oblige Israel to desist from implementing the agreement.

Ramifications of the Military Evacuation

Since 1967 the IDF has transferred a considerable portion of its routine activity into the territories. This was done to ensure IDF operational deployment designed to counter threats from Israel's eastern front — hence IDF POMCUSes (emergency depots) were relocated in the West Bank — and for reasons of convenience: military training schools and firing ranges were relocated to enable forces in the area to take part in operational-cum-training missions.

It is difficult to envisage an agreement that stipulates the evacuation of the area by Israel and the IDF without also calling for the removal of these facilities. For one, the Arab side would refuse to countenance the existence of these bases in its sovereign territory. Then too, both sides would share a desire to reduce to a minimum possible points of friction and sources of provocation after the signing of the agreement.

The evacuation of these facilities would give rise to several interrelated problems. Alternative locations for the facilities and firing zones would have to be found and readied inside Israel. This would take time, and would be costly. Even allowing for some expansion of Israel's borders in the course of a settlement, pre-1967 Israel is now too small to handle the IDF's deployment and training needs in their present format. Training grounds that were at the IDF's disposal prior to June 1967 have since been taken over for civilian development needs, while the size of the army and the composition of its units have also changed drastically since then. It would be difficult in the extreme to squeeze all the IDF's facilities and training sites into the Negev. Moreover, the Israel Air Force has no substitute for the air space over Judea and Samaria, access to which is a fundamental condition for intelligence and early warning as well as for training.

The time required for relocating is an equally complex issue. Locating alternative sites and constructing new facilities might require no more than a year or two. But some facilities simply could not be transferred due to a lack of room in Israel. The problems engendered would require development of new technologies for simulation systems, intelligence and early-warning devices, and so forth. It is impossible to estimate the time involved before the Israeli defense establishment examines the subject and draws up preliminary plans. Five years would be a rough estimate.

Nor has the cost of the military evacuation been worked out. It might range anywhere from two to four billion dollars. Were Israel to opt to seal the new border with fortifications and electronic devices, another one billion dollars or so would be called for.

Table 1. Eastern Front-Israel Military Balance--Personnel (thousands)
(Full participants: Jordan, Syria, Lebanese militias, Palestinian forces;
Partial participants: Kuwait, Libya, Saudi Arabia)

1982	Army			Air Force & Air Defense			Navy			Total		
	Reg	Res	Total	Reg	Res	Total	Reg	Res	Total	Reg	Res	Total
Eastern Front*	386	155	541	103	37.5	140.5	10	2.5	12.5	499	195	694
Israel	130	310	440	30	50	80	10	10	20	170	370	540
Ratio 1982	3:1	0.5:1	1.2:1	3.4:1	0.75:1	1.8:1	1:1	0.25:1	0.6:1	2.9:1	0.5:1	1.3:1

*Excluding Iraqi forces.

1987	Army			Air Force & Air Defense			Navy			Total		
	Reg	Res	Total	Reg	Res	Total	Reg	Res	Total	Reg	Res	Total
Eastern Front**	440	155	595	105	33	138	13	1.2	14.2	558	189.2	747.2
Israel	130	310	440	30	50	80	10	10	20	170	370	540
Ratio 1987	3.4:1	0.5:1	1.4:1	3.5:1	0.7:1	1.7:1	1.3:1	0.1:1	0.7:1	3.3:1	0.5:1	1.4:1

**Excluding Iraqi forces.

1992	Army			Air Force & Air Defense			Navy			Total		
	Reg	Res	Total	Reg	Res	Total	Reg	Res	Total	Reg	Res	Total
Eastern Front***	601	159	760	107	33	140	13.4	1.6	15	721.4	193.6	915
Israel	130	310	440	31	50	81	10	10	20	171	370	541
Ratio 1992	4.6:1	0.5:1	1.7:1	3.5:1	0.7:1	1.7:1	1.3:1	0.6:1	0.8:1	4.2:1	0.5:1	1.7:1

***With substantial Iraqi Army & Air Force participation.

176

Table 2. Arab-Israel Military Balance--Personnel (thousands)
(Full participants: Egypt, Jordan, Syria, Lebanese militias, Palestinian forces;
Partial participants: Algeria, Kuwait, Libya, Morocco, Saudi Arabia)

1982	Army			Air Force & Air Defense			Navy			Total		
	Reg	Res	Total	Reg	Res	Total	Reg	Res	Total	Reg	Res	Total
Arab Coalition*	752	650	1402	216.5	62.5	279	30	25	55	998.5	837.5	1836
Israel	130	310	440	30	50	80	10	10	20	170	370	540
Ratio 1982	5.8:1	2.1:1	3.2:1	7.2:1	1.25:1	3.5:1	3:1	2.5:1	2.75:1	5.9:1	2.3:1	3.4:1

*Excluding Iraqi forces.

1987	Army			Air Force & Air Defense			Navy			Total		
	Reg	Res	Total	Reg	Res	Total	Reg	Res	Total	Reg	Res	Total
Arab Coalition	920	662	1582	222	123	345	25	15	40	1167	810	1967
Israel	130	310	440	30	50	80	10	10	20	170	370	540
Ratio 1987	7.1:1	2.1:1	3.6:1	7.3:1	2.4:1	4.3:1	2.5:1	1.5:1	2:1	6.9:1	2.2:1	3.6:1

1992	Army			Air Force & Air Defense			Navy			Total		
	Reg	Res	Total	Reg	Res	Total	Reg	Res	Total	Reg	Res	Total
Arab Coalition	923	664	1587	222	123	345	25	15	40	1170	802	1972
Israel	130	310	440	31	50	81	10	10	20	171	370	541
Ratio 1992	7:1	2.1:1	3.6:1	7.1:1	2.5:1	4.3:1	2.5:1	1.5:1	2.0:1	6.8:1	2.2:1	3.6:1

Table 3. Eastern Front-Israel Military Balance--Formations & Weapons Systems 1982
(Full participants: Jordan, Syria, Lebanese militias, Palestinian forces;
Partial participants: Kuwait, Libya, Saudi Arabia)

Army

	Divisions				Independent Brigades Inf./Para./Com./Terr.	Tanks	APCs & ARVs	Guns & Mortars	ATGM Launchers	SSM Launchers
	Armor	Mech.	Inf.	Total						
Arab Coalition	7	5	-	12	19	4865	5120	3150	2850	42
Israel	11	-	-	11	20	3600	8000	1000	+	+
Ratio 1982	0.6:1	*	*	1.1:1	0.95:1	1.4:1	0.64:1	3.2:1	*	*

Air Force & Air Defense

	Interceptors		Strike & Multi-Role Aircraft		Total Combat A/C	Helicopters			Military Airfields	Long-Range SAM Batteries
	High Quality	Others	High Quality	Others		Attack	Transport & ASW	Total		
Arab Coalition	70	310	226	234	840	80	168	248	27	171
Israel	40	-	445	185	670	42	133	175	8	+
Ratio 1982	1.8:1	*	0.5:1	1.3:1	1.3:1	2.9:1	1.3:1	1.4:1	3.4:1	*

Navy

	Submarines	MFPBs	Missile Destroyers, Frigates & Corvettes	Gun Destroyers, Frigates & Corvettes	Landing Craft	Naval Bases
Arab Coalition	4	26	6	1	10	11
Israel	3	23	-	-	13	3
Ratio 1982	1.3:1	1.1:1	-	*	0.8:1	3.7:1

Table 4. Eastern Front-Israel Military Balance--Formations & Weapons Systems 1987
(Full participants: Jordan, Syria, Lebanese militias, Palestinian forces;
Partial participants: Kuwait, Libya, Saudi Arabia)

Army

	Divisions				Independent Brigades	Tanks	APCs & ARVs	Guns & Mortars	ATGM Launchers	SSM Launchers
	Armor	Mech.	Inf.	Total	Inf./ Para./ Com./ Terr.					
Eastern Front	7	6	2	15	15	4680	5350	2616	3450	86
Israel	12	-	-	12	22	3790	8000	1200	+	12
Ratio 1987	0.6:1	*	*	1.3:1	0.7:1	1.2:1	0.7:1	2.2:1	*	7.2:1

Air Force & Air Defense

	Interceptors		Strike & Multi-Role Aircraft		Total Combat A/C	Helicopters		Military Airfields	Long-Range SAM Batteries
	High Quality	Others	High Quality	Others		Attack	Transport Total & ASW		
Eastern Front	95	280	50	380	805	154	222	30	199
Israel	173	-	24	485	682	77	143	11	+
Ratio 1987	0.5:1	*	2.1:1	0.8:1	1.2:1	2:1	1.6:1	2.7:1	*

Navy

	Submarines	MFPBs	Missile Destroyers, Frigates & Corvettes	Gun Destroyers, Frigates & Corvettes	Landing Craft	Naval Bases
Eastern Front	9	46	6	1	11	10
Israel	3	28	-	-	13	3
Ratio 1987	0.3:1	1.6:1	-	*	0.8:1	3.3:1

Table 5. Eastern Front-Israel Military Balance--Formations & Weapons Systems 1992
(Full participants: Jordan, Syria, Lebanese militias, Palestinian forces;
Partial participants: Iraq, Kuwait, Libya, Saudi Arabia)

Army

	Divisions				Independent Brigades (Inf./Para./Com./Terr.)	Tanks	APCs & ARVs	Guns & Mortars	ATGM Launchers	SSM Launchers
	Armor	Mech.	Inf.	Total						
Eastern Front	12	8	10	30	7	6180	7750	3370	4470	146
Israel	13	-	-	13	22	3790	8000	1200	+	+
Ratio 1992	1:1	*	*	2.3:1	0.3:1	1.6:1	1.1:1	2.8:1	*	*

Air Force & Air Defense

	Interceptors		Strike & Multi-Role Aircraft		Total Combat A/C	Helicopters			Military Airfields	Long-Range SAM Batteries
	High Quality	Others	High Quality	Others		Attack	Transport	Total & ASW		
Eastern Front	210	-	125	805	1140	305	400	705	39	220
Israel	200	-	55	425	680	77	143	220	11	+
Ratio 1992	1.1:1		2.3:1	1.9:1	1.7:1	4:1	2.8:1	3.2:1	3.5:1	*

Navy

	Submarines	MFPBs	Missile Destroyers, Frigates & Corvettes	Gun Destroyers, Frigates & Corvettes	Landing Craft	Naval Bases
Eastern Front	9	52	6	-	10	11
Israel	4	26	-	-	13	3
Ratio 1992	2.3:1	2:1	6:1	-	0.8:1	3.7:1

Table 6. Arab-Israel Military Balance--Formations & Weapons Systems 1982
(Full participants: Egypt, Jordan, Syria, Lebanese militias, Palestinian forces;
Partial participants: Algeria, Kuwait, Libya, Morocco, Saudi Arabia)

Army

	Divisions				Independent Brigades	Tanks	APCs & ARVs	Guns & Mortars	ATGM Launchers	SSM Launchers
	Armor	Mech.	Inf.	Total	Inf./Para./Com./Terr.					
Arab Coalition	10	-	3	23	40	8065	8470	6050	4550	54
Israel	11	-	-	11	20	3600	8000	1000	+	+
Ratio 1982	0.9:1	-	-	2.1:1	2:1	2.2:1	1.1:1	6:1	-	-

Air Force & Air Defense

	Interceptors		Strike & Multi-Role Aircraft		Total Combat A/C	Helicopters			Military Airfields	Long-Range SAM Batteries
	High Quality	Others	High Quality	Others		Attack	Transport &ASW	Total		
Arab Coalition	130	620	496	354	1635	161	324	485	98	304
Israel	40	-	445	185	670	42	133	175	8	+
Ratio 1982	3.25:1	-	1.1:1	1.9:1	2.4:1	3.8:1	8.4:1	2.8:1	6:1	-

Navy

	Submarines	MFPBs	Missile Destroyers, Frigates & Corvettes	Gun Destroyers, Frigates & Corvettes	Landing Craft	Naval Bases
Arab Coalition	16	50	7	8	36	17
Israel	3	23	-	-	13	3
Ratio 1982	5.3:1	2.1:1	-	-	2.8:1	5.7:1

181

Table 7. Arab-Israel Military Balance--Formations & Weapons Systems 1987
(Full participants: Egypt, Jordan, Syria, Lebanese militias, Palestinian forces;
Partial participants: Algeria, Kuwait, Libya, Morocco, Saudi Arabia)

Army

	Divisions				Independent Brigades	Tanks	APCs & ARVs	Guns & Mortars	ATGM Launchers	SSM Launchers
	Armor	Mech.	Inf.	Total	Inf./Para./Com./Terr.					
Arab Coalition	17	15	9	37	23	7990	10050	5120	5724	129
Israel	12	-	-	12	22	3790	8000	1200	+	12
Ratio 1987	1.4:1	*	*	3.1:1	1:1	2.1:1	1.3:1	4.3:1		10.8:1

Air Force & Air Defense

	Interceptors		Strike & Multi-Role Aircraft		Total Combat A/C	Helicopters			Military Airfields	Long-Range SAM Batteries
	High Quality	Others	High Quality	Others		Attack	Transport & ASW	Total		
Arab Coalition	210	590	150	355	1305	224	304	528	64	365
Israel	173	-	24	485	682	77	143	220	11	+
Ratio 1987	1.2:1	*	6.3:1	0.7:1	1.9:1	2.9:1	2.1:1	2.4:1	5.8:1	*

Navy

	Submarines	MFPBs	Missile Destroyers, Frigates & Corvettes	Gun Destroyers, Frigates & Corvettes	Landing Craft	Naval Bases
Arab Coalition	17	77	12	-	22	17
Israel	3	28	*	-	13	3
Ratio 1987	5.7:1	2.8:1	*		1.7:1	5.7:1

Table 8. Arab-Israel Military Balance--Formations & Weapons Systems 1992
(Full participants: Egypt, Jordan, Syria, Lebanese militias, Palestinian forces;
Partial participants: Algeria, Iraq, Kuwait, Libya, Morocco, Saudi Arabia)

Army

	Divisions				Independent Brigades	Tanks	APCs & ARVs	Guns & Mortars	ATGM Launchers	SSM Launchers
	Armor	Mech.	Inf.	Total	Inf./ Para./ Com./ Terr.					
Arab Coalition	16	15	11	42	15	8490	11050	5320	6020	184
Israel	13	-	-	13	22	3790	8000	1200	+	+
Ratio 1992	1.2:1	*	*	3.2:1	0.7:1	2.2:1	1.4:1	4.4:1	*	*

Air Force & Air Defense

	Interceptors		Strike & Multi-Role Aircraft		Total Combat A/C	Helicopters			Military Airfields	Long-Range SAM Batteries
	High Quality	Others	High Quality	Others		Attack	Transport & ASW	Total		
Arab Coalition	350	-	235	1070	1305	244	304	548	64	365
Israel	200	-	55	425	680	77	143	220	11	+
Ratio 1992	1.8:1		4.3:1	2.5:1	1.9:1	3.2:1	2.1:1	2.5:1	5.8:1	*

Navy

	Submarines	MFPBs	Missile Destroyers, Frigates & Corvettes	Gun Destroyers, Frigates & Corvettes	Landing Craft	Naval Bases
Arab Coalition	17	77	12	-	22	17
Israel	4	26	1	-	13	3
Ratio 1992	4.3:1	3:1	12:1	-	1.7:1	5.6:1

Appendix 2

Israeli Public Opinion on Security and the Palestinian Question

A central feature of Israeli public opinion during the late 1980s has been deep division over the question of the future of Judea, Samaria and Gaza. The country is bitterly divided between supporters of a territorial compromise — who are willing, in return for peace, to withdraw from most of the West Bank and Gaza — and adherents of a Greater Israel, who reject withdrawal from or transfer of any part of Judea, Samaria or Gaza to non-Israeli rule. This picture is supported by a look at election results during the past decade. The outcome of the last two elections was a near dead heat between the Right and Left, with the issue of the territories the main focus of disagreement. The following brief analysis and presentation of opinion poll findings is intended to elucidate the sources of this division.

Social psychology recognizes that there are two dimensions to every attitude. The first is the attitude itself; the second is one's ego-involvement in the attitude. Measurements of this second dimension are the intensity and the salience of the attitude. The second dimension is no less important than the first: when assessing the effect of an attitude on actual behavior or its potential social and political consequences, it may be even more important.

The Israeli national debate over the territories is not reflected solely by the even split between the main political blocs regarding their future. It runs deeper, reflecting the intense emotional involvement of many segments of Israeli society. It involves not merely a question of foreign or defense policy; it goes to the very heart of Israel's self-image. In this sense we are dealing with a historic and existential national decision. Since the advent of the *intifada* in late December 1987, the debate has become yet more intense, and with it the growing polarization of Israeli society, to the extent that the question of the territories is now the dominant factor of the Israeli socio-political scene. It has already brought about a political stalemate, and is threatening the country with political and national paralysis.

A second major feature of Jewish public opinion in Israel is a deep mistrust of the motives, goals and aims of the Arabs in general, and the Palestinians in particular. Six wars in 40 years, and 70 years of Arab terrorism, have left their mark on the collective subconscious of Israeli society. To all this must be added the Israeli perception of the uncompromising attitude of the Palestinian leadership — at least as it has been expressed publicly until recently, particularly in the Palestinian Covenant and in declarations of hatred and hostility toward Israel, Zionism and the Jewish people. Further, Israeli suspicion of the Arabs and their motives is grounded in a more fundamental Jewish suspicion toward the non-Jewish world in general. This basic mistrust is well rooted in the bitter lessons of Jewish history. In this context the Holocaust experience is an essential element of the collective subconscious of the Jewish People.

There is a definite interrelationship between these two central features of Israeli public opinion: attitudes regarding the future of the territories, and lack of trust and deep suspicion of the Arabs. The opinion that "territories should not be given back even for peace" — held by half of the Israeli Jewish population — is given to two different interpretations, with widely divergent psychological and practical implications. One possible interpretation is that for ideological reasons an Israeli may be unwilling to give up parts of Judea, Samaria or Gaza because he/she indeed prefers the preservation of a Greater Israel to peace. An alternative interpretation is that an Israeli would prefer peace over a Greater Israel, and for peace would indeed be willing to give back territories, but he/she simply does not believe in the viability of the peace that is contemplated. This type of respondent is convinced that even if the Arabs sign a peace treaty they have no intention of honoring it. As he/she assesses the Arab attitude toward a peace treaty it is not the end of the conflict but rather a ruse aimed at the destruction of Israel in stages. In this sense the term "in return for peace" does not mean the same thing, from a psychological-cognitive point of view, to all Israelis.

185

It is difficult to determine what percentage of those opposing a territorial compromise are motivated by an ideological commitment — religious or otherwise — to a Greater Israel, and what percentage are motivated by suspicion, perhaps even hatred, of the Arabs. We are not aware of any research data that might cast light on this question. In its absence, we can only attempt to reach a very rough estimate on the basis of general knowledge and indirect indicators. It would appear that 25-33 percent of the Jewish population — more than half of the supporters of Greater Israel — oppose giving up territory not for ideological reasons but rather for psychological reasons, namely grave mistrust and deep suspicion, bordering on hatred, toward the Arabs in general and the Palestinians in particular.

Clearly, were this sector — one-quarter to one-third — of the Israeli Jewish population to change its attitude, it would have a farreaching effect on overall Israeli attitudes toward peace (since around half the Israeli Jewish population already are prepared to exchange territories for peace). This could come about as a result of some very dramatic act or event. The late Egyptian leader Anwar Sadat understood this only too well. He was aware that in order to achieve a breakthrough in the political stalemate he had to prepare Israeli public opinion, or in his own words, break down the psychological barrier, and that this could only be done through a dramatic, exceptional and far-reaching act. Israeli hostility and suspicion toward the Palestinians exceeds by far that which existed toward the Egyptians. Yet perhaps here, too, a dramatic, unexpected and far-reaching act could bring about a significant and meaningful change in Israeli public opinion.

Alternatively, there exists the possibility of a gradual change in public opinion, resulting from the cumulative effect, over time, of moderate statements emanating from Palestinian spokesmen: voices calling for peaceful coexistence with Israel. We cannot exclude such a possibility, although it is clearly a much more tortuous and uncertain road.

An additional major feature of the Israeli scene — one which introduces a sensitive and complex dimension to the public debate over the territories — are the Jewish settlements in the West Bank and Gaza. In Judea, Samaria and Gaza there are around 100 settlements — cities, towns and villages — in which over 60,000 Jewish Israeli citizens reside. These settlements are spread throughout the area and are organized into six regional councils and seven local municipalities. Maalei Adumim numbers over 10,000 people and the population of three other cities is approximately 5,000 each. If the sharp debate within Israel over the future of the territories is essentially an ideological one, for the Jewish settlers in the territories it is a personal issue of the utmost gravity: a fight for their very homes.

These Jewish settlers, along with their extended families and supporters inside Israel, form a strong special interest group. They are a highly organized and cohesive lobby, with strong internal discipline, and possessing an extensive network of political, economic, educational, commercial, media and security institutions. Their central authority is the Council of Judea, Samaria and Gaza, composed of the heads of the local and regional Jewish municipal councils in the territories.

★ ★ ★

Following are findings culled from two public opinion polls conducted on representative samples of the adult Jewish population in Israel. Most of the data relate to a poll taken during late December 1987-early January 1988, based on a sample numbering 1,180 Jewish respondents representing the adult Jewish population within Israel proper (excluding the Jewish population in the territories). These data are supplemented by data from a poll conducted simultaneously on a representative sample of the adult Jewish population living in Judea and Samaria, numbering 99 respondents. In some instances, results from the main poll are compared with data from a comparable poll undertaken two years earlier, in January 1986, on a representative sample of 1,172 respondents. All polls were designed by Professor Asher Arian and his assistants, of Tel-Aviv University's Department of Political Science, within the framework of the Jaffee Center Project on Israeli Public Opinion regarding National Security Issues. The polls were administered by *Dahaf*. All figures are percentages.

1. There are three long-range solutions for the territories held since the 1967 war. Which one do you agree with most?

	Dec '87	Jan '86	Judea & Samaria Sample
A. In exchange for peace, I would be willing to give up the territories as long as Israel's security needs were provided for.	31	30	10
B. Annexing the Territories.	29	23	44
C. Leaving the situation as it is.	40	47	46

Those who answered that they agreed most with "leaving the situation as it is" were then asked:

2. And if Israel had to choose between the first two alternatives, which would you choose?

	Dec '87	Jan '86	Judea & Samaria Sample
A. Giving up the territories.	39	32	30
B. Annexing the territories.	61	68	70

Combining both questions, we get the following division between the first two alternatives for the entire Jewish population:

	Dec '87	Jan '86	Judea & Samaria Sample
A. Giving up the territories.	47	45	24
B. Annexing the territories.	53	55	76

188

3. What is your opinion of the way the government is handling security matters in the territories?

	Dec '87	Jan '86	Judea & Samaria Sample
A. Too harsh.	11	5	5
B. Just about right.	36	50	24
C. Too soft.	53	45	71

4. In your opinion, should autonomy (self-rule) be established in Judea, Samaria and the Gaza Strip, or not?

	Dec '87	Judea & Samaria Sample
A. Definitely.	18}	13}
	}45	}41
B. I think so.	27}	28}
C. I don't think so.	29}	28}
	}55	}60
D. Definitely not.	26}	32}

5. In your opinion, should Israel accept or oppose the creation of a Palestinian state in Judea, Samaria and Gaza?

	Dec '87	Judea & Samaria Sample
A. Definitely accept.	7}	3}
	}21	}7
B. I think it should accept.	14}	4}
C. I think it should oppose.	27}	16}
	}79	}93
D. Definitely oppose.	52}	77}

189

6. Regarding the northern border, do you think that Israel should be prepared to return the Golan Heights to Syria in exchange for a peace treaty?

	Dec '87	Jan '86	Judea & Samaria Sample
A. Should return the entire Golan Heights.	6	14	-
B. Should return only part of the Golan Heights.	26	not asked	21
C. Should not be ready to return any part of the Golan Heights.	68	86	78

7. Under the present circumstances, do you think that Israel should or should not be ready to hold negotiations with the PLO?

	Dec '87	Judea & Samaria Sample
A. Israel should be ready to do so.	34	16
B. Israel should not be ready to do so.	66	84

8. And if the PLO undergoes basic changes and announces that it recognizes the State of Israel and will completely give up acts of terror, do you think that then Israel should or should not be ready to hold negotiations with the PLO?

	Dec '87	Jan '86	Judea & Samaria Sample
A. Israel should be ready to do so.	66	50	41
B. Israel should not be ready to do so.	34	50	59

9. Are you in favor of or do you oppose, in principle, the death sentence for terrorists?

	Dec '87	Judea & Samaria Sample
A. In favor.	79	92
B. Oppose.	21	8

10. There are three basic opinions about the future of the territories in Judea, Samaria and the Gaza Strip if Israel comes to discussing peace with Jordan. Which opinion do you support?

	Jan '86
A. In exchange for a peace agreement, I would agree to return all the territories, with minor border modifications and with a special arrangement for Jerusalem.	16
B. In exchange for a peace agreement and for acceptable security arrangements, I would agree to return all the territories heavily populated with Arabs (about 2/3 of the territories).	35
C. No territories should be returned, even for a peace agreement.	49

11. To what extent do you agree or disagree with the following opinion: "We must enter into a political process of peace treaties immediately, even at the cost of territorial concessions."

	Dec '87	Jan '86	Judea & Samaria Sample
A. Certainly agree.	17}	14}	10}
	}48	}45	}22
B. Agree.	31}	31}	12}
C. Don't agree.	36}	40}	30}
	}52	}55	}78
D. Certainly don't agree.	16}	15}	48}

12. And with the following opinion: "Israel should encourage the emigration of Arabs from Eretz Yisrael."

	Dec '87	Judea & Samaria Sample
A. Certainly agree.	35}	39}
	}69	}71
B. Agree.	34}	32}
C. Don't agree.	24}	23}
	}31	}29
D. Certainly don't agree.	7}	6}

13. And with the following opinion: "Under no circumstances whatsoever may we return parts of the Land of Israel."

	Dec '87	Judea & Samaria Sample
A. Certainly agree.	17}	28}
	}46	}55
B. Agree	29}	27}
C. Don't agree.	40}	38}
	}54	}45
D. Certainly don't agree.	14}	7}

192

14. What do you believe to be the Arab aspiration in the final
    analysis?

	Dec '87	Jan '86	Judea & Samaria Sample
A. To regain some of the territories occupied in the Six-Day War.	7}	5}	5}
	}30	}27	}17
B. To regain all of the territories occupied in the Six-Day War.	23}	22}	12}
C. To conquer Israel.	30}	36}	29}
	}70	}73	}83
D. To conquer Israel & annihilate a large portion of the Jewish population.	40}	37}	54}

15. To what extent is each of the following factors a reason
    for Arab opposition to the State of Israel?

They harbor hatred for the Jews.

	Dec '87	Jan '86	Judea & Samaria Sample
A. It is a reason.	87	87	90
B. Not a reason.	13	13	10

Israel is viewed as a foreign
element in the Middle East and
as a "thorn in the side."

	Dec '87	Jan '86	Judea & Samaria Sample
A. It is a reason.	87	81	93
B. Not a reason.	13	15	7

193

Appendix 3

Maps:
The Arab and Jewish Populations
of the West Bank and Gaza

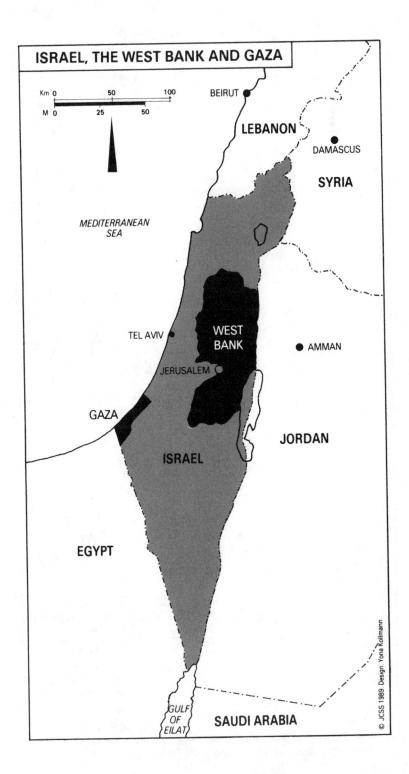

ISRAEL, THE WEST BANK AND GAZA

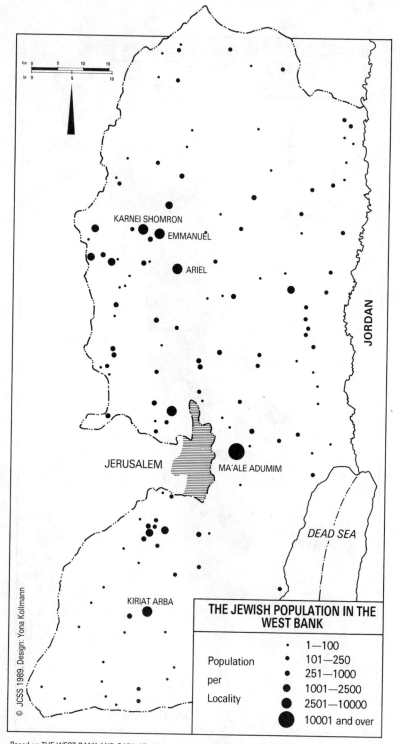

KARNEI SHOMRON
EMMANUEL
ARIEL

JERUSALEM
MA'ALE ADUMIM

JORDAN

DEAD SEA

KIRIAT ARBA

THE JEWISH POPULATION IN THE WEST BANK

Population	· 1—100
	· 101—250
per	● 251—1000
	● 1001—2500
Locality	● 2501—10000
	● 10001 and over

Km 0   5   10   15
M 0   5   10

© JCSS 1989. Design: Yona Kollmann

Based on THE WEST BANK AND GAZA ATLAS, Benvenisty and Khayat, Jerusalem Post 1988.

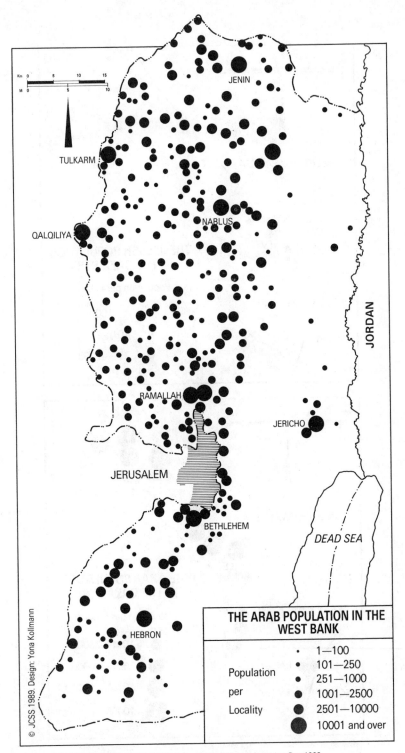

THE ARAB POPULATION IN THE WEST BANK

	1—100
	101—250
Population	251—1000
per	1001—2500
Locality	2501—10000
	10001 and over

JENIN

TULKARM

QALQILIYA

NABLUS

JORDAN

RAMALLAH

JERICHO

JERUSALEM

DEAD SEA

BETHLEHEM

HEBRON

Km 0   5   10   15
M 0   5   10

© JCSS 1989. Design: Yona Kollmann

Based on THE WEST BANK AND GAZA ATLAS, Benvenisty and Khayat, Jerusalem Post 1988.

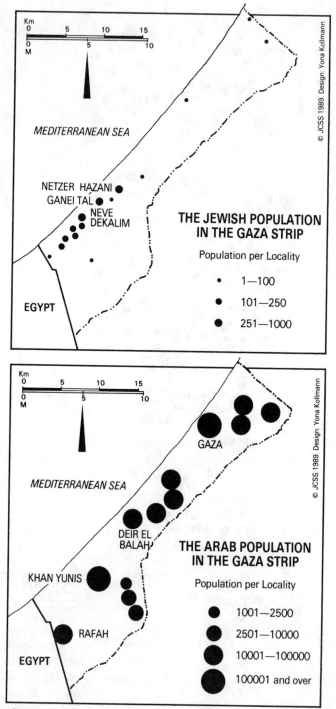

Km
0   5   10   15
0   5   10
M

MEDITERRANEAN SEA

NETZER HAZANI
GANEI TAL
NEVE
DEKALIM

EGYPT

**THE JEWISH POPULATION
IN THE GAZA STRIP**

Population per Locality

•   1—100

●   101—250

⬤   251—1000

© JCSS 1989. Design: Yona Kollmann

Km
0   5   10   15
0   5   10
M

MEDITERRANEAN SEA

GAZA

DEIR EL
BALAH

KHAN YUNIS

RAFAH

EGYPT

**THE ARAB POPULATION
IN THE GAZA STRIP**

Population per Locality

●   1001—2500

⬤   2501—10000

⬤   10001—100000

⬤   100001 and over

© JCSS 1989. Design: Yona Kollmann

Based on THE WEST BANK AND GAZA ATLAS, Benvenisty and Khayat, Jerusalem Post 1988.

The West Bank and Gaza: Geographic and Demographic Background

The physical and human geographical characteristics of the territories are an important component of the present aggregate pattern of the Palestinian problem. Any option for a major solution of the problem should be examined against the backdrop of the existing geographic and demographic attributes of these territories.

According to our assessments and observations, the territories are very poor in natural resources, and are subject to a rapidly growing state of over-population. The basic resources on which the population of these regions subsisted up to the middle of this century, namely arable land and water, cannot support the present population, which has more than doubled since. The development of agriculture as well as of other sources of livelihood within the territories over the last 40 years has fallen far short of minimal requirements resulting from population growth, to say nothing of that expected within the next decade. Projections based on present population estimates, the territories' demographic characteristics, and growth trends, suggest that the population of Judea, Samaria and the Gaza Strip will grow by nearly 50 percent up to the year 2000, when it will number 2.3-2.4 million.

The West Bank (Judea and Samaria)

Judea and Samaria extend over an area of 5500 sq km (2130 sq miles). Over 80 percent of this area is deeply bisected mountainous country with extensive areas of barren limestone. The eastern parts of this region, nearly half its area, are desert or semi-desert. Only 30 percent of the area is classified as agriculturally useful land, but much of this land is covered by patchy, poor, shallow, stony soils. Most of these soils produce low yields of field crops or support sparse plantations, mainly of olives. A substantial part of this agricultural land is made up of narrow terraces on hill slopes.

Only approximately 10 percent of the area, 54,000 hectares (135,000 acres), is reasonably good agricultural land. Water resources (springs, wells and cisterns into which rain water is collected during the rainy season) are scanty. The Jordan River, on the eastern boundary of the region, is the only perennial river, but few of its waters are utilized in Judea and Samaria. Exploitation of the Jordan and its tributaries by Israeli and Jordanian water supply and irrigation schemes leaves extremely limited possibilities for augmenting Judea and Samaria water resources.

All told, 261 of the 432 Arab villages in this region depend almost entirely for their water supply on catchment of rain water into small cisterns (storing 50-100 cubic meters per annum) with which each household is equipped. Only seven percent of the cultivated land is irrigated. Still, unused potential water resources are few, except for those of Western Samaria that feed the aquifers of the Israeli coastal plain and are vital for the Israeli economy. Any massive interference with the natural flow of these resources toward the coastal plain could not only deprive that densely inhabited and cultivated region of a substantial part of its water resources, but could also cause serious damage to the existing equilibrium vis-a-vis saline sea water in parts of the aquifer in the vicinity of the Israeli coastline.

In recent years Israel's water consumption has totaled an average of 1.8 million cubic meters per annum; of this, agriculture consumed approximately 1.3 million cubic meters. The aquifers of the coastal plain are fed to a great extent by rain water falling on the western slopes of the Samarian Highlands. These waters percolate through pervious rock formations westward into the groundwater resources of the coastal plain, and provide 300-350 million cubic meters, or 17-19 percent of the total annual water supply. Were a Palestinian Arab political entity to develop an effective modern system of wells on the western fringes of the West Bank (a few kilometers east of the present western boundary of the West Bank), Israel would have to find alternative sources for a large quantity of water that flows freely into its territory and upon which the population and agriculture of the Israeli coastal plain depend to a large extent.

The average annual household water consumption per capita in Judea and Samaria is estimated at 15 cubic meters (as against 80 cubic meters in Israel). Even full utilization of available water resources by West Bank Palestinians would not permit the substantial extension of irrigated agricultural areas upon which any significant increase in crop production depends. The limited resources of agricultural land and water and the ubiquitous limestone are, in fact, the only available natural resources of Judea and Samaria. Nor has extensive geological research produced any hope of finding additional resources. The mineral resources of the Dead Sea, which borders on Judea, are already fully exploited by Israel and Jordan.

Turning to population statistics, according to the Israeli Central Bureau of Statistics the population of Judea and Samaria is estimated to number 885,000 (September 1988). This figure is based on a census carried out by the Israeli military authorities in September 1967, estimates of natural increase since then, registration of population movements, sample surveys and research. Arab sources (Jordanian statistics, studies by various Arab scholars, PLO publications) put the figure much higher. These latter claims are based on the Jordanian 1961 census, Jordanian statistical publications from the years 1961-67, and individual studies by Arab and other researchers.

An assessment of all these sources, coupled with additional independent studies, leads to the conclusion that the 1967 census was not fully accurate, and that official estimates of the natural increase are slightly below their actual rate. Hence the actual number of inhabitants is probably somewhere between 950,000 and 1,000,000 (of which approximately 100,000 live in refugee camps). But an accurate figure can only be produced by a new census.

According to official Israeli publications, the annual rate of population increase (births minus deaths minus emigration) has been 2.8-3 percent. Emigration, mainly to the Persian Gulf oil states, was extensive in the 1960s and 1970s, but has declined sharply since the early 1980s as a result of the slump in the oil industry and saturation of the labor market in the Gulf. Indeed, in recent years there has been a growing movement of returnees from some of the Gulf states; additional tens of thousands of Judea and Samaria residents who went abroad for temporary or permanent residence are legally entitled to return to the territories.

In the absence of fully authentic registration of births and deaths, it is impossible to establish with certainty the actual rate of natural increase. Estimates range from 3.2 to 3.8 percent per annum. The percentage of young people in the reproductive age groups, 20-49, in Judea and Samaria has risen from 28 percent in 1967 to 32 percent in 1985 and is expected to rise to 36-38 percent by the year 2002. Therefore a rise in the absolute figures of annual natural increase can be expected at least until the end of the century, even if a downward trend develops in the birthrate.

As for patterns of work and residence, nearly half the Arab population of Judea and Samaria lived in urban areas in 1988, as against 33 percent in 1967. However, the actual extent of "urbanization"of this population over the last 20 years is not fully reflected by these figures. In the 1960s over 60 percent of the rural population of Judea and Samaria was engaged in agriculture in or near the village of residence. By 1987 this figure had fallen to 26 percent. Some 35 percent of the Judea and Samaria labor force (over 50 percent of the rural labor force) was by this time employed in Israel, and a few thousand Arab workers were employed in Jewish settlements and concerns in Judea and Samaria. Numerous workshops and small industries depend mainly on Israeli clients. Thus about half the population of Judea and Samaria is actually fully or largely dependent on earnings derived from Israel.

Judging by the percentage of the male labor force that commutes daily to work in and around Israeli urban centers, most villages in Western Samaria have lost much of their rural character. This development is having a far-reaching effect on the socio-economic structure and patterns of behavior of the rural population. There is a continuous decrease in the absolute number of villagers whose sole or main occupation is farming — a profession on which the majority in the territories depended for their livelihood before 1967.

The Gaza Strip

The Gaza Strip extends over 352 sq km (135 sq miles). It is a narrow 44 km-long strip along the Mediterranean coast, an undulating plain partly covered by sand dunes. It is a semi-arid transitional zone. Its northern sector receives, on the average, sufficient rain for rain-fed agriculture. Rainfall in the southern part is marginal, and in most years can support only low yield winter crops. Nearly half the area of the Gaza Strip is under cultivation, much of it under irrigation. Citrus plantations and market gardening, for marketing outside the Strip, are the main local sources of income. Water resources are scarce and are all drawn from numerous wells. Rain water, caught and stored in small cisterns, provides a portion of household requirements.

Continuous overpumping in many wells in recent years is causing serious damage to the volume and quality of water resources available in the Gaza Strip. Groundwater level has fallen seriously, and rising salinity of the water in many wells has rendered them useless for most types of agriculture. Large areas of citrus plantation have withered as a result of this development. The rise in water consumption as a consequence of the rapidly growing population and of efforts to expand agricultural production, is gradually rendering the water supply problem even more acute.

Official Israeli statistics put the number of inhabitants of the Gaza Strip at 581,000 (1988), approximately half of whom live in refugee camps. This figure is based on the 1967 census, and surveys and research carried out since. The pre-1967 Egyptian administration of the Gaza Strip estimated the size of the population in 1966 at 455,000 (as against the Israeli census figure of 354,000 in 1967). Extrapolating Arab sources, then, by 1988 the population exceeded 660,000. Here again independent research indicates that the 1967 census was incomplete, although by only a small margin; the actual figure is probably about 40-50 thousand higher than the official Israel one, or around 625,000.

The rate of population increase in the Gaza Strip over the last ten years has been substantially higher, and the emigration rate much lower, than in Judea and Samaria. According to official Israeli figures the rate of population growth over recent years has been 3.4 percent per annum. The excess of births over deaths is nearly 4 percent.

Gaza contains no natural resources other than agricultural land and water. According to official figures, 46 percent of the gainfully active labor force is employed in Israel. In actual fact this percentage is substantially higher. Moreover numerous workshops and small industries in the Gaza Strip work mainly for Israeli clients. Hence well over 50 percent of the gainfully employed inhabitants of the Gaza Strip derive their income from Israel.

General Population Trends

The total number of non-Jewish children born annually in recent years in Israel and in the territories together, substantially exceeds the number of newly born Jewish children. There are, at present, more non-Jewish than Jewish children under the age of six in Greater Israel. The Jewish natural reproduction rate is 13.1 per thousand annually, and has been dropping since the 1950s. The Arab rate is 34.2 per thousand. Only a major turning point in this demographic trend, either by virtue of a large wave of Jewish immigration or by emigration of non-Jewish inhabitants, could reverse this growing unfavorable gap (from an Israeli point of view) between Jewish and non-Jewish population growth. Merely in order to maintain the Jewish proportion of the overall population of Greater Israel at 60 percent by the year 2000, some 700,000 Jews would have to immigrate to Israel over the next ten years. To restore the existing ratio inside the State of Israel between Jews and Arabs (Jews form slightly over 80 percent) following annexation of the West Bank and Gaza, approximately eight million Jews (virtually the entirety of Diaspora Jewry) would have to immigrate to Israel by the year 2000, or nearly 800,000 Jews annually over the next ten years. This would increase the population of Greater Israel to nearly 16 million: 12.7 million Jews and 3.2 million Arabs.

Territorial Discontinuity

One key geographic factor likely to have a conspicuous impact on the future political fate of the territories is the territorial discontinuity between Judea and Samaria on the one hand, and the Gaza Strip on the other. They actually form two regions with different physical and human characteristics, totally separated from each other by a strip of Israeli territory approximately 40 km wide.

The only possible direct and easy access between Judea and Samaria and the Gaza Strip is through Israel. A political development that rendered this passage impossible would impose upon communications between these two regions an extremely difficult and lengthy detour — either via Jordan and Egypt (nearly 600 km) or via Jordan, Syria, Lebanon and the Mediterranean (550 km).

Appendix 5

The Palestinian Diaspora

There are no reliable statistics on world Palestinian population, which is variously estimated at four to five million, including Israeli Arabs (who are not discussed here). This population is generally assumed to be broken down approximately as follows:

Israel	800,000
West Bank and Gaza	1,600,000
Jordan (excluding Palestinians abroad)	1,000,000
The Gulf States (mostly Jordanian citizens)	500,000
Lebanon	275,000
Syria	250,000
Elsewhere (Europe, western hemisphere)	250,000
TOTAL	4,675,000

The socio-economic conditions of these Palestinians vary widely, as do the legal and political constraints under which they live. One major distinction concerns their refugee status. The distinction between refugees and non-refugees has potentially important ramifications for the durability of various policy alternatives. According to UNRWA statistics, about 2.2 million Palestinians are registered as refugees throughout the Middle East, of whom approximately 770,000 live in refugee camps (another 50,000 camp residents are not registered refugees). These figures are certainly exaggerated to some extent, but not by an order of magnitude that would produce a completely different picture. Approximately half of all Palestinians are registered refugees, which corresponds to the generally-accepted proportion of the Arab population of Palestine that became refugees in 1948-49 (500,000 out of 1.2 million).

Appendix 6

The Israeli Arabs: Basic Data

At the beginning of 1988 Israel's Arab citizens numbered approximately 670,000 persons (or 815,000 if we include the 145,000 residents of East Jerusalem and the Druze on the Golan Heights, who do not hold Israeli citizenship), and constituted about 15 percent (or 18 percent, respectively) of the country's total population. Their electoral potential stands at 13 to 14 Knesset seats. In the year 2000, Israeli Arabs will constitute around 23 percent (or 27 percent, respectively) of the population, and their electoral strength will grow proportionately. About 80 percent of Israeli Arabs were born and raised after the establishment of the State of Israel. As a result of their high natural birth rate (which has shown a gradual decline in recent years) the proportion of the younger age groups among them is quite high (e.g., the age group 0-14 makes up 43 percent of the Israeli Arab population, as against 30 percent among Israeli Jews).

Israeli Arabs constitute an absolute majority in some of their areas of residence in the Galilee and the "Triangle" (northwest Samaria). Many of them reside in villages located near the border between Israel and the territories; indeed, most of the areas in question are within the territory designated for a Palestinian state in the 1947 UN Partition Resolution.

A number of additional factors are of potential importance in assessing the impact of a Palestinian settlement on Israeli Arabs. For one, 85 percent of Israeli Arabs are Muslim, with Muslim homogeneity in the Triangle. Then too, most of the country's Arab population lives in large villages undergoing accelerated urbanization and modernization. This is accompanied by a rise in the qualitative weight of the individual at the expense of the influence once wielded by the clan and the extended family. While the Israeli Arab educational system is generally on a lower level than the Israeli Jewish system, there is a developing intelligentsia: about 14,000 university graduates, and another 5,000 students attending institutions of higher learning, many of whom cannot find employment in their specialties. Finally, Israeli Arabs have developed a unique pattern of media consumption in Arabic from both Israel and the neighboring states — in addition to the Hebrew media.

The Arabs of Israel are integrated into the various state systems — but not always to the degree called for by their proportion in the population or by their qualitative weight. Although the country's Arab citizens enjoy full legal rights and equality before the law (with the exception of the Law of Return), the fact that they do not fulfill the obligation of military service (or do alternative national service) is cited as formal grounds for depriving them of equal rights and opportunities, thus hindering their full integration into Israeli society. The budgetary crisis experienced by Arab local councils, which has been a focal point of public unrest in the Arab sector in recent years, is one example of the sense of discrimination felt by the Israeli Arabs, even though the law does not discriminate in this realm.

Despite great progress since 1948, the infrastructure of Arab settlements has not kept pace with natural population growth. It is still incapable of providing sufficient sources of employment, comprehensive local services, and other necessities of community life. Comparisons drawn by Israeli Arabs between their settlements and what they see in nearby Jewish settlements that have benefited from funds furnished by the Jewish Agency and the land-settlement movements (but also from government budgets that did not reach all state sectors in equal measure) generate feelings of deprivation and discrimination, and these reinforce nationalist trends.

The response to Palestinian efforts to recruit Israeli Arabs to terrorist activity has been negligible. Some 350 Israeli Arabs were arrested and tried for violating state security between 1967 and 1973, and since then there has been no significant increase in the number of Israeli Arabs accused of terrorism. The most acute disruptions of law and order (against a Palestinian nationalist backdrop) occur in the form of one-day protests (Land Day, Sabra and Shatilla Day, Equality Day), that are tolerable in nature. However even if Israeli Arab violence is limited and sporadic, its reverberations tend to be intense because it occurs in the center of the country (as distinct from the territories with their sparse

Israeli population). Particularly grave actions, such as the blocking of the key Wadi Ara highway, naturally impact even more powerfully on the general population.

Some members of the Israeli Arab population serve in the IDF. Besides the Druze and the Circassians, who have been serving since 1957, there are Bedouin volunteers in the career army and in compulsory service, as well as some Christian and even Muslim volunteers. The number of volunteers probably exceeds the number of those eventually recruited, as it is improbable that all the volunteers meet IDF recruitment criteria.

Appendix 7

The Economic Implications
of the Options

Economic ramifications are one of eleven issue areas according to which each option is discussed and evaluated in this study group report. However, while the main point of view of each of the other ten issue areas is Israel, the issue of economic ramifications reflects almost equally upon Israel and the West Bank and Gaza. The uniqueness of the economic analysis derives from the fact that during 21 years of Israeli rule over the territories, the two separate economies have turned into a single economic entity. This is particularly significant for the economies of the West Bank and Gaza, in view of their size.

Any analysis of the economic implications of the options requires quantitative and qualitative estimates of the relevant economic variables for each scenario. The analysis must therefore take into consideration the reciprocal quantitative relations between the Israeli economy and that of the territories.

The options were defined as broad political scenarios. This leaves a wide range for economic interpretation. From the economic standpoint the essence of the distinctions among the various scenarios lies in the nature of the relations that would evolve, on a continuum ranging from economic separatism to economic integration. Correspondingly, the main political variable is whether the borders between Israel and the territories stay open or are closed to the flow of workers, goods, services and capital. For example, in option III (Palestinian state), the authorities of that state may decide, for political or ideological reasons, to close the border with Israel to the flow of workers and goods, even though in the short run this may cause the Palestinian state considerable harm. The damages which would be suffered by Israel and the Palestinian state in such an eventuality can and should be quantified before the parties to the dispute meet at the negotiating table.

Here we offer a preliminary attempt to estimate future developments in the economy of the territories as a result of either of two extreme scenarios: the separation of the two economies, or the continuation of the process of integration. Ideally, this assessment should be based on an econometric model that describes the combined economic development of both the territories and Israel, in order to develop and analyze reciprocal implications. In the absence of such a model — which, to the best of our knowledge, does not exist — caution perhaps should have dictated the restriction of our analysis to qualitative dimensions alone. But this would have made it difficult to draw comparisons between the options.

On the other hand the presentation of quantitative findings might create a misleading illusion of accuracy. Quantitative economic estimation of the results of the political options is difficult not only due to the inability to foresee politico-economic developments. Even if it were possible to do so, to the best of our knowledge no orderly analysis of the economic implications of the various options has yet been made in Israel. Existing economic forecasts tend to assume that the present situation will continue. Thus we did not find, for example, any authoritative estimates by the defense establishment of the cost of removing military installations from the territories, or of the economic implications of allocating alternative training areas west of the Green Line. Nor are there official estimates of the economic implications of evicting Jewish settlers from the territories. Obviously, in the options examined here the cost of abandoning military installations and evicting Jewish settlers from the territories is of vital importance both for estimating the economic feasibility of the options and for assessing the economic implications of adopting them in terms of the future of the Israeli economy.

Methodology

In the first stage of our inquiry we describe the relationships between the Israeli economy and that of the territories at the time of the outbreak of the *intifada*. We also analyze the economic implications for Israel and the territories of two economic scenarios: separation versus integration of the two economies.

We then attempt to determine the relevant economic indicators of various political scenarios. These are external economic variables that affect essential variables of the economy, such as GNP, private consumption per capita and foreign debt per capita in Israel and the territories.

The following economic magnitudes were examined:

(1) Defense expenditure, including expenditure on current security, forcebuilding, training, military deployment and training areas. Our estimates on this subject are merely preliminary and are not based on official data, which are unavailable. Research findings in other issue areas indicate that some of the options are unstable and may engender progressively increasing hostility, of which one reasonable outcome is war. It is very difficult to estimate the cost of a war, since it depends on numerous factors. A planned war may cost the economy less than a surprise war. It may be necessary to assume the worst, i.e. that a surprise attack will be launched, as in the Yom Kippur War. The cost of such a war may amount to as much as $4 billion in the form of defense outlays and a 10 percent drop in GNP in the war year. Although this assumption is arbitrary, it is better to consider it than to ignore its possibility.

(2) The real cost of evicting Israeli settlers from the territories and resettling them. This cost consists mainly of the expense of providing alternative housing, infrastructure and employment, as well as loss of work days and production potential in the Israeli economy. Here too, our estimates are purely preliminary, since no reliable study has been made of this subject, but we attempted to account for certain dynamics that could increase the cost of eviction. For example, the question of the number of settlers relocated may have far-reaching effects on the economy: the cost of relocating 20,000 families is not proportional to the cost of relocating 1,000 families — there exist diseconomies of scale. Large-scale relocation may result in a major loss of work days and even in the emigration from Israel of some of the evicted families.

212

(3) The structure of the economic relations between Israel and the territories, including movement of workers and goods. Here we examine the two extreme options: separation of the territories from Israel and the closure of borders to the flow of workers and capital, compared to integration of the economies of Israel and the territories and the opening of borders to free flow of labor and goods. Since an econometric model that combines both economies does not exist, we once again had to suffice with preliminary estimates only.

(4) Economic cooperation with the territories may lead to greater Israeli cooperation with Jordan and Egypt and might in some options develop into cooperation with the entire region. The economic implications of these developments should therefore be considered.

(5) Trade between Israel and non-Arab countries, including trade in both goods and services (particularly tourism). Israel is highly dependent on its international trade (imports and exports), which approaches the size of its GNP. Some political options might lead to deterioration of international trade relations with Israel, including economic sanctions and abolition of trade agreements. Other options might improve trade relations with countries that in the past abstained from trading with Israel. Unfortunately, no authoritative estimates of this issue are available, so the treatment of the subject is principally qualitative in nature.

(6) Foreign aid to Israel and the territories. In some options, it would be necessary to obtain large scale aid for Israel, and in particular for the territories. It is therefore necessary to note the need for foreign aid and to indicate what amounts of aid would be required. Israel is presently the beneficiary of foreign economic and military aid of $3-3.5 billion per annum. Future amounts of foreign aid and the level of cooperation may depend on the political scenario chosen.

(7) A special problem is the shortage of water in the region. This must be solved in any option chosen by Israel, because there is currently not sufficient water to the west of the Jordan for both economies. It is therefore necessary to secure additional water from external sources, or to desalinate

water. The feasibility of the implementation of these two alternatives depends on the political scenario chosen.

In the second stage of the economic analysis of the options, we attempt to estimate the implications of these economic factors on the Israeli economy and on the territories. Again, since an econometric model that combines both Israel and the territories does not exist, and in view of additional constraints of time and funding, we employ a model that is highly aggregative but lacks detail. It is a variation of Professor Pinhas Sussman's model as described in Zvi Lanir, ed., *Israel's Security and Economy in the 1980's* (New York: Praeger, 1983).

The model describes the behavior over time of the following real economic variables:
(a) Gross national product
(b) The labor force
(c) Investments in the economy and accumulation of capital
(d) Private consumption
(e) Public consumption (civil and military)
(f) Balance of payments and foreign debt.

In this model, excess demand is immediately reflected in the foreign debt; this growth has a reciprocal effect on investment opportunities in the economy. According to the model, the size of investments in the economy depends on the ratio between foreign debt and GNP. When this ratio increases, it reduces investment in the economy. In addition, interest and capital repayments reduce real resources. However, even when one has a detailed econometric model, it is not possible to insert all economic factors into it in order to examine their effect on the various target variables, and it will therefore be necessary to consider some of them qualitatively.

The Economy of the Territories in Comparison to the Israeli Economy

We have noted that the economy of the territories is far more dependent on the Israeli economy than the Israeli economy is dependent on the economy of the territories. This stems primarily from the relative size and robustness of the two economies.

Table 1 shows a comparison between principal economic variables of the two economies. For the territories, the latest available statistics are for 1986, so the year examined by us is 1986.

It is obvious from this comparison that the economy of the territories is small in comparison to the Israeli economy, particularly with regard to public consumption and gross capital stock in productive sectors. This is particularly striking in view of the fact that the population of the territories constitutes between 30 and 40 percent of the population of Israel. The degree of integration of the two economies in 1986 is demonstrated by the indices shown in Table 2.

From these data it is evident that the territories are highly dependent on trade with Israel and on income from employment in Israel. On the other hand Israel's dependency on the territories appears weaker, although in some sectors (construction and agriculture) the dependence is large while in others (textiles and services) it is quite significant. Israel's dependence on Gaza is somewhat weaker in terms of labor force and significantly weaker in terms of exports and imports, relative to the West Bank.

The Economic Implications of Separation of the Economies

Implications on the Israeli Economy. In examining the implications of a perfect separation of the Israeli economy from that of the territories, we assume that this form of separation would involve the eviction of Jewish settlers from the territories and the removal of civilian and military installations. According to our estimate, the cost of the removal and transfer of military installations, and particularly the construction of fortifications and security systems along the new border, would be $3-5 billion, spread over a period of 2-3 years. We estimate the cost of evicting some 20,000 settler families from the territories and relocating them inside the borders of Israel after a peace settlement, at $3-5 billion — the equivalent of $150,000-250,000 per family. This represents the real cost to the economy, at the expense of productive investment and reduction of the growth of productive capital in the economy. Civilian relocation investments would also have to be made within a short-term period of 2-3 years.

This information was introduced into the econometric model, resulting in ranges of various macro-economic indicators such as GNP, private consumption and foreign debt, in each year of the following decade.

The damage to Israel's GNP that would result from the civilian and military relocation and from total economic separation, taking into account a decline in the work force by over 100,000 workers from the territories, would be reflected in a fall of some 3 percent of GNP in the first year. The GNP would subsequently return gradually to positive growth, although at a lower rate than would have been possible had the economies remained integrated. Again assuming a situation of relocations and separation, per capita consumption would fall by 4.5 percent in the first year and would not return to the 1988 level (assuming 1988 as the base year of the option) in less than four years. Foreign debt per capita would continue to rise over the next decade, as compared to the situation of continued integration in which the upward trend would have ceased within a few years. Obviously, increased foreign aid to Israel would reduce these damages to the Israeli economy. Extra aid on the scale of $5 billion per annum during each year of relocations would eliminate the damage caused by the relocations but not the damage caused by economic separation.

Severe damage would be caused to the construction industry and to some extent to the agricultural sector as well. In the building sector, 40 percent of all workers come from the territories. Separation would initially lead to an increase in construction time and a reduction in building starts. In the short run, workers from the territories would be replaced by Israeli workers and perhaps even by workers from abroad. In the longer run, the construction industry would have to adopt labor-saving technologies — mechanized construction methods. During the adjustment period, prices in the construction sector would probably rise. A similar process would take place in the agricultural sector, where prices are also expected to rise during the adjustment period. In this regard, it would be necessary to identify and eliminate bottlenecks in the construction industry caused by simultaneous relocation and separation, in order to complete the relocation within the time and at the costs mentioned above.

Implications on the Economy of the Territories. The effect of separation on the economy of the territories would be critical. Here we describe it in terms of maintaining per capita consumption and total resources at the 1986 levels. Since the population of the territories is growing at the rate of 3.5 percent per annum, consumption and resources should also grow at the same rate merely in order to maintain per capita characteristics even at their present low levels. We have assumed the need for an additional increase of 2 percent per annum in per capita consumption. Hence the macro-economic variables would have to grow at a rate approaching 6 percent per annum.

The year 1986 is the latest for which data on the economy of the territories are available. Total resources of the territories in 1986 in millions of dollars are shown in Table 3, and per capita uses in the territories and in Israel (for comparative purposes) in Table 4.

Following separation of the economies, receipts in the territories from foreign countries (effectively, income from work in Israel) would disappear. If these receipts are deducted from total exports, the export figure would be $425 million (a drop of about 47 percent). A large proportion of exports from the territories is presently shipped to Israel; closure of the borders would generate a serious problem of finding alternative markets for these goods and services. A very high proportion of the imports of the territories is also derived from Israel, and alternative sources would no doubt be more expensive. Accordingly, there may be a real decline of some 40 percent in imports and exports, while the remaining 60 percent would suffer less favorable terms of trade, i.e. imports would derive from more expensive sources and exports would go to less profitable destinations. As a result, the trade deficit is expected to reach $1-1.3 billion.

In 1986 public consumption in the territories was very low ($110 per capita) as was gross local investment ($360 per capita). Private consumption per capita was also rather low ($1,250). The territories may obtain additional resources from an increase in GDP or a reduction in the trade deficit. An increase in public consumption and gross local investment, which is vital, would generate a trade deficit of almost $2 billion per annum. This is 1.3 times the GDP of 1986 and would therefore be very difficult to maintain, even for a few years.

To avoid the necessity of providing aid on the scale of $2 billion a year over time, it would be necessary to direct resources into investment in the territories. Investment would be mainly in the industrial sector rather than in agriculture, because the water problem in the territories would persist. Investment in industry must ensure employment for workers cut off from the Israeli economy, who would probably not be able to find employment in the Gulf countries because of the fall in oil prices, and for those who were engaged in production for export to Israel — a total of some 200,000 workers. Even assuming a conservative estimate of capital requirements per worker — $15,000 (in Israel, gross capital stock per worker in 1986 was approx. $42,000) — this still means an investment of $3 billion.

The success of the industrialization of the territories would depend not only on large investments but also on the ability to introduce unfamiliar technologies and to find markets for goods to be produced by those industries. Many developing countries have difficulties introducing modern manufacturing technologies. Palestinians, however, pursue higher education in large numbers, and there is a large reserve of qualified academics currently employed in other countries. This may make the process of adoption of technologies somewhat easier.

The problem of developing export markets for industrial products is extremely severe. Jordan has only a limited ability to absorb industrial products, due to the poor state of its economy. Other Arab countries, and particularly the Gulf nations, constitute potential markets, but it will also be necessary to develop markets in Western and Eastern Europe and in other parts of the world.

Integration of the Economies and its Economic Implications

By maintaining the integration of the economies of Israel and the territories, it may be possible to accelerate the development of the territories without harming the standard of living of its population, provided that investments are made there in industrial enterprises. The high natural population growth rate and the increase in the proportion of participation of men and women in the work force on the one hand, and migration back to the territories from Arab countries on the other, would create permanent pressure on the labor market in the territories, generating an estimated 3.5 percent per annum growth in the number of work places required. If the new employers continued to be divided between Israel and the territories by the same ratio as in 1987, Israel would have to absorb 3.5 percent more workers from the territories each year. Their addition to the Israeli economy in a situation of full employment might lead to an annual growth rate of the GNP of 4.6 percent, and correspondingly to an average annual growth of per capita consumption in Israel of 2.5 percent and an annual reduction of per capita foreign debt of 2.7 percent.

Notably, the proportion of workers from the territories relative to the total work force in Israel would increase, due to the fact that the Israeli work force would grow by only two percent per annum. In some sectors, workers from the territories would become predominant and dependence on them would increase progressively. Hence sudden political unrest might cause the complete shutdown of some sectors in Israel, with a spinoff effect on other sectors as well. In such an event the process of adjustment would be more difficult and expensive. Israel must consider the ramifications of this risk if it decides (assuming it has the option) to support integration of the economies.

The Water Shortage Problem

Whatever option is chosen, it must address the problem of the shortage of water in the region. In options in which economic integration were possible, or which are acceptable to Jordan and Egypt, it might be possible to supplement water supplies from external sources, both natural and artificial. In options not predicated on full cooperation among Israel, the territories and the Arab countries, solving the water problem in Judea, Samaria and Gaza would bring about a significant reduction in the amount of water available to Israel, thereby requiring a structural change in the Israeli agricultural sector.

A reduction in the amount of water available to Israel of, say, 100-200 million cubic meters, would not be marginal. Hence it should be attributed a higher cost than the marginal product value of water in agriculture. The marginal product value is about 15 cents per cubic meter (for irrigated cotton, which is the marginal crop). To estimate the damage to the economy of a shortage of 100 million cubic meters, we will assume an indicator of double this value, i.e. 30 cents per cubic meter. For a shortage of 200 million cubic meters, we will use an indicator which is three times the marginal product value, i.e. 45 cents per cbm. The cost to the Israeli economy of a shortage of 100-200 million cubic meters of water per annum would thus be $30-90 million.

A cost of 45 cents per cubic meter makes desalination justified (particularly if it is combined with cogeneration of electricity), where the cost of capital is included in the water production cost. Moreover, the political options involving agreement and cooperation among Israel, the territories and the Arab countries would probably require the transfer of similarly large quantities of water from Israel to the West Bank and the Gaza Strip. Here Israel would be compensated by the supply of water from alternative sources, such as the Nile or the Litani Rivers or desalinated water.

Summary of Quantitative Data

The economic ramifications for Israel of each of the political scenarios depend upon the costs, the sources of finance and the magnitude of financing by external sources.

The ramifications are also dependent on the degree of economic interaction after the scenario is established. Figure 1 describes the ranges of potential integration and the rating of the various options according to each category of costs. Each category of costs is bracketed between conceivable maximum and minimum levels. Each option can move within this range. Because of the unique importance of water, its anticipated deficit by option is also presented. By ranking, rather than assigning a specific number, we seek to reflect the uncertainty and the wide range of absolute values over which each option could move.

The various degrees of economic integration/separation of each option are also emphasized. A Palestinian state, for example, could separate its economy from the Israeli economy or, alternatively, could reach a state of almost perfect integration with the Israeli economy. The same holds true for a Jordanian-Palestinian federation, whereby integration would include the Jordanian economy as well. On the other hand the options of annexation, status quo and autonomy could all involve perfect integration, but could also be predicated on partial integration — were, for example, the Arabs in the territories to decide to boycott products made in Israel.

Summary of the Six Options

In economic terms, the range of the options examined in this study group report extends from continuation of the status quo, which involves partial economic separation resulting from the uprising, to a Palestinian state or federation with Jordan, involving total economic separation. Between the two extremes are the options of annexation and perfect economic integration, limited autonomy and extended autonomy with perfect economic integration, and withdrawal from Gaza involving perfect economic separation from Gaza but not from the West Bank. In the Palestinian state option, both perfect separation and almost perfect integration are possible, while in the Jordanian federation option perfect separation and partial integration constitute the limits of the range of feasible economic relations.

Ideally, the economic implications of various forms of projected economic relations should not be examined at some point in time that is close to the present, but rather at a time when the process of adjustment of the economies is completed and the system is stabilized on its new path. This reservation should be born in mind when examining our assessments of ramifications of the options on the Israeli economy (see Table 5). We have used 1988 as the base year for comparison of conditions, have deliberately ignored the possibility of war (in spite of its relatively high probability in some options, such as annexation), and have assumed a population growth rate of two percent for all options (although this constancy, too, is debatable). Using the Zussman model for various ranges of the costs that are implied by each option yields results that are overlapping for variables like per capita personal consumption and per capita external debt.

The results in Table 5 further emphasize the stability of the Israeli economy and its weak dependence upon the economy of the territories. Thus in all six options the annual average growth rate of per capita consumption is within the 1.3-2.5 percent range for the 1988-98 period. The annual average rates of change of per capita external debt are in the -2.0 to +1.0 percent range. These results stem partially from the nature of the model — it channels the gap between uses and resources into external debt, while feedback on domestic uses is relatively small. A different econometric model is likely to yield a different ranking of the options and different magnitudes of annual average changes.

With regard to the territories, however, the critical issue remains the question of integration or separation from the Israeli economy. Separation without massive economic aid, either for transfer payments or for investment and higher public consumption, would generate an economic disaster: in Gaza, a drop down to only 20 percent of the economic activity of 1986; in the West Bank a milder decline, to 60 percent of the 1986 activity level. In contrast economic integration, though not perfect, would help during the first years to establish a sound economic system and facilitate its gradual adjustment to separation from the Israeli economy. In the long run, too, the possibility of integration holds out mutual benefits to both economies.

All told, then, the Israeli economy is relatively non-sensitive to the various political options, while the economy of the territories is extremely sensitive. This predicates a strong link between the success of the political option, on the one hand, and the framework of economic relations with Israel selected by the Arab partner to a settlement, on the other.

Conclusion

In view of the usual practice of ignoring economic issues when examining political scenarios, the mere raising of the question of the economic implications of the six options implies significant progress. However, there are disadvantages alongside the advantages. The economic analysis should provide not only information on general indications of the effects of the scenario, but also quantitative answers to decisionmakers in terms of costs and benefits. But to do so, the scenario must be properly defined in economic terms, there must be quantitative data on every relevant economic factor, and there must be a calibrated model into which the relevant data can be introduced and which can be solved so as to obtain results. Naturally, these requirements sound exaggerated to political decisionmakers who are not economists. Yet history — even very recent history — appears to demonstrate that politicians' failure to recognize these requirements leads them to fail to demand compensation for the costs involved as a condition for entering into an agreement.

Table 1

PRINCIPAL MACRO-ECONOMIC INDICATORS IN THE TERRITORIES
IN COMPARISON TO ISRAEL IN 1986 (%)

	ISRAEL	JUDEA & SAMARIA	GAZA	JUDEA, SAMARIA AND GAZA
GNP	100	6.6	2.8	9.4
Private consumption	100	6.4	2.7	9.1
Public consumption (not including direct military imports)	100	1.4	0.6	2.0
Investment	100	6.6	2.0	8.6
Exports	100	2.3	1.4	3.7
Civilian imports	100	5.0	3.5	8.5
Gross capital stock	100	1.5	0.5	2.0
Population (*)	100	19.5	12.7	32.2
Workforce	100	11.8	6.5	18.3

(*) Estimates of the Central Bureau of Statistics. In
regard to the territories, there are indications that
these estimates are downward biased.

Table 2

INTERDEPENDENCE INDICES, 1986, PERCENTAGES

JUDEA, SAMARIA AND GAZA:	Judea & Samaria	Gaza	Judea, Samaria and Gaza
Workforce employed in Israel out of total employed	31	46	37
Income from employment in Israel relative to GNP	18	54	27
Exports of goods and services to Israel relative to GNP	15	41	21
Imports of goods and services from Israel relative to GNP	50	126	68

I S R A E L:

	Judea & Samaria	Gaza	Judea, Samaria and Gaza
Employees from the territories relative to the total workforce	3.8	3.4	7.2
Employees from the territories relative to total employed in construction			40.0
Employees from the territories relative to total employed in agriculture			18.0
Employees from the territories relative to total employed in industry			5.5
Exports to the territories relative to total exports	8.0	5.0	13.0
Imports from the territories relative to total imports	1.6	1.4	3.0

Table 3

<u>RESOURCES OF THE TERRITORIES IN 1986 ($ MILLIONS)</u>

Total resources	2,738
Imports	1,187
Gross domestic product (at market prices)	1,551
Net receipts from work abroad	484
GNP (at market prices)	2,035
Total exports	909
Total imports	1,197
Trade deficit	288

Table 4

USES PER CAPITA IN THE TERRITORIES
AND IN ISRAEL IN 1986 ($)

	JUDEA & SAMARIA	GAZA	AVERAGE	ISRAEL
Private consumption	1,440	954	1,249	4,049
Civilian public consumption	130	86	114	1,034
Gross domestic investment	463	216	365	1,242
Investment in fixed assets	382	216	317	1,110
Investment in inventory	80	0	47	132
Total domestic demand	2,033	1,257	1,728	*6,325
Exports of goods and services	319	296	310	2,644
Total uses	2,353	1,553	2,039	*8,969

(*) Not including direct military imports

227

Figure 1

THE SIX POLITICAL SCENARIOS ON AN AXIS OF
MAJOR ECONOMIC COSTS (CONSISTENTLY)

1. Economic scenarios:integration/separation

```
Complete separation                            Complete integration
------------------------------------------------------------------->
Palestinian state    }      Exit        {  Annexation
Jordanian federation }-----> from <------{  Status quo
                     }      Gaza        {  Limited autonomy
                                        {  Expanded autonomy
```

2. Military costs ($ billions), in addition to present costs (not considering a war)

```
 0                                                            3-5
------------------------------------------------------------------->
Status quo        Limited          Expanded     Palestinian state/
                  autonomy         autonomy     Federation with
----------        --------------                Jordan
Annexation        Exit from Gaza
```

3. Eviction of Jewish settlers, $ billions (presently 0)

```
 0                                                            3-5
------------------------------------------------------------------->
                 same as military costs
```

4. US aid and military cooperation, $ billions (total amounts)

```
 0                                                            3-5
------------------------------------------------------------------->
Annexation     Status quo     Limited      Expanded     Palestinian
                              autonomy/    autonomy     state/
                              Exit from                 Federation
                              Gaza                      with Jordan
```

5. Present and future deficit of water west of the Jordan River (MCM)

```
 0                                                            200
------------------------------------------------------------------->
Palestinian state/     Expanded     Exit from     Status quo/
Federation with        autonomy     Gaza          Annexation/
Jordan                                             Limited autonomy
```

228

Table 5

Average annual rates (percentages) of change in per capita personal consumption and per capita external debt in Israel, 1988-98, in the various options.

	Personal Consumption (per capita)	External Debt (per capita)
Status quo	2.0-2.5%	(-0.5) - 0.5 %
Autonomy	1.5-2.5	(-1.0)-(-2.0)
Annexation	1.5-2.5	1.0 - 1.5
Palestinian state	1.3-2.0	0.5 - 1.0
Unilateral withdrawal from Gaza	1.5-2.5	(-0.5) - 0.5
Federation with Jordan	1.3-2.0	0.5 - 1.0

About the Members
of the Study Group

Aharon Yariv

Major General (res.) Yariv's long and distinguished IDF career included postings as founder and commander of the Command and Staff College, and Director of Military Intelligence (1964-1972). He was a Member of Knesset from 1974 to 1977, Minister of Transport (1974) and Minister of Information (1974-1975). He established JCSS in 1977, and has headed the Center ever since.

Joseph Alpher

Mr. Alpher joined JCSS as Executive Editor in 1981, after 16 years service as an officer in the IDF Intelligence Directorate and as a senior official in the Prime Minister's Office. He has published extensively in Israel and the US on Middle East strategic affairs, and has edited several works on the subject. He has been Deputy Head of Center since 1986. He was coordinator of the JCSS study group and coeditor of its report.

Jona Bargur

Dr. Bargur heads the economic division of the Interdisciplinary Center for Technological Analysis and Forecasting at Tel Aviv University. He specializes in resource economics, public policy and regional planning, and most recently worked on developing an energy policy for Israel. He participated in the ICTAF team that prepared preliminary drafts on economic issues for the study group, as well as Appendix 7.

Yehuda Ben-Meir

Dr. Ben-Meir is a Senior Research Associate at JCSS. He headed the Bar-Ilan University Psychology Department until 1971. From 1971 to 1984 he was a Member of Knesset for the National Religious Party, and from 1981 to 1984 was Deputy Foreign Minister. In 1987 he published *National Security Decisionmaking: The Israeli Case* (JCSS Study no. 8). He wrote the preliminary drafts on the Israeli domestic setting for the study group, as well as Appendix 2.

Abraham Ben-Zvi

Professor Ben-Zvi is a Senior Research Associate at JCSS. He is past Chairman of the Department of Political Science at Tel-Aviv University. He has published extensively on the issues of surprise attack, cognitive theory in international relations, and US foreign policy. He recently wrote *The American Approach to Superpower Collaboration in the Middle East, 1973-1986* (JCSS Study no. 5, 1986).

Moshe Brawer

Prof. Brawer has taught for more than 25 years at Tel Aviv University, where he has been Chairman of the Department of Geography and Dean of the Faculty of Humanities. He is a prolific author of articles and books on the geography of the Middle East. He is former President of the Israeli Geographical Society and a Fellow of the Royal Geographical Society. He wrote the preliminary drafts on geography and demography for the study group, as well as Appendix 4.

Zeev Eytan

Dr. Eytan is a Senior Research Associate at JCSS. He served as a Colonel in the IDF unti 1980. He specializes in military forces in the Middle East. He has written extensively on Israeli military affairs in *Ma'arachot,* the IDF Journal. He supervises the JCSS military data base, and writes the data sections in the *Military Balance.*

Shai Feldman

Dr. Feldman is a Senior Research Associate at JCSS. He specializes in nuclear proliferation, US Mideast Policy, and Israel's national security policy. From 1984 to 1987 he headed JCSS's Project on US Foreign/Security Policy in the Middle East. He is the author of *Israeli Nuclear Deterrence: A Strategy for the 1980s* (Columbia University Press, 1982). He coedited the study group report.

Gideon Fishelson

Professor Fishelson is in Tel Aviv University's Department of Economics. He is also university Dean of Students, and serves as Scientific Coordinator of the Armand Hammer Research Project on

Economic Cooperation Toward Peace in the Middle East. He specializes in labor economics, resource economics and the economy of Israel. He participated in the ICTAF team that prepared preliminary drafts on economic issues for the study group, as well as Appendix 7.

Shlomo Gazit

Major-General (res) Gazit is a Senior Research Associate at JCSS. He is a former Coordinator of Israeli Government Operations in the Administered Territories and former Director of IDF Military Intelligence. He served as President of Ben-Gurion University in the Negev from 1981-85, and Director General of the Jewish Agency from 1985-88. His book *The Stick and the Carrot* (in Hebrew) deals with aspects of the Israeli policy in the West Bank and Gaza. He wrote the preliminary drafts on Israeli security for the study group, as well as Appendix 1.

Dore Gold

Dr. Gold is a Senior Research Associate at JCSS. He heads the Center's Project on US Foreign/Security Policy in the Middle East. His most recent publication is *America, the Gulf and Israel: CENTCOM and Emerging US Regional Security Policies in the Middle East* (JCSS Study no. 14, 1988). He contributed to the Washington Institute's preliminary discussions of its drafts on the United States for the study group.

Mark A. Heller

Dr. Heller is a Senior Research Associate at JCSS. He served as Deputy Head of Center from 1984 to 1986. In 1983 he published A *Palestinian State: The Implications for Israel* (Harvard University Press). He wrote the preliminary drafts on the Palestinians for the study group, as well as Appendix 5.

Martin Indyk

Dr. Indyk is Executive Director of the Washington Institute for Near East Policy, and principal author of *Building for Peace* (1988), the Institute's Presidential Study Group Report on American strategy for the Middle East. He chaired the discussions at the

Washington Institute of the preliminary drafts on the United States for the study group.

Efraim Karsh

Dr. Karsh is a Senior Research Associate at JCSS. He teaches international relations at Tel Aviv University. He specializes in Soviet military issues and Middle Eastern and European affairs. His most recent published work is *The Soviet Union and Syria* (Routledge 1988). He wrote the preliminary drafts on the Soviet Union for the study group.

Anat Kurz

Mrs. Kurz is Acting Director of JCSS's Project on International Terrorism. She recently edited *Contemporary Trends in Terrorism* (1987, Praeger/Greenwood). She wrote the preliminary drafts on terrorism for the study group.

Ariel (Eli) Levite

Dr. Levite is a Senior Research Associate at JCSS. He specializes in international security and military strategy. His study on Offense and Defense in Israeli Military Doctrine is being published by JCSS in 1988-89. He collaborated with Shlomo Gazit in preparing the initial drafts on Israel's security for the study group.

Bruce Maddy-Weitzman

Dr. Maddy-Weitzman is a Research Associate at the Dayan Center for Middle Eastern and African Studies at Tel Aviv University, and a Post-Doctoral Research Fellow at the Jewish-Arab Center, University of Haifa. He specializes in inter-Arab relations, the Arab-Israel conflict and modern Middle East history. He wrote the initial drafts on the Arab states for the study group.

Shemuel Meir

Mr. Meir has been a Research Associate at JCSS since 1983. Previously he served as an IDF officer. His most recent publication at JCSS is *Strategic Implications of the New Oil Reality* (JCSS Study no. 4, 1985). His areas of specialization include Israel's national security, issues of defense and economy, and the US-Soviet strategic balance.

Yoram Peri

Dr. Peri is Executive Editor of *Davar* daily newspaper, and a Visiting Research Associate at JCSS. His book *Between Battles and Ballots: Israeli Military in Politics* was published by Cambridge University Press in 1985. He wrote the preliminary drafts on sociopolitical ramifications in the IDF for the study group.

Yoel Raban

Dr. Raban is a Research Associate at the Interdisciplinary Center for Technological Analysis and Forecasting. He specializes in the economics of innovation and marketing. He participated in the ICTAF team that prepared preliminary drafts on economic issues for the study group, as well as Appendix 7.

Yitzhak Reiter

Mr. Reiter served from 1978 to 1987 as Senior Research Officer in the Prime Minister's Office, Deputy Adviser to the Prime Minister on Arab Affairs, and Director of *Al-Anba* daily Arabic newspaper. He is currently a research fellow at the Harry S. Truman Institute for the Advancement of Peace, at the Hebrew University in Jerusalem. He wrote the preliminary drafts on the Israeli Arabs for the study group, as well as Appendix 6.

Aryeh Shalev

Brigadier-General (res.) Shalev is a Senior Research Associate and past Deputy Head of Center at JCSS. He served for 33 years in the IDF, where his final posting was Military Governor of the West Bank. At the Center, his most recently published work is *The West Bank: Line of Defense* (1985, Praeger/Greenwood). He is currently researching the strategic importance of the Golan Heights, and the *intifada*. He wrote the preliminary drafts of the options definitions for the study group.

Harvey Sicherman

Dr. Sicherman is a consultant to the State Department and an Adjunct Scholar at the Washington Institute. He served as Special Assistant to the Secretary of State, 1981-82. He is the author of *Changing the Balance of Risks: U.S. Policy toward the Arab-Israeli Conflict* (Washington Institute Policy Paper #11, 1988). He participated in the Washington Institute discussions of preliminary drafts on the United States for the study group.

Steven Spiegel

Dr. Spiegel is Professor of Political Science at UCLA. His 1985 volume *The Other Arab-Israeli Conflict* won a 1986 National Jewish Book Award. He was principal author of the Washington Institute's preliminary drafts on the United States for the study group.